WHY MEN FALL OUT OF LOVE

OF LOVE

THE SECRETS THEY DON'T TELL

Electronic and soft-cover print versions published by
Wellness Institute/Self-Help Books, LLC
500 West North Street
Pass Christian, MS 39571

*Cover design and artwork by
Jason Ladner and Don Curry*

SelfHelpBooks.com *is a division of the*
Wellness Institute/Self-Help Books, LLC

ISBN 1587411326

Printed in the United States of America

WHY MEN FALL OUT OF LOVE

OF LOVE

THE SECRETS THEY DON'T TELL

by

Michael French

Foreword by
Herb Goldberg, Ph.D.

This book is for Patricia,

with love and affection

Acknowledgements

Foremost, I want to thank the men who were willing to share their lives with me for this book. I applaud their courage, openness and honesty.

I am indebted to Frank Baca for his encouragement throughout this project, and to John Webber and Joe Terrell for offering free lessons in coping. Also, thanks to a half-dozen friends, men and women, who read this manuscript in its various evolutions and made suggestions, many of which were gratefully incorporated.

For Harold Dawley, publisher of Wellness Institute/Self-Help Books, my gratitude for his editorial insights and structural changes to the manuscript. He made my job easier and this book more illuminating. As did Annie Lux with her multi-colored pens.

Finally, my infinite thanks to my wife and children for the love and patience they've shown me in good weather and bad.

Foreword

Men today are clearly in the process of making significant changes. At the same time, they are being torn apart by the deeper pressures created by centuries of toxic, overpowering conditioning that dehumanizes them and severely damages, if not destroys, their capacity for personal and intimate relating, as well as their awareness of, and desire for, a different, expressive, connected way of being. While traditional conditioning still tends to overpower the fragile, tender shoots of growth, men are clearly becoming aware of, and are on their way toward, a dramatically new way of being and defining themselves.

A primary building block in the process of men's healing from their past conditioning, and movement towards a transformation in the direction of a personally connected sense of themselves as full persons, is the open and expressive communication, exploration, analysis, and reflection of their personal selves through sharing the stories of their relationship histories. For myself, as a psychologist and writer on the topic of gender and the male experience, a core dimension of a man's personal liberation involves his willingness and ability to be fully and unashamedly transparent about disclosing his inner life. Once men come out of hiding about their inner experiences, they have overcome critical obstacles to their personal growth, namely shame, secretiveness, and denial of what it's like to be a man.

In this remarkable book, *Why Men Fall Out of Love: The Secrets They Don't Tell*, Michael French has made a significant contribution to the growing body of literature about the realities of masculinity and manhood by presenting, with remarkably vivid and compelling detail, nuance and sensitivity, the life and relationship histories of ten men of various ethnic and religious backgrounds. All share the struggle to survive and thrive as men

The men whose stories are shared in this book are men who had the courage to unmask themselves, remove their façades, and share their often painful, highly personal struggles and the ways they went about trying to change themselves. In this way, this book is a vehicle for men's healing and transformation. Bringing the deeper realities of being a man out into the open for other men to read and learn from is a noble gift that gives the men who have not yet begun to acknowledge, understand, explore and change themselves a map with which to begin their journeys, as well as the comfort of discovering that their experience, indeed, has much in common with that of other men. Most men feel damaged and self-hating, yet these stories help us to see how this is every man's psychological heritage.

Michael French's book is a unique gift to all men. He has succeeded in doing something that few have been able to do: namely, eliciting from a wonderful sampling of men their intimate relationship histories. Considering how closed most men are about revealing their true selves to others, the personal stories in this book are told with amazing candor, revelation, and no-holds-barred honesty. It is a significant accomplishment. Reading this book might be the crucial first step many men need in order to take the journey from secret and furtive self-destruction to an open and joyous journey toward self-discovery and personal liberation. With this book, Michael French has done all men a major service. For this excellent contribution, we owe him profound thanks!

Herb Goldberg, Ph.D.

Dr. Goldberg, a licensed psychologist, is the best-selling author of *The Hazards of Being Male, The Inner Male, The New Male, The New Male/Female Relationship*, and *What Men Really Want.*

TABLE OF CONTENTS

Part Six – What Every Couple Should Know

Bibliography

PART ONE

RELATIONSHIP BUSTERS

Chapter One

When Men Stop Loving

*The great tragedy in life is not that men perish,
but that they cease to love.*

—*W. Somerset Maugham*

According to the U.S. National Center for Health Statistics, one in three first marriages end in divorce, and two out of three second marriages meet the same fate. While at any given time 59 percent of the adult population are married, 10 percent are divorced and seven percent widowed, another 24 percent have never taken wedding vows. What is unknown is how many relationships the average man or woman goes through before finding or not finding that special person. What percentage of relationships simply implode, disintegrate, or fall by the wayside without anyone really understanding why?

About three years ago I was having a drink with a friend, a successful entrepreneur in his early thirties, when he suddenly volunteered, in a tone approaching despair, that he thought he had fallen out of love. It wasn't just that he had lost interest in his long-time girlfriend, he said. Something deeper was going on, something that made him sad. He and his partner weren't connecting for a *reason*—but he couldn't put his finger on it. Why couldn't he figure it out? Why was talking to his girlfriend about his emotions so difficult? What were his real feelings, anyway? And why did so few men open up to each other on this critical subject?

His frustration was brimming over, and he kept looking at me as if I held the answers. My friend knew I was neither a psychologist nor relationship expert—I am currently president of an on-line sales company and on occasion a writer and editor—but I was almost twenty-five years his senior. In addition to any wisdom he thought I had acquired from being "successfully married for many years," as he put it, he seemed to prefer my layman status, as if that made him feel safer. When I admitted I wasn't sure how to advise him, he was unfazed. He knew I would come through, he said, and he made me promise we would talk again.

Over the next few days I found my thoughts returning often to my friend's problem, pondering the ups and downs of any intimate relationship, including my own marriage. On the domestic front I too was in rough waters, though I hadn't told anyone except a close friend at the gym. Now that our son and daughter were grown and gone, my wife and I were arguing more frequently, usually over inconsequential things, and both of us intuited a deeper rift. Was I stumbling through a garden-variety mid-life crisis, or was this something more? Like my friend, I wondered if I was still in love. Perhaps the spark of "being in love" had been replaced by habit and convenience. My friend, wanting help in solving his relationship issues, had unwittingly pushed me to delve into my own emotions, including not a small amount of anger. I likened that anger to a low-grade fever that had been slowly rising in me over the years. Where had it come from, I suddenly wondered, and where was it taking me?

Within a week I found myself visiting my city's largest book store. After passing multiple aisles of self-help books for women, I found in one corner a clutch of books espousing a male view on relationships, masculinity and emotions. I had skimmed Robert Bly's *Iron John* decades ago, but the message had failed to resonate on any personal level. I had thought nothing more about that book, until now. Suddenly, I was reading everything I could find in that forlorn corner, including the landmark *The Hazards of Being Male: Surviving the Myth of Male Privilege* by Herb Goldberg, Frank Pittman's insightful *Man Enough: Fathers, Sons, and the Search for Masculinity*, and Terrence Real's *I Don't Want to Talk About It: Overcoming the Secret Legacy of Male Depression*. I soaked up all the insights about men that I could, especially about their emotional growth and what they looked for in their relationships. As much as I learned, I came up hungry for more.

When I visited the section of books for women, I was impressed not only with the sheer quantity of titles but the depth of the subject matter. In particular, the number of stories about women leaving their significant others to pursue new passions and disciplines, or simply to take a sabbatical "to find themselves," so outnumbered chronicles of male pilgrimages that a couple of conclusions seemed inescapable. First, men were not "allowed" this same luxury of self-discovery. Whether it was their own prohibition or that of their culture, running off somewhere to "soul search" for a couple of months seemed frivolous and irresponsible. My second conclusion was that men were leery of confession. When they enter the adolescent world of competition, males grow cautious about showing their feelings or making themselves vulnerable. They come to prefer, as I certainly did, to bury their emotions like a dog would his bones, digging them up when the occasion demands it.

In the books I read, I also saw that women shared their stories of courage and self-discovery like coins of the realm, and even if they were sworn enemies they still rallied to each other's side in times of crisis. They could talk about the most intimate subjects without a shred of self-consciousness. Openness seemed to be a primary definition of who they were. While a lot of women will admit to being catty, devious, jealous and vindictive, they do so with apology, as if this isn't who they really are, and they define their gender more along the axis of solidarity and sharing. There is no equivalent community of men, certainly little openness. Unless the danger is obvious, such as in war, men do not band together to share emotions. Sports is another prominent exception: the universal male outlet for fearless opinions, aggression, competition, bonding, affection, and hero worship. Religion too invokes shared emotions. All three are safe, institutionalized outlets, "approved for men," as it were. Yet in general men keep their internal lives—and their more complex emotions—a closely guarded secret. That is the unwritten code. Out of some weird male logic, I concluded, men assume that the less they reveal of themselves, the more power they have and the less they have to be afraid of. Over the next three years, I would find that assumption to be not just wrong but the very opposite of the truth.

When I visited with my friend a month later, little had changed. His agitation had not diminished. He was no closer to a decision about his relationship, and he had not whispered a word to his girlfriend about what was bothering him. In typical male passive-aggressive fashion, he admitted, he had procrastinated any action that would bring confrontation and emotional pain. What *had* changed was his willingness to confess to me about his past relationships, as well as to share stories about his successful but angry, repressed father, an overindulgent, fearful mother, and how his parents' relationship had impacted his attitude toward women. He also admitted he was afraid of leaving his girlfriend, even though he no longer had feelings for her. There were multiple levels of frustration in his story, centered on an inability to put the pieces together. Finally opening up about my own relationship, I told him I shared the feeling of being in the dark. We both talked up a storm, particularly about our childhoods.

"More guys should be candid about this stuff," my friend said as we parted, and we promised to meet again.

Yes, I thought, we should. The idea that other men who faced frustration, unhappiness or confusion in their relationships might want to talk about it had an immediate appeal to me. If nothing else, it would let me know that my friend and I weren't struggling alone. If I could find other men willing to be honest, I would encourage them to write down their stories. If those stories were interesting enough, maybe I would shape them into a book. I thought that a lot of men and women might want to learn more about the chemistry of emotions in men when they stopped loving or called it quits on their relationships.

What started as a simple launching turned into a rigorous sea crossing. Even with the promise of anonymity (all names and physical descriptions in this book have been changed, along with most professions and cities), asking men to write about their relationships made it crystal clear why there are so few books on the subject. There is no shortage of articles on men's views on sex (often written by women, even in so-called men's magazines) as well as on the qualities that a man looks for in a woman. But for men to be confessional on the subject of their darkest fears and most intimate emotions was another matter. Either in person, by e-mail or phone, I approached more than forty candidates—in the end, friends of friends of friends—asking each why his relationship, despite the most brilliant beginning, might have turned stormy in the end.

The experience was like trying to drag someone with stage fright, kicking and screaming, in front of a microphone. A few insisted they had no such failures. Others were honest enough to say that if they were too confessional, they might shock their partners and lose their respect or even their love. Despite a twelve-page questionnaire I had prepared to guide them, still more men complained that they felt lost before they put a single sentence on paper. A few admitted they lacked the courage to revisit their painful pasts, or were concerned about hurting their partners, current or former. Another declined my offer because he said "he would get in trouble." I asked if he meant with his girlfriend or wife. He blushed, perhaps ashamed, and then, like many others, politely dismissed me as an interloper. Even my entrepreneurial friend who had helped start me on my quest (and who finally did break up with his girlfriend) couldn't be convinced to bare his soul on paper.

This fits-and-starts process took almost three years before I garnered and edited nine good oral histories. I added my own (making it ten) because I thought it fit well into the themes and insights of the book, and because I promised several men that if they committed to this project, so would I. In the beginning, courage had to be stoked. In the end, I got the honesty I had hoped for. None of us looks particularly heroic. We are not always the men that women would like us to be. While ten stories is hardly statistically significant, I suspect that the issues and problems we raise are representative of a much broader population of men in the United States. Other countries and cultures might or might not be similar.

Much of what I learned these last few years, including from those willing to talk extensively—if not write—about their lives, caught me by surprise. First, while men are generally perceived as the uncommunicative gender, often stewing in their unhappiness, it is the women on these pages who are sometimes remote, angry and silent. Rage, guilt, anger, self-hatred and feelings of powerlessness are not gender specific, and can push anybody out of love with themselves and their partners.

Second, women are often accused of being disingenuous about their fears, doing everything to rationalize around them, but I came to believe that men are even more secretive. Even when they are being as honest as they can, there is something self-protecting, even self-censoring about men. It's as if, having been impostors for so long, many can't always tell the difference between the multiple masks they wear and their true identities.

Third, while many of these men fall out of love with their partners, sometimes their partners also fall out of love with them. Other men simply fail at keeping their relationships together. They lose the handle. Often it is for a very fundamental reason: they don't know how, or were never taught—or never took the time to learn—to relate to a woman in a day-to-day, intimate context. The socialization of women and their ability to process and communicate is often taken for granted by women. What comes naturally to them has to be learned by men.

Fourth, no matter whose behavior is the principal cause of a couple's unhappiness, it is usually the woman who leaves the man, and if married, initiates the divorce. Women are more likely to act to change their unhappiness while men tend to live with it. Men usually leave their relationships only when they've found another woman.

Fifth, struggling to understand why their relationships implode—and dealing with that pain—is not always a purely negative experience. For many men I spoke with, their journeys turned out to be a roller coaster of unimagined loops, twists and G-force curves, but by the end they were emotionally stronger and wiser. With new insights into themselves and their partners, their attitudes and behaviors became more positive.

Finally, one overall conclusion became clear: *if you understand why a man struggles with the notion of romantic love, why his relationships sometimes disappoint him, why he becomes unhappy and sometimes falls out of love—you gain some profound insights into men themselves.*

It can be argued that the origins of the emotions of disengagement start in childhood or early adolescence—perhaps at the same time young men first experience the emotions of falling *in* love. Falling in love is more than infatuation. It is the need to feel whole, to be healed, and to join together with someone heart and soul. In time, however, that same need can transform itself into the desire to tear apart, to reject, and to return to one's independence. The search for identity and happiness can mean a 180-degree turn on life's path.

9

Despite common belief, men don't fall out of love because one's girlfriend puts on thirty pounds, or a husband fights continually with his spouse over money, or someone's sexual needs are greater than his partner's. These kind of things are just the trip wires. Dig under the surface and one discovers in at least one of the partners (and sometimes both) feelings of abandonment, powerlessness, anger at one's caregivers, covert depression, a quest for validation, or a need to control. In addition, for some men any intimate bond is stressful—women make demands that they are unable or unwilling to meet—and except for their dependency on their partners, emotional and sexual, their relationships are inherently brittle. Whenever that dependency fades or vanishes, men are likely to fall out of love.

For many men, living with a controlling partner is one of love's principal assassins. Men are equally guilty of trying to control, but their efforts are rarely as sophisticated, subtle or pervasive; they are not as embedded in their gender "language" as they are for women. Possessing a mountain range of emotions, women have the ability to turn their feelings on and off, and jump from one to another, in the blink of an eye. Their control comes through interference, judgment, guilt, fault-finding, shaming or withholding affection—any of which can be conveyed in a tone of voice, a hand gesture, a hurt glance or a pregnant silence, just as much as with words. Yet many women are unconscious of what they do and the effect they have on their partners. That they can be intimidating to men comes as a surprise to them. Their self-image is so positive, and they are so supportive of one another, they think, how can strong men possibly be intimidated by caring women?

Are men, under the surface, just wimps? Perhaps few women have an in-depth understanding of masculinity, and even men aren't always sure how to define the "M" word. Women might think masculinity means guys crunching abs, having rugged good looks, acting like a gentleman, exhibiting confidence and independence, being competitive and successful, showing leadership, owning the skills of a great lover, or being emotionally strong. Men might add to that list being a fearless warrior, a survivor, a problem-solver, or just a breadwinner. The correlation between masculinity and fear is harder to grasp. If a man is honest, he will tell you that masculinity—a multi-dimensional reality that is passed from father-figure to son—is confusing, contradictory, and fraught with unrealistic expectations. Wanting to be "a man" leads one down the slippery path of repressed emotions, deceit, frustration, a fear of failure and, in some cases, a fear and distrust of women.

The ten men in this book, despite differences in the cultures in which they were raised, their ages, professions and socio-economic backgrounds, exhibit strong similarities in the way their emotions evolved. In telling their stories, they all said they learned something new about themselves and their partners. For the purpose of meeting a publishing deadline, these stories have an ending, but in real life they still go on. Growth is a constant.

While this book largely focuses on men and their views on relationships, the last two chapters are written for couples and, in particular, for women.

Not everyone will agree with what these men think and feel. Readers will have their own interpretations, just as I did, of the themes and issues presented in their stories. Perhaps this experience should be more about listening and understanding than judging or taking sides. I hope, however, that most readers will agree on one premise: conflicts that seem to come out of nowhere lie inside us, dormant from childhood, long before the first confrontation with our adult partners. So many men (and women) are emotional time bombs and don't know it.

Chapter Two

The Tyranny of Masculinity

For each man kills the thing he loves.

—*Oscar Wilde*

In the opening scene of Martin Scorcese's film *Aviator*, the nine- or ten-year-old Howard Hughes is being given a bath by his beautiful Victorian mother. They are alone in the room—he is standing naked before her—and the sensuality of the moment is palpable. As the mother caresses her son's chest and arms with a bar of soap, whispering to him, we sense his vulnerability as well as their mutual adoration. The mother seems in total control of the boy's emotions, and what she is telling him—to be afraid of people who have typhus and cholera—is reinforced when she asks him to spell the word "quarantine." After making sure he understands the danger of disease and germs, she adds, "you are not safe." The same bath scene is reprised at the end of the film, in the memory of the adult Hughes as he stares into a tarnished mirror. Here, his own faith in his ambition and genius is revealed. But his mother has already transfigured him with another message, something deeper and more primal than her faith and love. She has filled him with fear.

Hughes's adult life is a chronicle of one brazen accomplishment after another, proving to the world and himself that he is a superhero. Ever the perfectionist, he is as hard on himself as on those around him. He also tries to be perfect in order to push away his fears. At his core, however, the dark message from his mother prevails. He *is* afraid—of germs, of losing his mind, of rejection by those he loves, of having his weaknesses exposed to the public—but he can't make himself tell anyone. He tries with his principal love interest, Kate Hepburn, who reminds us in some ways of his mother. But Hughes is never totally candid with her. He thinks his problems will ultimately go away because, after all, he is the genius and hero who can conquer anything.

In the end, as in a Greek tragedy, Hughes's fears destroy him. The bar of soap he carries in his pocket (and uses on his hands until they bleed) is more than evidence of an obsessive/compulsive disorder or germ phobia: it is an ironic message that his problems are internal. Like many men who are boxed in by their fears, Hughes feels alone in the universe. He can't love any of the women he so badly wants to connect with because he can't trust them. He is afraid they will abandon him. Overwhelmed by his fears, he retreats emotionally and physically from the world. In his heart he kills almost everything he has loved. Only the beautiful, shiny planes he designs and flies are safe for his affection.

Like a lot of men, Hughes, rather than admit his fears, preferred to hide behind his women, his bravado, his achievements, and his definition of masculinity, which was to be a man of action. Any display of weakness, any admission of confusion, was quickly camouflaged by acts of reckless courage, indifference or denial. Any emotion that reflected vulnerability was the enemy. His life was not unlike the movies he made, which were essentially dramatizations of male fantasies.

As Goldberg, Real and Pittman all point out in their books, most men, until they reach a crisis—such as losing their jobs or marriages, becoming seriously ill, or being humiliated by scandal—will never seek help or in any way hint something is amiss. If a critical mass of desperation *is* reached, the real

13

problem begins. For some, experiencing a serious failure means the unraveling of their masculinity. Because most men have never fully developed or understood their emotions, too often they have no resources to draw on, no safety net, no knowledge of how to heal themselves. Women often turn to each other in a crisis while men stand alone because it is the "manly" or heroic thing to do. But behind their stoicism they feel backed into a corner. They don't know what to do with their pain. Cynicism, running away, shutting down, rage, depression, paranoia, drugs, alcohol, or even suicide become tempting escapes.

Men who know they *don't* have to stand alone are the same ones who refuse to shove their emotions under the table. They believe that their needs, while different from women's, are just as complex. Part of that complexity comes from their masculinity, whose multiple meanings and overarching importance cast a long shadow. Poorly understood, rarely challenged, full of taboos, masculinity is the cause of much misery—and hypocrisy. If it's all right for women to be afraid or anxious, or to talk about their failures, or seek help from one another, why shouldn't men do so with equal openness?

But for many men the territory of emotions is covered with "no trespassing" signs. They believe that women appropriate emotions from men to make feelings *their* club, from which, intentionally or unintentionally, men are excluded. (Many women have another point of view: in addition to their neurological and processing differences, their reliance on emotions is role playing that is handed down from their mothers, generation after generation, as part of the socialization process.) If men feel inadequate about accessing their emotions, perhaps it's because, generation after generation, they have consistently denied a basic truth: the first step on any journey of self-knowledge—any search for happiness—begins with admitting their weaknesses and fears.

The male taboo against confession, however, is a powerful one. Men usually confess to their partners only to quickly patch up their relationships (after all other strategies have failed), to get something in return, or to be dramatic and win attention—not to reveal their weaknesses. The same goes for men talking to men. Male friends who trust one another will often share their fears and anxieties, but most men prefer the safer, neutral ground of "guy talk." Analyzing why Peyton Manning is a better passer than Johnny Unitas, or comparing the new Cannon digital camera to the Sony, offers the comfort of familiarity and avoids conflict and the need for self-revelation.

Most men view the Women's Movement that was launched thirty-five years ago as an unprecedented vehicle for women, giving them power, confidence and upward professional mobility. Still, men have largely observed this phenomenon from the sidelines with clay feet. Some aspects of feminism—the values of caring, indulging and nurturing, for example—have positively influenced men as fathers. The so-called "softer male" who connects to his children is a huge advancement over the emotionally absent or stern father figures of a generation or two ago. Yet overall, feminism seems like a new planet in the solar system, spinning on a unique axis, its esoteric laws of gravity known only to half the population. Men usually have no idea what to do about it or where they fit in. Even though male-bashing appears on the wane, and there is a kinder, gentler post-feminism in the air, men still cling to the sidelines, nursing their questions like a bruise on the jaw. Will feminism ever go away? Who's behind the movement? What are "they" planning next? Why does it feel like women have taken power from us? But men think these thoughts in silence. Perhaps they fear ridicule if they speak up. All their questions, all that male inertia and passivity, may come from fear.

Due to the same passivity, stereotypes of male behavior and attitudes have not been challenged either. In most sitcoms and commercials, men are portrayed as they have been for decades: as adolescent skirt chasers, sports-obsessed beer drinkers, car fanatics, action movie addicts, gamblers, jealous competitors or, lately, preening metrosexuals. Except for sex, supposedly nothing gets men more aroused than the NFL or NBA playoffs, or how fast the new Porsche goes from 0 to 60. Popular culture would have us believe that men are predictable and easy to understand. In humorist Dave Barry's book, *Complete Guide to Guys* (as well as the movie based on the book), men live close to the surface, in the land of external pleasures, subject to the rogue waves of their testosterone and other male impulses. When they get in some kind of trouble, which is often, it is usually a woman who has to come to their rescue. Poor, dumb men can't seem to do anything right.

Humor is based on truth: a lot of men do like sports, cars, motorcycles, beautiful women, sex, guns, gambling, tinkering and fixing, and electronic gadgets. But when exaggerated or told too often, a joke becomes a stereotype. Barry's book, written ten years ago, seems today little more than a string of dated and often inaccurate clichés. But does anyone notice or object? It doesn't help men that no matter how they are portrayed, too many shrug off the barbs and caricatures to prove how stoical or superior they are. They want to show the world they are bullet-proof. These same men listen docilely when women claim they are still the underprivileged gender, fighting the unending battle for equality of one kind or another. Not to react is not to care, these men believe. In the end, their indifference and lack of awareness put them at a distance from reality. Except for in the workplace, most men I spoke with felt that women have already won the gender battle. Under the premise that control and leverage in any relationship is rarely 50/50, the vote went overwhelmingly in favor of women.

Those who *are* aware know how popular culture and the more radical brands of feminism have pigeonholed men for decades. They also know that even male "supremacy" in the office is an uncertain assumption. Excepting the power/money worlds of Wall Street, Hollywood, the military, government, sports and entertainment—male bastions to the bitter end, perhaps—the glass ceiling may one day be history. Equal pay for equal work, as well as sharing positions of authority—starting with white collar tiers and working down—depends to a great degree on women. How aggressively in the post-feminist age will they pursue a career path and, specifically, which careers? It's not hard to imagine the psychological barriers that would be lifted if a woman becomes President of the United States. But the seeds of change are already here. According to the U.S. Department of Education, for the last ten years colleges have bestowed more diplomas on women than on men, and the "diploma gap" only appears to be widening. In most graduate schools, including law and medicine, women are at parity with men or close to it. While feminist educators beat the drums that grade school and junior high school girls are still imperiled, the victims of curriculum or teacher bias, virtually every national test reveals that it's boys at this critical age who are slipping academically and are "the behind gender."

In the last twenty-five years, there have certainly been efforts by men's groups to speak up about who they are and what they think. Remember all those shirtless men beating drums in the woods, and later the Million Man March in Washington, D.C.? Herb Goldberg and Frank Pittman, among others, have advocated dismantling old stereotypes and building a more realistic, healthier model of male needs. Today, more men than ever gather to talk about issues and problems relevant to men—yet I suspect not nearly enough. No effort has been sustained that is remotely equivalent to the collective consciousness of the Women's Movement. Can it ever happen? To say that a full-fledged Men's Movement is impossible because men are too competitive, fearful, jealous and distrustful of each other begs the question. Those emotions and behaviors are their prison, the very problems from which a movement or group consciousness would liberate them. Perhaps it's time for men to step out of their cells, reevaluate what makes them happy, be more assertive about their feelings, and begin to help, not isolate, each other. That is the formula for self-healing, and a prerequisite to the birth of any movement.

Chapter Three

The Hidden Lives of Men

When we step into the family, by the act of being born, we do step into a world which is incalculable, into a world which has its own strange laws, into a world that could do without us, into a world we have not made. In other words, when we step into the family we step into a fairy tale.

—G. K. Chesterton

The ten stories in this book offer a variety of opinions on why men struggle with love. One insight, hardly ground-breaking but seminal, is that once they are in a committed relationship, many women find their core emotional needs have been met. Until significant problems arise with their partners, they will think twice about abandoning the nest, particularly if it includes children. For a man, however, the nest and its boundaries send a mixed message almost from the beginning. On the one hand, there is the idea of "growing up" and "settling down" and having a family—a primary definition of masculinity. On the other hand, most men, at some level, are inherently uncomfortable in a committed relationship, even if they are content with their partners.

As feelings of being in love give way to the daily routine of living together, many men become conscious of the limitations on their freedom. What a woman may happily define as "security" and "comfort" often come without the consent of a man's hormones. Perhaps he understood the theory of giving up his freedom before entering a serious relationship, but the reality is another matter. For many, suppressing their attraction to other women comes at the price of finding fault with their partners or themselves, retreating into passive-aggressive behaviors, or wanting to escape from their relationships whenever possible. Men like this may simply not be emotionally ready for a serious commitment, but even when they are ready, their hormonal and psychological differences mean a need for exploration and a certain amount of freedom.

As hoary a stereotype as it may be, this is a basic definition of a hunter-gatherer. This does not imply a license to pursue relationships with other women, but it does mean finding healthy outlets for independence, self-assertion and emotional fulfillment. Whether that outlet is creative, spiritual or physical, men in this endeavor need to be held *not* accountable to their partners. They need to have *their* world, private and unfettered, where they are not judged or stereotyped. Psychologists have written for years on the need for men and women to keep growing emotionally outside of their primary relationships. In the last generation or two, women have learned the value of growth through independence, but men appear to be far less confident and adventurous, as if they don't trust their instincts or have a fear of screwing up. Do they do this to themselves, or do they allow their partners to restrict their freedom? If opportunities for self-assertion and growth are cut off by an overly controlling relationship, or simply by a lack of awareness on a man's part, falling out of love may be the result.

While they may appear confident and in control, many men, based on their childhood and adolescence, have significant abandonment issues. Some are so sensitive to rejection that they have a latent fear that the women they fall in love with will ultimately turn against them, or simply change and become a stranger to them. In order to avoid rejection, some will emotionally disengage from their partners before their partners do the same to them. Our fear of abandonment is nothing new. In the Bible, Job, a good man who was afflicted with one ill fortune after another, felt deserted by God. In *Aviator*, it can be argued that because Hughes had a dysfunctional connection to his mother, his descent into madness was fed in part by repeated rejections from women. That men can go mad if they don't find love is not an exaggeration, but losing love may be even more painful. The adage that "it is better to have loved and lost than never to have loved at all" would be disputed by a lot of men.

While they rarely admit it, most men do not deal well with pain, emotional or physical. Neurologically, they are simply not equipped in the same way women are. In the film *Million Dollar Baby,* one of the themes is how the characters cope with the pain of isolation and abandonment. The trainer, Frankie, and his protégé boxer, Maggie, gravitate to each other from pasts filled with rejection. The love and respect they find for one another— he becomes her father figure, and she becomes his surrogate daughter—is ultimately tested by a tragic ring accident. Physical suffering, especially for Maggie, is not easy, but the emotional pain for each of the characters is what is most devastating. "Girlie tough ain't enough," Frankie says to Maggie at the start of the film, but by the end of the story we know that girlie tough is a lot more formidable than male tough. Maggie can handle her suffering. Her death is noble because she's found her redemption—she knows who she is, and she did what she wanted with her life—while Frankie remains passive and tormented, unsure that his life has amounted to anything. He may be a Catholic buried in the ritual of suffering, but first and foremost he is a man struggling with his emotions. Feeling more abandoned than ever after Maggie's death, he sends himself into exile, looking for redemption.

When a man fails in his relationship, he too looks for redemption. Initially, out of anger, he may fault his partner for the breakup. But in the end he points a finger at himself. He wonders what he did wrong and what he can do about it. It can be argued that women are less likely to accuse themselves of making a mistake, and if they admit it, they are more forgiving of themselves, or they seek out friends to exonerate and support them. Otherwise, many women tend to blame men, and why not? It is not difficult to jump on the bandwagon of male-bashing if men are already in the driver's seat. A common scene in movies and books is the repentant male bearing flowers and asking forgiveness of his partner for an argument that was surely his fault. But how often do women bring flowers to men?

Why do men beat themselves up? If no one is going to offer support or forgive them (unlike women, men do not usually rally around another man in trouble; instead, they isolate him), they have to atone by themselves. The more *mea culpas*, the better. The fact that a man doesn't understand what went wrong in his relationship doesn't mitigate self-blame. If anything, his ignorance only makes him feel more guilty. For a lot of men, any kind of failure is their fault. A man thinks he has somehow let himself down or someone he loves, or in his mind disappointed his childhood caregivers, or failed some test of masculinity. Surely he is guilty of something.

Feelings of inferiority or inadequacy are not uncommon in men. Despite outward displays of confidence, some secretly brand themselves losers. This feeling starts in adolescence when boys are first out to prove themselves and are the most vulnerable. Determined to "become a man," they will often set impossibly high standards for themselves. As they experience the inevitable failures of trying to measure up, they devise intricate, often ingenious schemes to be judged a success by their peers and particularly by girls. Males learn to be cover-up artists, even con artists, at this hyper-competitive, hyper-sensitive age. "Winning" a girl over even by artifice and deceit is condoned because without a girlfriend many boys feel stigmatized. It's the kind of stigma—and pain—that sometimes leads to isolation and depression, so lies, or stretching the truth, are easy to rationalize. More than being a sports star or having money or being good looking, having a girl on his arm can mean the ultimate peer approval for a young man.

Behind his "victory," however, he often has a nagging feeling that he doesn't really know what he's doing, that he's a fake, that it's wrong to lie, and that at any moment his doubts and duplicity will be exposed to the world. Many men carry this fear and self-doubt into their adult lives, their professions and their relationships, no matter how successful their lives appear to be. Some are driven to succeed by the very fear of being exposed.

Like my friend who thought he had fallen out of love, a man can feel woefully inadequate when things go wrong and he tries to "fix" his relationship. He often has no clue where to start. As almost every child psychologist recognizes, male children and adolescents are not encouraged to indulge their emotions. They're encouraged to achieve, including, eventually, a successful adult relationship. If that relationship fails, no matter whose fault it is, a man's entire world can come to a grinding halt. Feeling dejected and isolated, he may, like many men in this book, see a therapist and be given a strategy to unravel the mysteries that overwhelm him. Left to his own devices, however, anger, guilt and frustration usually take over. Most men, rather than admit their pain and unhappiness, would rather joke about their "confinement" and doubts about having chosen the right partner than deal with any problem straight up. If they do find the courage to confront their partners, they prefer an instant, linear and rational solution—a traditional masculine approach to problem solving. To struggle with nuance, introspection, and the multiple dimensions of "emotional reasoning" that women employ is perceived by most men as a waste of time. The truth is that it's not a waste of time but that men are simply not good at it. "Emotional reasoning" is a skill that is natural to women but has to be learned by men. Unfortunately, most men are unwilling or unable to learn it.

Without the natural flexibility and patience to problem solve, many men just give up on their relationships. They would rather walk out and lock the door to their pasts than be scrutinized by their partners, or dive into their private ocean of anger, pain and guilt. Women give up on their relationships too—perhaps more often than men—but usually without suffering the same stigma. Women are liberating themselves; men are seen as being irresponsible. In fact, the problem is both more simple and more complex: a man who does not understand or feel comfortable with himself, who was never nurtured as a child, will almost inevitably wilt under the responsibility of a relationship or a family. He may not necessarily run away, but neither will he find deep satisfaction or meaning in his most intimate relationship. Men will often live with their unhappiness and confusion, sometimes unaware there even is a problem, until their partners let them know. Men are the emperors of denial.

There are many stories by women about why they leave their husbands, partners or lovers, but few by men who head for the exits. Are they moving on simply to be with another woman? Are they just tired of their partners? Are they filled with so much anger, depression or confusion that they don't know what else to do but leave? Maybe they just never got the approval they were looking for. For men, falling *in* love seems relatively straightforward. It usually starts with physical attraction and infatuation, followed by an emotional connection, then attachment, trust and, as the relationship matures, a sense of responsibility. Falling out of love is usually more gradual, complex, and deeply unsettling, not just for its emotional impact but because of the subtle, dimly understood reasons behind it.

The thief who steals love is another being who lives inside us. Perhaps he is the child we once were and then abandoned without his consent. In my case, it was the child who was never given the time, opportunity or encouragement to speak for himself. The thief is also the prison of our masculinity; the values of popular culture; our passive willingness to accept male stereotypes; our struggle to find healthy role models; the conscious and unconscious behavior of our women partners; and, not least, the difference between how men and women think and communicate.

* * * * *

So why *do* men fall out of love, or simply fail to maintain their relationships? These *six key reasons* are explored in depth in the chapters that follow.

- *Childhood issues of anger and loss, and the need for reconnection*
- *Masculinity issues of identity, power and fear*
- *Popular culture's emphasis on conformity, happiness and commercialism*
- *Male stereotypes that contradict who we really are and what we want*
- *Behaviors and attitudes of our female partners*
- *Processing and communication differences between men and women*

In the next ten chapters, we meet ten men who tell the stories of how their most intimate relationships ran into trouble. After each chapter is a *summary and interpretation* of the points they raise. Most of the interpretation is my own, and sometimes extends beyond the stories to gender issues. Because the reasons for falling out of love are inevitably layered and overlapping, each story is hard to categorize by a single theme. Nevertheless, here are four shoals on which relationships, like rudderless ships, tend to flounder and sink:

- *Sex and intimacy*
- *Validation and self-esteem*
- *Control and perfection*
- *Loss of attraction*

No doubt there are other danger zones, but these four *relationship busters*—and the two or three stories in each category—help illuminate the *six key reasons* listed above.

PART TWO

SEX AND INTIMACY

Chapter Four

Steven's Story

Sex is one of the nine reasons for reincarnation.
The other eight aren't important.

—Henry Miller

It's a fall Saturday night in southern New Mexico, crisp and cool with a dusting of snow on the mountains. Steven, twenty-eight years old, facing yet another argument with his girlfriend, Renee, has simply walked out of the house, refusing to deal with her. A real estate agent with a college degree in history, Steven has well-defined shoulders, an olive complexion, and wavy black hair. His grin is infectious, as is his personality. He's normally happy and outgoing, but tonight he's ready to throw in the towel over Renee. They have been living together for several years, getting to know each other and building their relationship, but lately the issue of physical intimacy has become a battleground. Renee is a bubbly, cute brunette with pensive blue eyes and a sexy giggle. She talks often about wanting to get married, an idea Steven first agreed to—indeed, he was the one to bring it up—but now he's not so sure. He feels there's been

27

a major change in Renee over the last year. Her interest in sex has almost disappeared. Not like the early days, when neither could wait to jump into bed. Now Steven has to beg Renee to take a shower together or to devote Saturday night to fun and games. When he asks what the problem is, Renee says the only problem is that Steven is too demanding—sometimes he even intimidates her. When they get into a really serious argument she makes the charge that he's oversexed, as if it's a disease, which makes Steven feel self-conscious, almost ashamed. He wonders if Renee, having gotten the promise of marriage, was only using sex as a lure and basically gets no pleasure from it. He also had an affair early in their relationship— during a period when he and Renee had broken up—but he told her the truth when they got back together. Even though he apologized, he thinks this is something for which Renee has never completely forgiven him.

"I need sex not just because I'm horny," he told her tonight before leaving, "but because it makes me feel good about myself, as a man, as a lover, as someone who hopefully has the gift of bringing pleasure to a woman. When you won't have sex with me, how do you think that makes me feel? How am I supposed to stay in love with you if there's no intimacy?"

* * * * *

Steven was born and grew up in a tiny, mostly Hispanic town in southern New Mexico. It's the kind of place where everyone you pass on the road raises his hand off the steering wheel to wave. Today the town has "swollen" to around 5,000 but the native culture remains virtually unchanged. Steven's family has lived in this small town for five generations, and Steven is the first to earn a college degree. His mom is a housewife and his dad is an auto mechanic. Thirty years ago his dad was a dashing Hell's Angel on a chrome bike who swept Steven's eighteen-year-old mom off her feet. Their domestic life has had its ups and downs, Steven says. After graduating from college, Steven moved to a larger city where he eventually went into real estate sales and earned a six-figure income. For a self-described "small-town boy," he is understandably proud of his successes, including buying his first home while still in his twenties. He makes friends easily, and women in particular find him intuitive and sympathetic. In his past relationships, he's always seen himself as someone willing to learn from his mistakes. In his committed relationship with Renee, however, he now faces tests he's never had, and wonders what lessons he still has to learn.

* * * * *

"Life in my hometown is slow, easygoing and friendly, but with a great suspicion of outsiders. Children are encouraged not to leave when they grow up. Traditionally, your parents will give you a small parcel of land, cutting off a piece of their own, and you're expected to buy your own doublewide, have babies, then repeat the whole cycle with your kids. In the Hispanic culture the past is more important than the future. My parents still live in the same mobile home where I was born. I would say that about seventy or eighty percent of the families who live in my town have been here for five or six generations. Hunting elk and deer in season, fishing, drinking with your buddies—that's what men have always done around here.

"I could say a lot about the values of 'my people,' good and bad, but I've learned to accept their resistance to change, their strong family ties, and their utter lack of ambition. I like to tell the story of one girl from a local family who

29

was an academic star, got almost perfect SATs, and was accepted at more than one Ivy League school. This is a rare, almost unheard of achievement for anyone from my town. Her parents and relatives viewed her success with great suspicion and discomfort. Instead of commending Linda for her odds-defying accomplishments, the general attitude was, 'What, Linda, going to a fancy college, you think you're better than us? You want to shame your brothers and sisters? You want to leave us…why? What's wrong with you?' She didn't shame her family, obviously, they shamed her. To Linda's credit, she left for college and rarely came home again. Fundamentally, mine is a closed, jealous, and insecure culture. Like a bunch of crabs in a bucket. When one tries to crawl out, the others grab it and pull it back in.

"My relationship with my dad was one more of intimidation than intimacy. He was definitely not someone 'in touch with his emotions.' I remember when I was around ten I accidentally shot the window of a passing truck with my BB gun. Dad witnessed the event and grew furious. He was sure I had done it on purpose. He broke the gun over his knee, hit me with it, and then threw the barrel at me as I was running away. 'It was an accident,' I screamed. But he didn't see it that way, or maybe his anger came from embarrassment. He had little patience for my mistakes and misbehavior, and believed that swift and strict punishment was the most effective way to teach a lesson and to make a boy into a man. At the time I feared and disliked him, especially when he drank and came home late at night. Then the most petty thing could set off his temper. But I didn't know enough to judge him. I thought all fathers in my town did this kind of thing.

"When I went elk hunting with dad, sometimes he deliberately left me in a distant valley and expected me to find my way back to camp. That was his test of manhood for me. I had to prove I was self-sufficient. I remember breaking down in tears more than once, yet after a number of these episodes I learned that it was pointless to wallow in self-pity, and I knew I had to be tough and help myself. That was the extent of my intimacy with my dad—his teaching me 'life's lessons.' He didn't do a lot of talking. Once in a while, spirits bolstered by a few beers, he would open up and tell me he loved me. Yet the next day he was back to his rigid, remote self.

"My mom was just the opposite. She was open and honest and purposefully nurturing. She gave me dolls for gifts, put me to work in the kitchen, and because I was an asthmatic she would rub my chest with Vic's and make sure I always had a humidifier in my room. This drove Dad crazy. He didn't mind me learning to cook, but washing dishes was 'women's work,' and he accused Mom of babying me with my asthma. While my mom disciplined me when I misbehaved, it was always a constructive kind of punishment—consistent and in control—and she would give explanations about what was right and wrong. She didn't spoil me, but I definitely developed my feminine side from the honesty and tenderness she shared with me. To this day I'm much closer to her than my dad. I also learned compassion and respect for women, though that message would get buried under my father's narrow interpretation of male-female relationships, especially during my adolescence.

"When I was around fourteen, my mom and I found out Dad was having an affair. Mom was hurt and shaken. When I asked why she didn't ask for a divorce, she said, 'Oh, I wouldn't do that, I love your father.' Maybe that was true, or maybe she was just afraid to leave Dad, or she didn't want a confrontation with him, or she was just too dependent on him. I'm still not sure. But what had the biggest impact on me was her reaction of acceptance. This

31

gave me the impression that it was okay for men to be disloyal to women—including me with my girlfriends—because either you'd be forgiven by the girl, or your behavior just wasn't that important to them.

"Around the same time, one night my dad, drunk, took me aside to tell me about 'the birds and the bees.' Being a hunter, he chose the metaphor 'bucks and does.' I don't know why he suddenly felt this need to be my sex education instructor—Mom had already told me everything—but he went on and on about how I needed to be 'the big buck,' and that way I could 'get all the does I wanted, and that would teach them respect.' This was Dad's attitude toward women. Just be the buck. Don't worry about any subtle communications, or kindness, or sharing emotions. Just dominate and you won't have any problems.

"The compassion and values I learned from my mom were quickly challenged by my junior high school peer group. Most of my friends were more like my dad. Women were objects put on this earth for the pleasure of men. If you were a teenage boy, this meant a lot of 'grabbing' girls wherever one could find temporary privacy. In general, I caved in to my friends and followed their lead. Incredibly, I thought, the girls didn't mind. They seemed to expect and want this crude behavior, as if they had been brought up with the same values and attitudes as my father. I didn't wonder about it then, but now I think this was the behavior they'd seen with their older sisters and girlfriends, and their fathers simply condoned it while their mothers stayed silent.

"In my high school, sports was the major rite of passage for boys and could be either a salvation or a curse. Salvation because they're a testosterone release, and they also teach teamwork and strategy, skills you definitely can use as an adult. Also, in many ways they are a validation of male values: skill, power, success, and the importance of winning. For a young man, these become the benchmarks of self-esteem. I was gifted athletically so that's where my self-esteem came from. Consciousness of emotions— beyond the 'high' you get from winning—plays no useful role in this scheme, and this is the dark side of sports. Those who aren't good enough to make a team are often ostracized or labeled as losers; those who do make the team are continually judged and under pressure to live up to expectations. Another downside is you can't show vulnerability or pain. Instead you learn to suck it up. Contrast this with 'female values' and the perception that emotions are the fundamental way of communicating. Women let you know right away that emotions are their domain and men are simply not equipped to communicate on this level. Men get the message—so a lot of us don't even bother showing our emotions. I think this reticence has a lot to do with sports and competition. If a man knows he can't win in one area, he is conditioned not to complain (he'll be judged a wimp) but simply to try something else where he will be successful.

"Because I was a major jock, yet pretty down to earth, I was popular with both guys and girls. I particularly enjoyed hanging with girls. By the time I reached high school I dropped my old male friends because they were still behaving immaturely. I adopted a whole new image. Part of being popular in my school was to have as many girlfriends as possible; consecutively or simultaneously, it didn't seem to matter. Of course, the ultimate achievement was to take a girl to bed. Yet as much as I wanted to have sex, there was something in me that just wasn't ready. Maybe it was a lack of understanding of what a girl wanted; maybe it was a fear of my untested sexual abilities. There was another inhibition that plagued me as well. I would walk away from easy opportunities to sleep with a girl because I'd suddenly have this incredible guilt. Because of my mom, I wanted to do the honorable thing with a girl, and exploiting her for sex didn't meet that definition.

"In the end, however, I lost my virginity to a girl who was crazy about me, and no doubt I exploited that devotion. After all, adoration is a kind of hedge against your own insecurities. We were both drunk and virgins so I didn't have to fear being ridiculed for being any more inept than she was. While the sex seemed exciting at the moment, the next day there was regret on both our parts. We decided to try it again, sober, but this time the experience was dry, awkward and mechanical. We never dated again. Looking back, I know now that a lack of emotion can make sex seem almost like punishment.

"Each of my parents had a voice in my head. The tension from listening to both of them at the same time could be paralyzing. By the time I graduated from high school, however, my dad's view of relationships—the great buck standing supreme—was winning the day. My pursuit of as many girls as I could attract was such a strong impulse that even then I saw I would have difficulty in the future with commitment to one partner. Part of this came from my enormous need for validation, which, I think now, stemmed from a fear that had unintentionally been instilled by my dad. I didn't have confidence that I could do anything in my life unless Dad had specifically taught me that skill, like fixing a car, or hunting, or building a shed. On the one hand, he had made me tough and independent, yet that world of 'street smarts' was so circumscribed that I had little confidence to try anything new. Dad had never taught me, or I had never learned, to understand the intangibles and subtleties of life: like how and when to take risks, or knowing the limits of ambition, or believing that the universe outside my small town was worth exploring. My dad's world was almost completely tactile; the emotional, the abstract, and the world of ideas were of no use to him.

"Even though I was a basketball star, I didn't get enough validation from sports. You could be a god one moment, but if you screwed up there was always someone to replace you, and suddenly you were feeling bad about yourself. Girls were the ultimate source of approval, the ones that truly counted. Maybe I wanted more of the nurturing emotions that my mother gave me. Most men I know are hungry for emotion. It's really why they're attracted to women. They think the attraction is to physical beauty—and at first it might be—but ultimately they want and need emotional support, and the more the better. If you ask me, that's the main reason you fall in love.

"My relationships took on a pattern. Bursts of bliss followed by disappointment. I would bask in a girl's admiration, exploit that admiration, get her to make out passionately or take her to bed, then be clueless about what to do next. I didn't know how to communicate emotionally, though I was intuitive enough to understand that this is what it took to sustain a relationship. But rather than make that effort, I simply went on to another girl, thinking that this time it would be better.

"During my senior year I got into a relationship that opened a new door to self-understanding. Lizzie was from North Carolina—an exotic fact in its own right if you're from New Mexico—and more mature than I. The excitement to me was that Lizzie became my emotional anchor, more of a friend than a romantic interest and, most importantly, a link to the outside world that I definitely wanted to join. I'm not sure what made me want to turn my back, at least partially, on the cultural values of my small town, but I've always had this inherent curiosity about the world and what makes people act the way they do. Lizzie fed me volumes of information about the South and its values. I was more attracted to her than any girl I had slept with. I didn't exactly open up to her about my deepest feelings, but I could hang with Lizzie and not think about other girls. She made me think about the future and what I wanted out of life.

"At the end of my senior year, I entered into another relationship with a girl named Trisha. I was beginning to see how emotions worked for girls. It was like a universal language for them. I couldn't explain the specifics of the language—what was the equivalent of an alphabet or rules of grammar—but just from intuition I could decode parts of it. Trisha was even more mature than Lizzie, and almost immediately pulled me into her life with the message that she needed me. She never said it specifically but I felt it. She didn't care that I'd been a big jock or that I had a sense of humor or that I was reasonably good looking. What counted was that I was the one who understood her. Without exactly saying so, she wanted me to provide comfort and reassurance to her whenever she needed it. Physically she was frail, and her eyes always hinted at an unspecified pain. And the mystery of that pain only made her more attractive and intriguing to me. She was choosing me, empowering me to help her. She was giving me a kind of power that didn't relate to my achievements or any other high school value. Even more alluring, she was asking me to give her the same kind of emotions that I wanted from her. I didn't mind. The act of giving satisfied me on a very deep level.

"The lesson for me was that the more a woman needs you, the better you feel about yourself. Maybe I was susceptible to this kind of thinking because I had such large validation needs, but Trisha was also a master at showing her affection and appreciation at the right time and in the right way. The sex was incredible because it came from a deep emotional place, at least for me. Was this love or manipulation on Trisha's part? I don't know. I don't know if Trisha even knew. This pattern was just part of her nature. As we dated that summer, I began to think she really loved me and would never abandon me. I began to think I was indispensable to her, that she would always be part of my life. And the more she needed me, the more I needed her. She had created dependency.

"That fall Trisha went off to college, and within a month she wrote me that she had met someone else who was more mature, more exciting to her and, by implication, better served her needs. And she stopped communicating with me. Period. Just like that. It was my first 'Dear John' experience and I was totally caught off guard. I was devastated, in fact. I had taken for granted Trisha's devotion to me—taken for granted there was something wonderful and special about me—but suddenly I questioned everything. Had Trisha just used me? Was I really so special? I began to wonder who I really was, how I should define myself, beyond being a jock and a guy who easily attracted women. How could I trust any relationship unless I knew who I was?

"One thing was clear. I could no longer live off the fumes of high school success. The second thing, even clearer, was that while I had an inkling of how powerful the language of emotions was for women, how well it served their needs, it seemed to me that men were at a disadvantage. We didn't know the language. Soon I had another insight: one reason women ended relationships was because they didn't get the emotional support they needed, or they suddenly got their emotional needs met by someone new in a different way. What was less obvious was how and when their needs changed. Trisha didn't drop a clue that I was going to be out of her life. Did she know ahead of time, or did her needs just change one day, surprising even her? She never shared her emotional processing with me, so how was I supposed to figure it out? It seems to me that instead of explaining themselves to men, women prefer to complain about how unemotional and uncommunicative men are, and that becomes their excuse for jumping to another man.

"It took almost a year to get over losing Trisha. One day I ran into a former classmate, Melinda, who had always been a friend. I asked her to lunch and we talked about our lives. Out of high school now, I had my first full-time job. While I was enjoying being independent, socially I was pretty lonely. Over the next few months, as I started dating Melinda, I began to develop deeper feelings for her. I was so comfortable, so trusting. One night, kissing her in the car, I thought I was falling in love. At times she could be negative, and never once did she pay for anything—that was the man's job, she said—but I didn't care. The more Melinda said she needed me, the more secure I felt and the more I opened up about my past, including plenty of details, such as the times I took advantage of girls in high school. I wanted to be totally honest. I thought that the act of confession was the only way to get rid of my insecurities and fears, and to create a bond between us. Our lovemaking was unbelievable, but our conversations afterwards were even better. I was hoping that Melinda would be just as candid with me, but as the months went on I noticed I was doing more talking and Melinda was doing most of the listening. Something felt wrong.

"Then Melinda gave me a not-so-subtle hint. I had been too candid with her, she implied. I was giving her more information than she wanted to hear. But it was too late. I couldn't take it back. Melinda was judging me by my past, not by the fact that I was changing from a misguided teenager to someone trying to develop into a well-rounded human being. She was thinking, hey, is this the type of guy I can trust and rely on as my permanent partner? She finally came out and admitted that my volatile past and old values were a turn-off, and she ended the relationship.

"I was beside myself. I was in love with this woman, and here was another rejection. I cried on and off for days. I even thought of suicide. I couldn't talk to anyone without feeling monstrously betrayed by Melinda, or just stupid. Both Trisha and Melinda had come on to me as vulnerable and fragile—yet in the end they seemed to have grown stronger while I was the fragile one.

"My mom tried to console me, but it was months before I felt half-way normal. I later learned that Melinda had done some pretty crazy things in her past, which really threw me. Not because I didn't approve. I just wondered how Melinda could have remained silent about her past when I had been so candid about mine. Maybe she had too many fears, or she felt too ashamed.

"Two failed relationships in a row made me look at myself even more critically. I always had the habit of blaming myself when things went wrong—whether it was a basketball game or a fight with my father. I think a lot of men are inclined to think this way because that's how they're brought up. You're told you're 'the man of the house' and therefore responsible for everything. At least that's the way it is in my culture. Somehow I had screwed up these opportunities with these women. Now I had to re-examine myself and my values. To change my life I enrolled in college. Five years later I had earned a degree in history.

"One afternoon I met a woman, Renee, at the college fitness center. She asked me to help design an exercise program for her. I was 23 and she was 27, but I didn't think of her as an 'older woman.' First, Renee looked younger than I, and second, she was beautiful, which seemed to transcend any age issue. In my typical pattern, I also intuited something vulnerable about Renee. As we got to know each other better, I learned that she was recently divorced, had a four-year-old son, and was in an unhappy relationship with her current boyfriend. She had also lost her father the year before. The message I got was that she was emotionally alone in the world—and here I was, ready to play hero again. That made me nervous. I didn't want to set myself up for more disappointment and pain. But Renee was a great flirt, sweet, bubbly, kind. There were sparks between us right away. I began to wonder: was I a magnet for this kind of woman, or was it the other way around? Or was it both?

"My resistance soon crumbled. Here was a woman whose emotional 'scent' was even stronger than Melinda's and Trisha's, and I got totally drawn in. She would sneak out on her boyfriend to meet me for dinner or a drink, then she finally broke up with him. Soon we were having sex, and the next thing I knew, Renee told me that she was in love with me. This was only two months after we'd met. I wasn't sure if I was in love with Renee. But when a woman says she loves you and you don't want to lose her, you'll end up telling her that you love her too. I mean, you can't say, 'hey, let me think about it.' You could lose the girl in a second. So you hedge your bet. A lot of guys I know do that. It happened to me in high school when I was trying to get a girl into bed and she said, 'I know you love me.' You end up saying more or less what she wants to hear. Women don't always seem to understand a man's mentality. When it suits their purpose, women will take your words literally, even when they intuit that you might be lying. They'll take those four little words—'I love you too'—and infer a deep and complex system of commitment to them, way beyond what you're feeling.

40

"As I got to know Renee, I found her more and more irresistible. I was always proud to have her on my arm in public. Other men were jealous of me, and that jealousy just validated my taste. I know I have a hang-up about approval, and I like adrenaline, and when that combination comes in the form of a beautiful, sweet, admiring woman who whispers in your ear and takes you to bed, you are, by definition, in a state of bliss. Everything about Renee seemed spontaneous and innocent. But looking back, I think she knew how she was presenting herself. It wasn't as spontaneous as it felt. She would tell me almost anything that she knew would 'hook me.' Because of Trisha and Melinda, I'm sure I was conscious of Renee's manipulation on some level, but my doubts paled compared to the emotions that Renee aroused in me. I accepted her female aura. When a woman wants something, her ability to communicate that need, including through her sexuality, is an incredible gift. I sucked up all her love and adoration with delirious gratitude. I also liked her son, Joey, even though my male friends warned me about dating someone with a young child. If there's a fight between Renee and me over her boy, I was advised, don't expect Renee to take my side.

"The more I became involved with Renee, the more I realized I couldn't live without her. I was falling in love again, and unlike Melinda, Renee was a positive person. She urged me to continue with school and supported my ambition to become a real estate agent. She didn't care about my immature past. She seemed to love me for exactly who I was. She was a strong, confident, moral woman who I respected. I decided that it was Renee I wanted to marry.

"So one romantic evening I suggested the idea of marriage. Renee just looked at me, gave me a kiss, and said no. I was stunned. How could this be happening? Was this a

41

repeat of Trisha and Melinda? She wasn't rejecting my proposal for any emotional reasons, I soon learned, but for practical ones. Renee was about to leave her job and go back to college and had little money, except what she borrowed from her mom. How was I going to support her? Where were we going to live? Did I really love her son Joey? She had thought this all out. I was an impulsive romantic—anything to lock her in place, just like my dad had done with my mother—a sort of a 'tie them up' mentality. But Renee wouldn't have it. Burned in her first marriage, I figured, she was a lot wiser and more cautious now.

"I deferred to her wisdom. I wanted Renee, so I thought I would wait till I had my degree and a job. I wanted to make her happy. But as time went on and Renee started school, we settled into a routine that I found frustrating. I had begun working in real estate and had no problem attracting clients. Suddenly I was making good money. It was time to get married, I told her proudly. But Renee kept adding qualifications. She wanted to finish school, wanted Joey to get closer to me, wanted us to know each other inside out. Then she suggested a certain type of engagement ring. I told her I would love to give it to her but I couldn't afford it just yet. Renee insisted the ring was an important statement—it proved my commitment to her—so she would wait. Clearly, she didn't want to marry me. I wouldn't figure out why for another year.

"Time passed. Every day I was growing more confident about my work and the prospects of a solid financial future. Renee seemed to be on cruise control. She graduated from college but she was no closer to tying the knot with me. If anything, she wanted to slow things down. I think, looking back, that she saw my growing confidence, my interaction with new clients, including single women, and felt threatened. She was beginning not to trust me.

She was also becoming defensive. She tried to make me jealous by talking about guys she had met in college, but after my experiences with Trisha and Melinda I had built up immunity to that ploy. Renee would also find reasons not to have sex with me, as if she thought that would make me more dependent on her. But all it did was make me angry. Whenever I suggested that she had a problem with sex, and maybe it had something to do with trust, and that she should get some help, she would walk out of the room.

"What Renee didn't realize was that the more defensive and distrusting she grew, the less attractive she was to me. But I had a hard time telling her. By nature I don't like confrontation or delivering bad news. I think I got that quality from my mom. It's one of my major weaknesses, getting my emotions out—especially my anger—in a constructive way. I don't want to get out of control like my father, get drunk, and blow up at somebody. At this time Renee and I were also having serious discussions about Joey: how he should be raised, forms of discipline, activities to do together. I pointed out that while Renee was a great mother in many ways, she was spoiling Joey by not enforcing some system of chores, and often letting him get away with petulant behavior. That upset Renee. She reminded me that Joey was her child. I suddenly remembered what my friends had told me. She thought I was attacking her for being a bad mother, but I was only trying to give her another perspective.

"Rather than argue with Renee, I would just leave the house. That always made her furious. I didn't realize then how deep Renee's fears of abandonment ran. The more I learned about her ex-husband—he was the one who initiated the divorce—and her previous boyfriends who had also split with her, I began to see how fragile Renee was. However, instead of this making me love her more, which was my usual response to a woman who had been hurt, I was getting turned off. Perhaps I was too conscious of my own needs. Renee was impressing me now as someone who, because of her fears, was becoming so self-protecting that she was giving nothing back to me. It got to a point where I couldn't say anything that was even slightly critical of her or Joey. And she was so possessive. One time I told her how my old friends were complaining that I never spent time with them, that I was always with her. Renee asked me if I was sure I had my priorities straight. I hated that kind of control.

"The issue about how to raise Joey came up repeatedly. I began to see something in Renee that I hadn't noticed in the beginning. Joey was Renee's security blanket. He was the one male in her life who would never reject her, and she didn't want anything to jeopardize that relationship. If Joey and I spent a lot of time together, I think Renee was afraid I might do something to pull him away from her. Little arguments began to mushroom into bigger ones. My emphasis was on exposing Joey to the real world, not harshly like my father had done with me, but with plenty of support. Renee, on the other hand, wanted to protect Joey from anything that she was afraid of. And Renee, it would turn out, had lots of fears.

"At some point I began to withdraw emotionally. I wasn't making any progress in the relationship. I felt I knew Renee as well as I'd known any woman in my life. There was a lot to love about her, but she hadn't made the same effort to get to understand me, or value what I had to say. I felt taken for granted. After four years together, I wanted to break up. I told Renee I was giving up too much of myself, too much of my freedom, in order to make her happy. She wasn't making me happy back. I was particularly frustrated in trying to help her with Joey. Renee was teary, and then in the blink of an eye she was furious. Hadn't I promised her that I loved her and wanted to marry her, she asked. This implied a deep level of commitment that morally I wasn't allowed to break. I was dumbfounded. I had tried to marry her but she kept putting me off. How long was I supposed to wait? It didn't matter what I argued back. Renee was convinced that by breaking up I was betraying her and her trust, maybe just like all the other men in her life.

"I know I made things worse when I started dating another woman, but why would I hang around Renee if she was only making me feel bad about myself? And, intentionally or not, she was a master at that. When Renee found out about this new woman in my life, she said I had broken my promise of commitment to her. I had taken advantage. I was letting Joey down. And hadn't she been the one to push me to get my college degree and go into real estate? Renee wouldn't stop. I began to feel terrible. The amazing thing about guilt is that it really works. If you're bombarded with it enough, you're inclined to surrender. And women can dish it out more effectively than men. Call it a method of control. It's such an effective weapon because a lot of men don't know how to deflect it.

"Renee and I stayed apart for about three months before reconciling. A year later we bought a house together and most of the time now we get along well. But I sense a strong undercurrent that still threatens to pull us apart. Renee remains riddled with little fears. Driving too close to another car on the freeway makes her anxious. If someone doesn't pay her a compliment at a party she is anxious. When I don't give her credit for the housework that she's done she gets anxious. If Joey is a few minutes late coming home after school she is anxious. You could say we both have validation issues, but Renee's seem more extreme and complicated. Or maybe she has an anxiety disorder.

"One of her biggest fears is sex. Despite our honeymoon period when we first met, it's become clear she doesn't really enjoy physical intimacy. This drives me crazy sometimes. One time I brought home a couple of soft-porn videos, hoping this might get her in the mood. I hid the videos in my desk, waiting for the right moment to bring them out. But Renee discovered them and exploded. She said Joey might have found them instead of her, did I ever think of that? And why would she ever want to watch porn? All porn meant was the exploitation of women. She said she was totally turned off by what I'd done. I couldn't get past her fury. When Renee is mad at me and threatens to withhold sex, it serves a dual purpose: it punishes me, and gets her off the hook.

"Renee is a beautiful women with a great personality, but once anyone lets fear rule his or her life, you can't sustain a successful relationship. I've told Renee several times I'd be happy to go to therapy with her. There has to be some reason she's afraid of sex and has so many other anxieties. If I'm being the unreasonable one, if I'm bullying her, or I'm doing something else wrong—maybe that 'buck and doe' metaphor is still subconsciously ruling my life—I'm open to finding out. But Renee refuses to get help. The problem is never her or us, she implies; it's me. I'm too pushy, too critical. I'm overwhelming her, she says, that's why she retreats. But when I back off she doesn't change or have any motive to change. She retreats, all right, into her fearful state. It's so frustrating to see this. Ultimately, I feel inadequate for not being able to do something to make her happy.

"When I talk to Renee about having our own child, she balks. One is enough, she says. I would really like to have a child, but if not, at least I want co-responsibility with Joey. One role a man is supposed to assume in a relationship is that of the father. I want to be a good father. I certainly want to be a more sensitive and caring father than mine was to me. But Renee keeps pushing me back. It's as if Joey were a movie or a book that she alone created, and she retains all rights to Joey.

"How do you respect someone if she doesn't respect you enough to grant you equal parenting powers with 'her' son? And if you don't respect her, how do you stay in love with her?

"Renee's hang-up about sex is also troubling to me. Maybe it all ties in with her lack of trust of me with Joey. Intimacy is all about trust, isn't it? Renee always tries to work around our lack of sex by offering romantic solutions—we could just cuddle, or take a hike in the mountains, or go dancing. I like to do all those things—romance is fine—but they're not a substitute for sexual intimacy. I know this is a crude example, but if a kid wants ice cream, and you try to pacify him with jelly beans or a candy bar, it only works for a while. Ultimately he still wants ice cream. Sex makes me feel good about myself. I want to be a great lover just like I want to be a great father. I want to be appreciated not only for my physical skills but for my ability to communicate on an emotional level. Sex is one way I can show my emotions without having to be the master code-breaker. Without a commitment to physical intimacy from her, I don't think my relationship with Renee has 'parity.' Something will always be out of balance. I won't feel that she loves me the way I love her."

Summary and Interpretation

- Steven's story demonstrates how determination can lift someone out of a culture that devalues personal growth and independence. His suspicion of his family values turns him to introspection at an early age, and helps him through some tough teenage relationships. At a relatively young age, he sees the mistakes he has made and how being manipulative with women is a losing game for men. From sports, he absorbs the positive lessons but is smart enough to understand the limitations of men who are always trying to prove themselves. As he grows older, he acknowledges the complex emotional language of women and gets frustrated trying to decode it. He's also frustrated by the conflict in his head—the sparring voices of his mother and father—about gender roles and particularly the meaning of sex and intimacy. While he is currently struggling in his relationship with Renee, he urges her to come to grips with her sexuality and the fears that limit it, which probably means delving into a painful past. According to Steven, Renee has put herself into a box that feels safe, but what she's keeping out are the fears she needs to deal with. She not only hurts herself, he says, but passes those fears on to her son, Joey, by being overly protective.

- While they rarely verbalize it as well as women do, many men, to be happy, like to feel needed by their partners. Steven makes this point several times. Being needed makes him feel important and helps define him in the traditional male role of "provider and protector." But there is an even deeper emotional reason why men covet this role. In looking for a life partner, there is an often subconscious search for one's mother in the sense of being loved, nurtured and needed. It is essentially a search for their deepest vulnerability, and a way to deal with that vulnerability by finding the right connection. Nurturing, which implies not just caring for someone but a bond of total trust and openness, is no small issue. It was Freud who observed that "no one who has seen a baby sinking back satiated from the breast and falling asleep with flushed cheeks and a blissful smile can escape the reflection that this picture persists as a prototype of the expression of sexual satisfaction in later life." Freud's explanation of sexual satisfaction illuminates the larger point of happiness in general. In the first months of life, happiness is synonymous with unconditional love, from infant to mother and mother to infant. Each needs the other to be fulfilled. Soon thereafter, as the demands of life intrude, love inevitably becomes conditional. For many men and women, what follows is a lifetime search for partners who will bring them back to that idealized state of unconditional acceptance and security.

• Many men are reluctant to ask for this nurturing, hiding behind a façade of emotional self-sufficiency. But if they did not get love and acceptance as a child, they want them more than ever as adults. Steven is upfront enough to say that he and a lot of his friends want that nurturing from their partners; it's one of the most important things in the world to them. Like women who tend to feel secure with partners who remind them of their fathers, many men will subconsciously seek out women who have many of the qualities—even negative ones—of their mothers. This is not just the search for a reconnection to childhood. In choosing a partner who in some way reminds him of his mother, a man has the security of familiarity. This becomes a buffer against what he *doesn't* know about his partner, the surprises that inevitably appear down the road.

• The unfamiliar is a great male taboo. The unfamiliar is a threat to a man's leadership, authority, power and security. Perhaps this is why most men do not like to venture very far from their emotional comfort zones or areas of expertise. They don't want anything to go wrong, especially if it's something they can't fix. In the matter of relationships, women often put down men who are commitment-phobic. What they may not understand is that a lot of men, like Steven, are reluctant to commit—even if they have strong affection for the woman—because they are leery not just of losing their freedom, but because they have a great fear of the unknown. It's the same reason men often stay in their unhappy relationships. They are afraid of leaving because they don't know what's waiting for them on the other side. They don't like risk.

- There is another reason for choosing partners who remind us of our caregivers, even when we recognize their negative qualities. There is the hope we can change our partners, or they will change themselves, into an idealized version of our caregivers. When that transformation inevitably doesn't happen, and the negative qualities overwhelm the relationship, the disappointment in a man is acute. He feels like a failure. And he often wants out of the relationship. Defining masculinity as always needing to be the problem solver, the "fixer," can be dangerous. Steven wants to deal with Renee's anxiety and fear issues in order to make him feel better about himself. But Renee wants to deal with her problems in her own way.

- When Renee tells Steven that he intimidates her, she has a point. She doesn't want to feel manipulated and pushed around. Steven claims that Renee doesn't want sex like she used to. But maybe what Renee doesn't want is what feels like an impersonal and perfunctory sex; she wants sensitivity and vulnerability. She wants sex her way, not his, and is struggling to communicate that. Steven, too conscious of his own needs, can't hear it.

- There is a control struggle between Steve and Renee. Many men, like Steven, end up blindsided in a relationship because it almost always starts out on a high note. At first the woman comes across as sexy, sweet, understanding, giving and caring. Based on first impressions, men believe women as a gender are delighted to be givers and pleasers (which, in Renee's case, may be defensive behavior over being abandoned and rejected in her previous relationships) and that they will always be givers and pleasers. This is rarely the case. Women give and please in order

50

to be accepted. Once accepted, they want to be listened to, and they want their own power. In addition, in Renee's case, behind her facade of sweetness and kindness, resentment may be building over feelings of loss of self and of being controlled by Steven, or by men in general. Women may suppress these feelings for years, but when they come flooding out, men are often surprised and wonder where those feelings come from. They wonder what ever happened to the woman they fell in love with.

- When Steven has his affair, and then gets back together with Renee and tells her about it, this is the masculine delusion about telling the truth and believing that women will always appreciate and respect a man's honesty and candor. Women have another way of viewing and communicating the truth. When Renee says Steven is "oversexed," or when she gets upset with his porn stash, this is her way of saying that she's still hurt over his affair. Renee feels, as many women might, that he wouldn't have found another woman if he really loved her. That's her truth. Men need to acknowledge not just the difference in how genders communicate, but how different their realities are. Women cannot be talked out of their perceptions and experiences with male logic.

- Women have the incredible power to bestow the mantle of validation on their partners through trust and physical intimacy. Steven is craving that validation from Renee but for the moment he can't get beyond their differences. For Steven and a lot of men, to be deprived of physical intimacy is a reason to fall out of love. And not because of the cliché that all men want from women is physical pleasure. What men also want and need are validation and emotion.

- Steven expresses classically defined male/female differences when it comes to sex and intimacy. For most

51

women, their sexual behavior reflects their feelings about the relationship; their behavior changes as the relationship changes. For men, the need for sex is often a constant, regardless of their feelings in the relationship. Specifically, for men, sex creates good relationship feelings. For women, good relationship feelings create their desire and interest in sex.

- What happens if the power struggle between Steven and Renee is resolved and Steven gets what he wants? In his relationships with Trisha and Melinda, he makes the point that initially they both seemed vulnerable and fragile, but in the end, when they left him, he was the vulnerable and fragile one. The truth is that once a man becomes dependent on a woman emotionally and sexually, he tends to fill up his emotional vacuum with her. She becomes his port for every storm. In so doing he becomes vulnerable. If a man doesn't have his own world of self-discovery and empowerment—whether it's physical or spiritual—and something goes awry in his relationship and his partner withdraws her love, the pain of what will be perceived as betrayal can seem insurmountable. According to Frank Pittman in *Man Enough*, a rejection by a woman can trigger such overwhelming anxiety that a man becomes desperate and will do almost anything to win her back.

- Besides a broken heart, a woman's rejection causes a feeling of failed masculinity. Steven experiences this with Trisha and Melinda. Because most men don't know how to heal themselves or look for support from friends, many will quickly look for another woman to salve their wounds and get their minds off their pain. If that fails, they might turn to their work, begin running marathons, or become super fathers—anything to restore a feeling of worth and authenticity. If they fail to find that self-worth, according to Herb Goldberg in *The Hazards of Being Male*, men become susceptible to extreme stress, illness, rage and even suicide. The blueprint of masculinity is perhaps embedded more deeply in our culture and our DNA than most men want to acknowledge. It may be more embedded than the need to find and sustain a successful relationship.

- Men and women can fall out of love when they lose respect for their partners. In the case of Steven, when Renee doesn't trust him to help her raise Joey, or when she's no longer interested in sex and won't explore or explain to him the reasons, he loses respect for her. From Renee's point of view, she may lose respect for Steven for always trying to solve her problems and not giving her space to breathe. Does Steven really know what women feel about sex? The behavior of a lot of women is influenced not just by their personal histories but by popular culture. In the media—from MTV videos to sitcoms to fashion ads—most women flaunt their sexuality. It's presumed by men that this is one of their power and pleasure centers, that in revealing their sexuality they know exactly what they're doing, and that sex is important to them. Yet, behind bedroom doors, there may be deep anxiety and uncertainty. A lot of women, like Renee, can be reluctant to share their fears because they think they'll be letting down their partners. They'll also be letting down themselves by not measuring up to what a woman is "supposed to be." The same goes for motherhood. Popular culture would have us believe there is no higher calling for a woman than to be a loving and devoted mother. It's also a biological mandate. Renee responds to both messages, and receives a heavy dose of validation, by always being there for Joey. In Steven's view, however, Renee is over-protective and over-controlling of her son, and, in the process, shutting Steven out of her life.

- If they feel insecure, women can easily hide behind their children, as Renee does with Joey, in order to avoid intimacy with their partners. A child becomes a huge security blanket. As Steven points out, a son is the one male in a woman's life that, deep down, will never reject her. Men should be sympathetic to a partner seeking validation from her child, but when the child becomes her main source of approval and emotional satisfaction, it may be a red flag. Steven wonders why he should give all of himself to Renee if she is holding her emotions back from him. Perhaps Renee picks up on Steven's attitude and perceives it as a threat, which makes her even more secretive. They both need to be better communicators. If Steven learned to be more assertive and was less afraid of confrontation, he could perhaps fulfill the male role of leadership that he desires.

- Steven makes the point that in adolescence the pursuit of girls and, in particular, successfully taking them to bed, means ultimate peer approval. The all-consuming goal of sexual conquest is conveyed in Tom Wolfe's novel *I am Charlotte Simmons,* where college boys in narcissistic heat believe themselves to be demi-gods; they grant themselves the power to do and say almost anything to seduce a woman. To keep the relationship alive, if it suits them, they find clever ways to cover up their deceit. The means—deception and lies—sometimes becomes an end in itself. Steven gives the example of trying to take a girl to bed when she suddenly says, "I know you love me." How many boys have the courage and confidence to say they really just want sex? Hopefully, there is affection involved, but the truth is a young man's hormones are on fire. Teenage girls should know that their power and self-esteem come from *not* confusing sex with love.

- Running out on a fight, as Steven does, is not uncommon for men. This "cut and run" defense is not just because they don't like confrontation or emotional pain. It's a male way of showing control. It's also a way men deny their dependency and vulnerability issues. While they secretly

54

want dependency, and to admit their vulnerabilities, men have to feel totally safe and comfortable when these critical subjects come up.

Chapter Five

Roddy's Story

Sex is hardly ever just about sex.

—*Shirley MacLaine*

Meet Roddy, thirty-three years old, divorced, a small business-man/entrepreneur who is not afraid to put in long hours to make a living. The oldest of three brothers, he enjoys boyish good looks, reddish-brown hair, a slim build, and a contemplative face that comes to life every so often with a knowing smile or a self-deprecating laugh. While his personality is laid back, he is observant and intuitive about what goes on around him. He describes himself as thoughtful and soft spoken as well as hard working, and some-one who always keeps his temper. He also believes he's a good judge of character, but admits to having blind spots about himself. Honesty and directness are what he respects most in his friends. He was married for almost three years to Laura, a pretty, petite woman with deep-set eyes and long red hair, and then endured a tramautic divorce. Though dating again, and in fact thinking of living with his new girlfriend, he is still hurt by his divorce, still analyzing the chain of events that unraveled his happiness. While he says he is no longer in love with Laura, they live in the same city and get together sometimes as friends.

In Roddy's case, one reason he fell out of love, he says, was that he felt deceived by Laura. Ironically, Laura levels the same charge at Roddy, believing that it was his involvement with another woman that sabotaged their marriage and pushed her out of love. Roddy has a different take on his extra-marital affair. Looking back today, he believes that neither he nor Laura looked deeply enough into their pasts to understand why deceit and abandonment were such deadly trip wires for them. At Laura's core, he says, was a mixture of fear and confusion about who she really was, and an inability to be honest and forthright about her past.

When he first met Laura, Roddy was in his late twenties and she was five years older. It was a tough time in his life because only months before his father had passed away unexpectedly, just two years after retiring from teaching at the local high school. He and his brothers did their best to console and take care of their mother, because that's what responsible sons always do. It's a definition of being a man, he thought. In retrospect, however, he wonders why he and his brothers had no one to console them. "It would have been nice to have support," he says. "I know men are supposed to be emotionally tougher than women, but while I can't speak for my brothers, I didn't feel tough at all." Roddy admits he was in pain for very clear reasons—unfinished conversations with his father, regret for their past misunderstandings, and empathy for a man who after years of hard work deserved something better than an early grave. He thinks of his father frequently.

* * * * *

"Despite our ups and downs, and a lot of frustration in trying to communicate, I always felt close to my father. He was born into a prominent Latin American family and admittedly was spoiled as a boy. One of his problems was because he was overindulged by his parents, he never learned to be truly independent. When he had a problem, it was too easy for him to go to someone else to solve it. He never fully learned how to set boundaries, or to deal with conflict or use his own judgment. Ultimately, in his twenties, he rejected his parents' lifestyle and came to the United States, where he met my mom. One of the upsides of indulgent, coddling parents, however, is that you're surrounded by love and affection, and you keep that love inside you. My mom fell in love with Dad, she said, 'because he was the most sensitive and gentle man' she had ever met, and she 'could connect with the childlike innocence he never gave up.' He was also a great dancer and witty conversationalist. My brothers and I could relate to Dad's childlike innocence as well, and no doubt his ability to understand teenagers made him a great teacher both for us and his high school students. He was bright and knowledgeable on many subjects. We had terrific intellectual discussions as we grew up. We were definitely a family of talkers.

"However, because he never learned to deflect or channel stress, or to set boundaries for himself, Dad could easily blow up and fill the house with his anger. All of us dreaded the moment when he came home from a long day of teaching. You could just see that expression of defeat or exhaustion in his eyes. As a child I was sometimes scared of him, but as an adult I felt very sorry for him—he was so bottled up—and to this day I make a conscious effort never to give in to my anger or to try to intimidate anyone with it. I simply put up a wall with people who are out of control or are abusive to me. I empathize with them just as I empathized with Dad, but when someone is out of control, I know to keep my cool and walk away.

"For a month after Dad's death, I was in a stupor and kept to myself. In my mind I kept going over conversations that I wished I had had with him. I felt we had so much unfinished business. About two months later I began to casually date several interesting, fun women. The ability to laugh and relax and forget my pain was great therapy. One night I ran into a group of women at one of the

58

downtown clubs, and made eye contact with Laura. I had no idea who she was, but something just clicked. No doubt for most people the initial attraction to someone is physical, and maybe you're inclined to fall in love with someone whose looks are at the same level as yours. I'm not Robert Redford, but I think I'm better looking than most men, and likewise Laura stood out from her girlfriends. An hour later Laura and I met by coincidence at another club. I half joked with her that this must be fate. We ended up sitting together for half the night, and she reminded me it was Valentine's Day and asked if it wasn't appropriate that I give her a kiss. The request was such a surprise that I instinctively complied, and the kiss lived up to all expectations. That one kiss began a journey of romance with all the typical cat-and-mouse play of any early relationship. At first Laura thought I was a 'player' and wanted little to do with me, but after several lunches and dinners I convinced her otherwise: that I found her interesting and pretty and sophisticated, and that I wanted to pursue a relationship.

"I am a great talker and listener because I need to communicate. All my life, receiving and giving information has been crucial to my happiness, or just my ability to function. One of my pet peeves in business is people who don't return voice mail or e-mail promptly. They just sit on your message, like it isn't important, having no sensitivity that it may be important to you. My parents had an open, candid relationship and it definitely rubbed off on me. I want a woman to know exactly where I'm coming from, who I am, and what I want for my future. I don't blurt it out all at once, obviously, but I move in that direction in any relationship—it's part of the excitement and chase for me. If you can't be totally candid with someone, what's the ultimate point of the relationship?

"Because of all the emotions and conflicts my father's

death dredged up in me, I was perhaps overly talkative with Laura as I got to know her in the next month or two. She was a great listener—empathetic, curious, and absorbed by my insights, even if she disagreed with some of them. I told her about my previous two-year relationship with a woman named Becky, a very independent, self-reliant woman with whom I had gone into business. The relationship had started out strong, but the strain of working and living with the same person put too much stress on us. It was painful—both the end of the relationship and my helplessness to change it. I like to think that I can fix problems. It's one of my roles, my definition of responsibility and, I suppose, manhood. But it didn't work with Becky. I couldn't fix a relationship that had become drained of romance and intrigue.

"Laura told me that her five-year relationship with her boyfriend had recently ended because he didn't give her the time and attention she needed. He would work at his job all day and get lost on his computer at night. She felt taken for granted. She tried to tell him how she felt but he blew her off. I empathized because this was how Becky ultimately treated me. Laura also told me that at her age it was time for her to be with someone who was real and serious and could make an honest, lasting commitment. She admitted she felt the pressure of being in her thirties and not wanting to be left behind. Not that she ever used the term 'old maid,' but I think for most women, not having a solid, permanent relationship makes them feel something is wrong with them, that they're a failure or an outcast. At least this is true where I live. Maybe in large urban centers where women are more assertive and independent it's different.

"When Laura said she wanted a commitment from me, I took that to mean marriage, even children. At first she was evasive about it but finally admitted that yes, a stable, loving marriage was what she coveted. My point of view was slightly different. I thought marriage was an historical institution of dubious relevance, but out of respect for the woman I was in love with, I told Laura I would honor her wishes. As for children, I don't have the ego that demands I reproduce my own gene pool. Laura was also mixed on having children—one minute yes, the next minute 'what's the hurry?' Yet the reasons for her hesitancy only became clear after we were married.

"We dated for two years before moving in together. Laura was a beverage manager at a prominent hotel, earned a good salary, and worked long hours. She had an incredible work ethic. I had my own business and my hours were equally long, but it was so much fun to meet at night and laugh and be silly over our crazy days. Being a small business owner was often a struggle, handling unending expenses and worries about cash flow. It meant lots of anxiety some months. Laura gave me the confidence that I would succeed. I still can't easily define the connection between us. In addition to the moral support she gave, and our mutual physical attraction, Laura had this certain style, a presence that I gravitated to, and we had great, stimulating conversations on lots of subjects. But I thought our deepest connection was a childlike bond, like the one my parents had had—open, innocent, respectful and candid. While growing up, even before puberty, I made friends with girls more easily than I did with boys. For me, establishing a friendship with a woman is a critical keystone for the relationship to advance. One definition of friendship is to hold nothing back from one another.

"And I thought I held nothing back from Laura. I told her that being in love with someone is not enough to sustain a long-term relationship, let alone a marriage. (I had fallen in love with three other women, and none of those relationships endured—either because I was immature, or the women had needs that I couldn't meet.) In addition to love, I suggested to Laura, there has to be the deepest respect for your partner, for his or her thought processes, moods, will and opinions, no matter how different they are from yours. You love someone for who he or she is as an individual.

"Laura and I got into an almost Socratic dialogue about this. Respect, we both agreed, is the opposite of control. Control in relationships, I believe, actually stems from the feudal idea of property rights and ownership. It's just been romanticized by the media. Think of Hallmark cards, the 'I am yours and you are mine' concept—as if you own each other. I have seen men and women find ways, large and small, unconscious and conscious, to control their partners. It's almost a priority with some people, maybe because our lives are so chaotic and we live in an age where nothing feels certain after 9/11. But it just doesn't work in a relationship. No one likes being told what to do or how to feel. Laura asked if I would ever try to control her in any way. I told her no, never, and she promised the same to me.

"I also told Laura that I thought respect should automatically be given to your partner, to everyone in your life, until the person betrays that respect. This holds particularly true for a parent to his or her child. That's where it all starts: if you don't respect your children, they'll grow up not respecting themselves or others. Trust, on the other hand, has to be earned. That may seem like a subtle distinction, but to me it's crucial that you don't give someone your trust until he or she earns it. Laura wanted to know what it would take to earn my trust. I told her just to be honest and open and uncontrolling with me, just as I would be with her.

"Sometimes I wasn't sure if Laura just found me incredibly amusing and eccentric or, as she later said, I was the most 'different' and 'interesting' guy she had ever dated. It reminded me a little of why my mother was attracted to my father. Laura certainly knew my thoughts and emotions well. I didn't hold back. She also let me know what she liked about me. Besides my confidence and work ethic, there was something stable and solid about me. She liked that I was always there for her. I wasn't coy or into hiding; I didn't duck any issue. I could be counted on.

"In turn, I was drawn to her independence and self-reliance and her strong sense of self. This, by the way, is almost always the type of woman that attracts me, and no doubt my mom is a role model for this. I feel that choosing a partner with those qualities validates the same qualities in me. I also enjoy, to a point, nurturing my partner if she needs some guidance. Maybe that's the 'male' side of me, the one that has to fix problems. But just to a point. I am not an enabler. I particularly don't care for women who are overly dependent on a man, are too needy, too clingy, or have too many problems that need to be 'solved.' That's why I'd fallen out of love with previous women. For me, independence in each partner is critical for sustaining a relationship.

"Laura didn't seem to have any problems, not major ones. She was used to being independent since childhood, she said. On the other hand, she was not nearly as forthcoming as I was about the past. She did tell me that when she was about two years old her mother divorced her father, and Laura ended up living with her mom, a free-wheeling hippie who eventually gave birth to two additional children from two different men. When she was old enough, it fell on Laura's shoulders to fix meals, give baths, and supervise homework for her younger half-siblings. Frustrated by not having a life of her own and fighting a lot with her mom, Laura moved out when she was twelve. She stayed with her dad in Washington,

D.C. until she was eighteen and then went to college. Life with Dad wasn't much easier than it was with her mom. He chased women, sometimes almost as young as Laura, just like her mother chased men. When I pressed for more details, Laura would become evasive, and while I was more than curious, out of our mutual pledge of respect for one another's privacy, I backed off.

"Even with the few details of her past she did provide, Laura's longing for a solid, stable relationship made all the sense in the world, and I wanted to give her that. Before we moved in together, and later, when we decided to get married, I told her I intended to be faithful and loyal to her, and hoped she would be to me. I went on to say that I hoped we could meet each other's needs. Even though I thought they were obvious, because they would be the same as Laura's, I listed mine: affection, companionship, emotional and physical intimacy, trust, openness, and having fun together. Laura agreed. But if somehow things didn't jive for us for a period, I told her, if one or both of us, for example, ended up having an affair, I thought it wasn't the end of the world so long as we were open and honest with each other and fixed the problem. I certainly wasn't intending to have an affair when Laura and I talked. My dad, as far as I know, never had one. But I knew many men who did 'stray' and the reasons could be quite complex.

"The two years Laura and I dated, before moving in together, were sexually quite incredible. Fireworks sex, spontaneous sex, playful sex, post-argument/healing sex. Sex in bed, sex in the shower, sex on the kitchen counter. Sex that means freedom and commitment and the ultimate trust-builder for a couple. I couldn't imagine being any happier physically with a woman. Once we moved in together, however, there were some subtle changes. Our daily lives, occupied with work, were the same, but

64

nights felt different. For one thing, the sex began to wane. Not from any lack of desire on my part, but Laura often complained of fatigue from work or said she wasn't in the mood. In addition, the stimulating conversations we'd had in our courtship were largely replaced with dull, repetitive exchanges about topical subjects. Was Laura somehow changing? Losing interest in me? Was there a problem I didn't know about? When I asked what was going on, she assured me that everything was fine and that she just needed her space. She reminded me that I'd promised to respect her boundaries. She was happy in her life and in love with me, she said, and everything was wonderful.

"But I wasn't sure how wonderful things were. Intuitively, something felt askew. Laura wasn't being open and honest with me, I thought, and I suddenly had some new insights. Except for the quite clear goal of a stable and lasting marriage—and the emotional satisfaction she didn't get from her previous boyfriend—Laura didn't seem to have any other dreams or goals. Whenever I asked her what she wanted out of life, she had no clear answer, except for vague references to starting a family sometime in the future, while I had definite financial, material and emotional goals. Laura suddenly struck me as adrift. She seemed to live off her spontaneous emotions, moment by moment, day by day, reacting more than planning. I got this feeling she had gotten what she wanted from me—a pledge to marry and settle down—and she wasn't prepared to delve into her life any further than that.

"I was disappointed because we'd talked a lot about the great adventure that life was, the importance of taking risks, self-discovery, growing and changing together. When I pushed her about that promise, Laura reaffirmed that she wanted to grow as a human being, but her words felt hollow. Maybe she did want to grow, but it felt like she was putting that responsibility on me, to lead and guide her. Was she simply burned out from a childhood of too much responsibility? Was I supposed to be the mentor or father she never had? This whole possible redefining of roles made me nervous about getting married. What was I getting into?

"In the end I pushed my doubts away and remembered my pledge to Laura of total respect, including respect for our differences. The wedding day arrived, we were with our closest friends, and Laura came into her own. My fears vanished. I'd never seen Laura so happy and I told her so. She blushed and agreed. We danced the night away. Going to our hotel room afterwards, we had decent but not great sex. I was a little surprised but I thought Laura was just wiped out from the day. The sad reality was that we did not make love again for another month, and then maybe only five or six times that entire year. Nothing came close to the passion and openness we'd experienced in the first year of our courtship. Laura seemed to fall back into a niche of mysterious self-absorption and emotional disengagement. At first I ignored the pattern, thinking we would adjust to marriage together. Instead, the distance between us grew. I was increasingly upset, and kept pushing Laura for answers. Was there something I'd done to her or hadn't done for her? Was there something in her past she hadn't told me? Had she been abused by one of her parents?

"Laura denied there was any abuse, but agreed she would see a therapist. Just to please me, she said, not because she was convinced anything was 'wrong' with her. In fact, she added, she was going to prove that everything was normal. After several visits with a therapist she announced that things were as she expected: maybe she was a wee bit tense, adjusting to a new work schedule at the hotel, but otherwise everything was fine. She was normal, just as she'd thought. Okay, great, I said, but why were we still not having sex? If it made me happy, Laura answered, she'd buy some sex toys for us, and maybe that would bring some sizzle back. She bought the toys but never used them. Our sex life remained on life support. On top of that, I was struggling with my business, and I told Laura how much pressure I felt. Instead of being sympathetic, as she was in the beginning of our relationship, she got defensive. Her business days were just as rough as mine, she said, and I should stop feeling sorry for myself. I had learned that it was not in Laura's character to admit that she did many things wrong, much less that something was her fault. But I wasn't blaming her for anything. I was just looking for sympathy.

"It also became clear to me that introspection and delving for psychological answers were not Laura's strong suit. Searching for answers meant there had to be problems, and Laura didn't want to admit there were any problems. While she found it interesting for me to talk about my past, I wasn't allowed into hers beyond the fragments she'd shared before we were married.

"The more I pressed her with my frustration and unhappiness, the more defensive she grew. She finally said she just didn't see why sex was so important to me or to men in general. Sex was way overrated, she insisted. She began to ape the attitude of popular culture, citing commercials and sitcoms where men are portrayed as klutzes, buffoons, immature adolescents who are perpetually horny. Women, on the other hand, are almost always depicted in the media as clever, resourceful, sophisticated, in control, and as skilled problem solvers. That's how Laura saw herself. From *The Honeymooners* and *I Love Lucy* to *Married with Children* and *Everybody Loves Raymond*, the stereotype persists that men may think they are the dominant partner in a relationship, including sexually, but in addition to being outsmarted by their women, they are more prone to get in trouble, and it's a woman who inevitably bails them out. Basically, this is what Laura believed. I was immature and overly demanding, even a troublemaker. She also thought most men, including me, were clueless about their more complex wives.

"I couldn't believe I was hearing this from Laura. It was as if she'd turned on me. One thing was true. She *was* complex, and I'm the first to admit I didn't understand her completely. But that was because she didn't provide the information to allow me to understand. I told her that most men are not as they are portrayed on television. We are not all testosterone-spewing adolescents or selfish cads. We have mature emotions and honest needs, especially about sexual intimacy. On television, the topic of intimacy seems to embarrass most men. They either joke about it or hide from it. Yet that wasn't me. My emotions were on my sleeve. I was deeply frustrated, feeling vulnerable, and I wanted answers from Laura.

"For awhile Laura insisted that simple romance should satisfy me. Who needed sex, really? What was wrong with just cuddling and holding hands? I like romancing a woman, but ultimately it's not true intimacy. I also explained to Laura that to reject a man sexually was a blow to his self-esteem, and if I'm struggling with my business and I'm worried about failure, sex takes on an even greater importance in terms of validation.

"I also reminded Laura how much I craved information, that it was part of the foundation of our relationship. Reluctantly, she finally told me specific stories about her parents, particularly her mom. Laura would come home from elementary school with friends only to find her mother walking around the house stark naked because she believed nudity was 'a natural state.' Her mother made no apologies to a badly humiliated Laura. There were numerous other incidents of exhibitionism, like bringing home strange men and making love to them while Laura was in the next room. It was the kind of behavior that eventually drove Laura out of the house and to D.C. Exposed to the libertine lifestyle of her dad, dating girls barely older than she, couldn't have made Laura any more comfortable. And she didn't go into all the stories that were on the tip of her tongue. But it was obvious to me that Laura, down deep, had come to associate sex with shame, lies and manipulation. She was afraid of it, I think, because it conjured up an image of herself as someone who, if she did enjoy sex, was therefore dirty or deceitful. Maybe that was already her self-image from our sexually intensive courtship days. I don't know for sure—she never shared with me the sessions with her therapist—but there was a palpable ball of fear in her when it came to intimacy.

"When I asked Laura why she hadn't told me earlier about the darker part of her childhood and adolescence, she said she was afraid that I would reject her. But isn't this worse, I asked her, keeping a secret that you've never dealt with? And what about your pledge to be honest with me? Laura said she didn't want to talk about it. She slammed the door on the whole subject. No more discussions about sex, no more talk of seeing a therapist, no more hints of wanting children. All she came to talk about in the next few months was her work. It was a blanket denial of our intimacy, as if it had never existed.

"I began to see that Laura really had issues not only with her parents' liberal lifestyles, but with the fact that she had to be the primary caregiver at a young age for her half-siblings. I think she internalized a lot of resentment for being denied the chance to be a carefree child and teenager. As much as she hated being put in that role of responsibility, however, it was the pattern she became comfortable with and carried with her into adulthood.

Part of the allure of hard work for Laura was not that she was so confident of her talents or craved independence, I think, but that work offered her the opportunity to get lost emotionally, or to avoid her feelings altogether. In her heart, she may have despised the burden of responsibility, which is why she looked to me for leadership, taking over even little things, including running most of our domestic errands. She wanted a break, a reprieve. When I suggested to Laura the obvious, that she needed to make the connection between dealing with her past in order to be happy in the present, she went even more on the defensive. I was trying to control her, she said. I was invading her space. Down deep, she said, I probably hated her.

"At this point I didn't know what to think. I wanted to seek out friends for advice, but my friends were also Laura's and I didn't want to embarrass her or us. The sex we once had—the fireworks sex, the knock-over-the-furniture passion—had that just been an act to win me over? What else had Laura been dishonest about? How about her relationship with her former boyfriend? Were her reasons for leaving him—his lack of attention to her—really true? And what about her mixed feelings about having children? Despite a fairly strong maternal instinct, I think Laura was afraid of being challenged not just by the work that kids can be but by the emotional connection she would have to give them. She would be reminded of her own childhood and playing the role of mother to her half-siblings at the expense of her own happiness and freedom. Maybe she was afraid of any deep connection. Did that mean our own relationship was a sham? Despite all our earlier talks and promises to one another, trust did not come easily to Laura.

"Fear can take over anyone's life, and if you hide it from yourself, maybe you think your partner won't see it either. But the partner always sees it. The partner sees it first. My deepest frustration was that on the one hand I was trying to be there for Laura, to help her, to 'fix' our problems, but on the other I was supposed to be respectful enough to give her space when she needed it and to accept her moods. The two turned out to be an irreconcilable contradiction.

"This all happened within the first year of our marriage. The second year was the final act. I had by now two powerful, conflicting emotions. One was that I was beginning to feel guilty and blame myself for not being able to help Laura. The second was pure anger toward my wife. She was being overly helpless and dependent on me when she should have been solving her own problems. Increasingly, she asked me to run errands, buy stamps, put gas in the car, as if she wasn't capable of doing even the most simple chore. Maybe she was clinically depressed, but how would I know if she didn't get help? In addition, she was making me feel insecure about my sexuality. Had I lost all my physical and sexual attraction? Did she know how she made me feel? No matter how agitated I was, because of my dislike of giving into my temper, I refused to blow up at her. But I had to do something. I began avoiding Laura by staying out late, lamely telling her I had office work while in reality I was with friends at clubs. If Laura suspected the truth, she didn't say anything. Maybe she didn't care. Maybe she was already falling out of love with me, as I was with her, but now neither of us talked about it.

"I'll give you my thoughts on why men have affairs. Usually it's not for control or power, or payback, or that they just can't keep their flies zipped. The emotional connection with your partner just suddenly goes dead, like a phone that's been pulled out of the wall. At least it feels that way, though of course it's not that sudden. There's a buildup of disbelief and frustration as you gradually become strangers to one another. Suddenly you aren't having sex at all, and the intimacy, not to mention trust and respect, between the two of you disappears. There's so much talk about how women are the emotional gender, but when they hold back, for whatever reason, when you feel you've been cut off from those emotions, there's nothing you can do about it. You're stranded. Suddenly something snaps inside you and pushes you over the line, and you make the decision to have a relationship with another woman. The first time you do it is a shock to your system. You're filled with guilt and anxiety, which is balanced by an adrenaline rush like no other. The rush of being loved and accepted by someone new, someone who says she understands you and is sympathetic to your problems—that's hard to match. Even if you think you might be making the biggest mistake of your life, emotionally you are so starved you will do anything to get your needs met.

"On the other hand, I think a lot of men, including myself, are cowards when they enter into an affair for not telling their wives. But there's a reason, besides not wanting to break up your marriage until you're absolutely sure it's beyond saving. You don't come home and confess because you're afraid of your woman's anger. No doubt this goes back to your mother when she shamed you or punished you. Some women can turn themselves into helpless victims or rage-aholics at the drop of a hat.

"As I began to stay away at night and meet other women at clubs, I was a sitting duck. Both men and women can smell someone's marital unhappiness a mile away, and they can exploit it before you know what's happening. But I wanted to be exploited. I knew I was trolling for women. I was desperate for a connection to someone who would understand me. A lot of women think that men's sexual needs are so simple. I've heard women say, 'I just give my husband a blow job once a week and he's happy.'

I just can't believe that. I don't think those women really understand men and sex, or the men they're with have no grasp of who they are. It's not about sex, *per se.* It's about intimacy and trust. Men need that just as much as women do.

"The woman with whom I became involved, Alice, was more than sympathetic to what I was enduring with Laura. I don't doubt Alice knew what she was doing—putting an even deeper wedge between Laura and me—but I was so hungry for a physical and emotional relationship that I couldn't stop seeing her even if I never stopped feeling guilty about betraying Laura. For every rush of adrenaline in being with a new partner, there is still a part of your heart that wants to work things out with your wife. But ultimately it's wishful thinking if she gives no indication of wanting to work things out with you. Laura left me in a vacuum. As long as I felt that Alice's love for me was genuine, I could rationalize our relationship. Night after night I would drown myself in the healing comfort of sex. Sex was this incredible ocean of relief, pleasure, self-discovery and rejuvenation. I can't think of a better definition of intimacy. I didn't even like to refer to what I was doing as 'having an affair' because of all the connotations of cheating and deceit. From Laura's point of view, no doubt, my betrayal could only be defined as deceit and cheating. But from my point of view, Laura had deceived and betrayed me first. And I came to have real feelings for Alice that I never had for Laura.

"I stayed away from Laura more and more. Sometimes I wouldn't come home at all. Laura had to have known what I was doing but, already schooled in the art of denial, she buried her head further in the sand. Not wanting to provoke conflict and anger, I fell into the same silence as Laura. Finally, my relationship with Alice became so obvious that Laura couldn't ignore it. One night she confronted me, and when I admitted I was in another relationship, Laura went ballistic, screaming and threatening me with more than divorce. In retrospect, I think a lot of her rage was directed at her parents, her half-siblings, at anyone who had let her down in the past. Despite all the people she might legitimately be disappointed with, including herself, she laid the blame for my infidelity one hundred percent on my shoulders. I certainly accepted part of the blame, but I threw some of it back at her for her lack of honesty and candor. Back and forth the spears went, reducing us both to tears.

"I don't know how many evenings we had like that before I moved out. Laura really didn't want to see a therapist again. She just wanted me out of her life, as if that would solve all her problems. It was the same drama, the same dilemma we'd always faced: Laura walling out my need for communication and sex because it touched a deep nerve of pain from her past, and me shutting out Laura because there's no hope of reaching my emotions or intellect through anger and blame.

"As we watched our relationship slip away, as much as I thought I understood my own emotional landscape, I questioned where my strong need for validation and approval came from. Your childhood is your best opportunity for building confidence and loving yourself. If that doesn't happen, I think sex becomes the 'make up' alternative for a lot of men, just to prove to yourself you're not a loser. Were my demands on Laura for sexual intimacy excessive and unfair because they reflected my own feelings of inadequacy? I did have my share of anger and fears while growing up, because I got rebuffed by people who I thought loved me. My inclination to seek out independent, strong-willed women, like my mother, was for a reason. If a woman was secure and confident about herself, I thought, she was less likely to hurt me.

"The reality, however, was that while I was attracted to this type of woman, once I got to know her I found her confidence and bravado were often a façade, and just under the surface, as in Laura's case, were problems that had never been dealt with. I got thrust into a role of rescuer and problem solver that I didn't really want. Ultimately, I got hurt because Laura's unresolved problems became mine, and perhaps my unresolved problems became hers. I am not unaware of the great irony of our relationship. For someone like me who craves giving and receiving information, I certainly dropped the ball with Laura.

Summary and Interpretation

- Roddy didn't fall out of love with Laura so much as give up on his relationship out of deep frustration and unhappiness. As he looks back on his marriage, I think what puzzles him most is why Laura withheld her past from him. But perhaps he doesn't understand the power of fear because he hasn't dealt with some of the fears from his own childhood. Laura may also have felt intimidated when Roddy insisted that she tell him what was "wrong" with her. When Laura finally does talk about the trauma of her adolescence, it's too late to overcome the damage caused by their loss of intimacy. Much of the self-worth that his marriage gave Roddy, making him feel like a winner, is taken away by its demise. Roddy mentions how men turn to women and sex to get away from the fear that they're not attractive or something is wrong with them. But women and the validation of sex can only cover up so much pain and insecurity. Men need to look into themselves for answers.

- The way Roddy and Laura met is crucial in understanding a masculine blind spot in relationships. They met at a club, made eye contact and, according to Roddy, things just clicked. She kissed him and that sealed it for him,

75

thus beginning his "journey of romance." Because most men lack real relationship skills, they are predisposed to believing in magical events, particularly when those events are accompanied by instant gratification of their needs for validation. Roddy, still grieving over his dad's death, and troubled by his worth as a dutiful son, had a strong need to feel good about himself.

- The seeds for future problems were planted when Roddy agreed to marry Laura even though he intuited he wasn't quite ready for this commitment. He said, "I wanted to honor her wishes." At that point, he should have insisted they both first work through their issues, rather than simply trying to make Laura happy. The man acting as the "rescuer" is a great male fantasy and one definition of masculinity. Many men have the misconception that if they give women what they want, even when it doesn't feel good to them, that love will bloom. The opposite may be true. Women can interpret male generosity as a kind of control—"I did something for you, now you owe me something"—and feel either powerless or turned off. Also, by accommodating Laura's desire to get married, Roddy may have been suppressing his own fear and resistance to the idea of commitment.

- Ultimately, Roddy's fear and resistance surfaced in the form of criticism of Laura. He gave something to her by marrying her, he thinks, but where is the reciprocity in the form of sexual and emotional gratification? Feeling pressured by Roddy, Laura shut down even more, which only gave Roddy more reason to be critical of her.

- Many of the differences between Roddy and Laura are really about men using linear male logic to talk women out of their intuitive, emotional understanding of a problem. When a woman doesn't quite believe or won't accommodate a man's proposed solution, he often sees her response as irrational, dysfunctional or crazy. Roddy thinks his frustration comes from Laura not hearing him, but a deeper frustration may be a result of him not hearing what Laura is saying, and projecting the idea that women should see things the way men do. Women will often agree with men to avoid conflict, but they resent doing so. Ultimately, that resentment turns to anger and a deeper unhappiness, and they walk out the door.

- If she hid the truth about her past from Roddy, did Laura think he simply wouldn't care or notice? Are a lot of women naïve about what sex really means to men? The cliché of "getting his rocks off" or "pulling a control trip" masks the importance to a man of tenderness, acceptance and trust. Being held in a woman's arms at the right moment can be a reconnection to childhood and the feeling of being safe with one's mother. Good sex is also a promise that one is holding nothing back from his or her partner. Men may have a hard time asking for it, but if they don't get enough intimacy, over time it's a reason to fall out of love. While Laura suggests that cuddling or holding hands or kissing is all the intimacy she needs, for most men romance is only a prelude to the special and deeper intimacy that sex confers. (For older couples, often the reverse is true: sex become less important as other acts of intimacy become more important.)

- It's helpful to be aware that a man's anger at being rejected sexually may be tied to non-sexual rejection during other vulnerable periods in his life. In Roddy's case, perhaps the death of his father became an abandonment issue that he projected onto Laura when she denied him sexually. With Laura, he did his best, as always, to suppress his anger and frustration at her rejection. Getting into any kind of argument is dicey for Roddy, as it is for a lot of men. They simply don't know how they will react, and they fear losing control. For both men and women, a harangue from a partner is often absorbed and tolerated out of the habit of silence they first learned as children because they were warned by their caregivers "not to talk back." Down deep, however, in the basement of resentment and anger, dwells a child who needs to speak up. When he or she finally does, as an adult, it sometimes comes out as rage that can seem inexplicable and frightening to those around them. The rage may quiet from time to time but it never dies. It simply transforms itself into profuse apologies, self-blame, or self-destructive behaviors.

- Though he was careful not to show it to Laura, a lot of pent-up anger from his childhood spilled out of Roddy as an adult, helping to push him into his affair. One of Roddy's blind spots may be the illusion that in keeping his temper at bay, he will not be "bottled up" like his father. In fact, he too has repressed his anger, despite his almost religious zeal in communicating what he thinks are all his feelings to Laura. As he finally recognized, just as Laura didn't come clean about her past to Roddy until it was too late, he wasn't completely honest with Laura.

- Roddy, by not having a chance to prove himself to his father before he died, may have a stronger need than most men for giving and receiving information. From his female partners (who, in terms of communication, become a surrogate for his father), he wants to know that he is important and that his feelings and thoughts really count. Otherwise, if he's kept in the dark, he finds it difficult to trust. He spelled out that need to Laura quite clearly early in their relationship. When she didn't meet his expectations, his own fears and projections took over. He just assumed the worst was going to happen. By embracing that defensive mindset, Roddy probably increased the odds of ending his relationship. It's like target fixation: the more one is afraid something bad will happen, the more things one does subconsciously to make *sure* it happens.

78

- If they want to grow emotionally, men have to learn to see themselves as people. Most men have not made growth in their relationships a priority because they think this is just something that happens in the course of time, that they can "relate" to their partner anytime they want, as if by flicking the "relate switch." In fact, relationship skills take years to build. It starts by listening to your partner without judgment or defensive behavior. Second, it means learning from your partner and admitting you may know less than she does about problem-solving, coping and getting along. Essentially, it's about a willingness to be vulnerable and not being afraid of making mistakes. Being defensive takes your focus away from your strengths. The Women's Movement is not something to be afraid of. It is something to learn from.

- Roddy and Laura struggle with the distinction between sex and intimacy. Ideally, sex is not just about validation but provides a connection to another human being. Many men, because they are poor at expressing their emotions, don't follow an act of sex, no matter how passionate it may be, with *talking* about their feelings—and so deny themselves and their partners an even deeper bond. In movies from the Forties and Fifties, off-screen intercourse ended with the man and woman lying in bed silently dragging on a cigarette, not even looking at each other. Today, we're more likely to see each partner diplomatically scoring the other's performance, like an Olympic dive, shrouding everything in humor. Or maybe they whisper a couple of "I love you's" and go back to watching television. The omnipresence of popular culture—and the pressure to conform—eliminates the incentive for many couples to think about what works best for them. They just assume that conforming brings happiness. For some couples, particularly as they age and restructure their relationship, an embrace or cuddling may be more intimate than any sexual act. In a happy, fulfilled relationship, each partner knows not only the right expression of intimacy but also the importance of timing.

- When women are asked why their relationships ended in disaster, a common response is "he was a liar, he deceived me, he was a phony..." They are full of righteous indignation. Laura thinks of Roddy as deceptive for both having his affair and then hiding it from her. What may not be obvious to a lot of women is that a man's "habit" of being less than honest, or stretching the truth—a behavior that usually starts in adolescence—is further encouraged by the struggle over control of a relationship. Because control is another (misguided) definition of masculinity—the perceived male requirement of being in charge—boys, and then men, have a second motive to deceive. Men will often subconsciously exaggerate, deflect the truth, or make excuses in order to keep that feeling of control. What an adolescent male learns as a "survival skill"—self-permission to lie—is soon embedded in his consciousness as acceptable behavior not just in his relationships but in all aspects of his life.

- Alexander Payne's insightful dark comedy *Sideways* is about two old college friends, Jack and Miles, who take a trip through California wine country, exactly a week before Jack's wedding. Women and sex are never far from their thoughts. Even if he's about to get married, Jack wants one last roll in the hay. Jack and Miles lie so often and in so many little ways, to themselves and to the women they meet, that the audience wonders if they're even aware of moral issues. They presumably know lying is wrong, but it's just part of who they are, and often necessary, in their minds, to accomplish their objectives. They also lie to get acceptance, pure and simple. They rationalize that life for a man can be pretty tough so they're entitled to take some ethical short cuts. Miles even steals money from his mother. Jack and Miles also lie for empowerment in the sense that they know they're "getting away with something." The egos of many men, and the strictures of masculinity, are based on the premise that a man must succeed at all costs, even if it means sometimes stretching the truth.

- As I left the theater after watching *Sideways*, two women behind me voiced criticism of the film. They found the behavior of the main characters despicable. "Can you imagine," one said, "if two women took off a week before one of their weddings and tried to screw a couple of guys?" Perhaps this judgment misses the point. Men and women behave differently not just because they are wired uniquely but because of cultural pressures and expectations. Jack says he wants to be faithful in his marriage. Whether he will or not we can't be sure, but he knows it's expected of him. He also knows he's going to miss sex with other women, so he makes the most of his last week of freedom—a typical male linear solution to a complex problem. This is what a lot of men do, or think of doing, before they marry. Women think and behave differently. If two women were taking the place of Jack and Miles, and one had a commitment fear, she might fall in love with someone she meets on the road. That, not sex with a random stranger, would be a credible solution to her anxiety.

- From Roddy's story, it's not clear how much pressure he received growing up to succeed financially and professionally as an adult. But the fact that he turned into a hard-working entrepreneur indicates pressure from somewhere. Most of the men I spoke with said they were given strong and clear messages from their caregivers that they had "to amount to something" or they couldn't respect themselves. When caregivers emphasize to boys the all-important goal of achievement, they often give a subliminal message that emotions are of secondary importance, or perhaps not important at all. How can men learn relating and partnership skills if they're not taught the importance of emotions? To get boys on the right track means nurturing them. This does *not* imply spoiling, coddling, pampering, overindulging or overprotecting. Such parental behaviors are actually controlling in nature, and often produce teenagers and adults who are filled with a sense of inflated entitlement. On the other hand, real nurturing means bestowing on a boy (or girl) a prudent amount of freedom, including permission to take risks; forgiveness of mistakes (this is not incompatible with discipline); appropriate physical comforting without self-consciousness; encouragement to be different; the right to talk about how he feels about himself and others; and the notion that "success" has as many definitions as there are people on the planet. If masculinity is to be redefined, either through a Men's Movement or a shift in cultural values, these are principles worth considering. Most male adolescents are simply not equipped to deal with their testosterone, peer pressure, rejection and failure—let alone to know when to control and when to reveal their emotions—because they were not given the resources, tools and lessons at an early age.

- Our cultural perception is that when a woman has an affair it's because she's not getting the attention, affection and passion she deserves from her partner. There is often a sense of entitlement underlining her actions. It's not to say that afterwards there's not guilt, remorse and confusion, but offsetting those emotions is the ability to forgive herself, to seek sympathy and help from friends, or to blame the man for hurting her. When a man has extra-marital sex, he's selfishly indulging his lust, betraying his partner's trust, and wreaking havoc on his family. When he feels guilt and remorse, he often doesn't look for support because he's afraid of being judged or shamed. As Roddy asserts, the truth may be that men have affairs for the very same reason that women do—to obtain that core affection and attention missing from their primary relationships. They want to know they are still deserving of love. They want to know they are not taken for granted. For those having affairs in their forties and fifties, they are also afraid of getting older, losing their looks and sex appeal; some have a strong fear of death. I think for most women, having affairs has little to do with wanting an equal playing field with men. It's mostly about validation, just as it is for men. Never mind that it's almost always a superficial validation—coming from without and not from within—but the pressure from popular culture that we deserve to be happy and to have our needs met can be irresistible.

- When either a man or woman cheats, perhaps the other partner needs to be more understanding and forgiving, and not immediately see himself or herself as a victim. The complexity of motives in the "offender" often needs time and therapy to sort out. While revenge may feel good, the Pavlovian rush to judgment and "kicking him (or her) out of the house" can obscure deeper issues in both partners. Regarding sex, Laura's dramatic and immediate shift from her pre-marital behavior leaves Roddy deeply frustrated. She owes him a full explanation rather than exploding in rage after depriving him of sex for so long. These are issues that will never be resolved if the cycle of revenge and vindication perpetuates itself. "The moment I found out about her affair, I fell out of love with her," is a statement I heard from many men. I wonder if what they really meant was that their trust was so fragile to begin with, and they had no idea how to repair it, or to deal with their pain, that it was just easier to kill all emotions and start over again.

- Men who cheat chronically are usually insecure Don Juans seeking to define their masculinity by bedding as many women as possible. One man in his late thirties told me that having sex with as many partners as possible was the only thing that made him feel good about himself. When I suggested that he might try delving into his childhood, he said, "Why look for pain when I have so much pleasure in front of me?" Basically, men like this are afraid of intimacy with a woman—of intimacy of any kind. The macho act of "conquering" helps them mask that fear, and to cover up any pain from childhood. Some men won't even risk dealing with pain because they think vulnerability is antithetical to masculinity. These same men can seem like terrific lovers, but they slip out of a relationship when anything more than superficial emotions come into play. That kind of façade is easy to spot when the man fails to open up about other important areas of his life, such as his childhood, previous girlfriends, or personal crises. As someone once said, women can fake an orgasm, but only men can fake a relationship.

PART THREE

VALIDATION AND SELF-ESTEEM

Chapter Six

Bill's Story

A man is a god in ruins.

—*Ralph Waldo Emerson*

On the same chilly fall night that we met Steven and Renee in New Mexico, it is a pleasant, balmy evening in Southern California. We find Bill, a successful lighting designer and museum curator, in his penthouse studio overlooking the glittering lights of downtown Los Angeles. Middle-aged, built like the football player he was in high school, he has broad shoulders and a trim waist. Of mixed race, his rugged features and deep brown eyes make him handsome. Bill has always liked the company of women, and women like him for his sensitivity, empathy, wit and humor. He has fallen in love many times, resulting in three marriages, each lasting about ten years. He was always the one to fall out of love and ask for the divorce. Why he fell out of love he's not entirely sure, but he believes it had something to do with a breakdown of trust, a feeling that his wife was no longer on his side—or could it be the way women can be so judgmental?

His relationship with his current girlfriend, a forty-year-old, pretty, quiet blonde named Alexandra, is on the rocks. After a big blowup, she and Bill haven't been in touch for three weeks. This has happened before—and they always seem to make up—but with each new fight Bill worries it will mean the end of the relationship. He is suddenly depressed as he gazes out on the city lights. He thinks of other couples having fun tonight, being in love, or just being happy. Why is he sitting up here, stewing? He suddenly wonders if he's ever been truly happy in his whole life. What's wrong with him? He knows women are his validation—women make him feel good about himself—but when something goes wrong, as it has with Alexandra, Bill falls into a black hole of loneliness and self-loathing. He just can't feel good about himself if there's not a woman who loves him. Instead, he almost feels rejected by the whole world. It's an emotional pattern he's had since adolescence after a traumatic childhood. He's been to countless therapists but nobody has really helped him. Looking out the window again, he thinks, almost obsessively, about Alexandra: how, when they first got to know each other, he knew she was "the one," the true love of his life that he couldn't live without. The more they fight, and the more times they walk out on each other, the more desperate he becomes to win her back.

Right now she won't answer his phone calls or e-mails, of which he's left dozens. One of the problems, he thinks, is that they are opposites. He loves people, parties, open energy; she prefers intimate moments with Bill, or just being alone. Bill, the communicator, lets Alexandra know his every feeling and impulse. She is revealing only when she's in the mood. He's sensitive and his feelings are easily hurt. Alexandra rarely acknowledges his pain or her own. Opposites or not, Bill is utterly dependent on her to tell him how much she loves him. But he also knows he can just as easily fall out of love if she ignores him too long. Then he'll be filled with anger and resentment and a sense of betrayal that goes back to his childhood and his mother—feelings that he believes helped sabotage his three marriages.

Bill pours himself a scotch. He doesn't usually drink alone, but things are going badly right now, so why not? While he is used to being whipsawed by his emotions, he sometimes has the sense that his life hangs by a thread and that at any moment his latest crisis with a woman will be his undoing. He wants badly to live on a planet whose orbit is stable, but he also knows that to some extent he creates his own chaos. He is highly conscious of the many contradictions that can rip at a man's life, including the rules of manhood, which he finds vague, antiquated, and misunderstood by both men and women. But where are the new rules, he wonders, to replace the old?

* * * * *

When Bill talks about having a traumatic childhood, he doesn't exaggerate. In his house there are two birth certificates hanging on a wall. The first, issued by the Texas county where he was born, identifies him as a boy but no name is given. In the box marked "race," the word "white" is checked. His second birth certificate, issued two-and-a-half years later by a special court decree when he was finally placed by an orphanage with his adoptive family, lists his name as "Bill Simms" and the race box is marked "colored."

Though he didn't learn all of his personal history until he was in his early forties, Bill was the product of an affair between a divorced East Indian mother and a man of Italian-Jewish descent. His skin color is latte—a very fashionable pigment today, he says, but fifty-five years ago he was an oddity in America. The day after his birth, his biological mother turned him over to a prestigious Houston orphanage, where he remained for thirty months. During this period he was "placed" with five different families and "returned" to the orphanage five times. Even when he eventually gained access to orphanage records and learned the identity of his biological mother (and got up the courage to call her), the information about his early years has always been sketchy. Why he was sent to five different homes without being accepted? Was it something besides his mixed race? What did the orphanage director say about him, if anything? Did anyone really care? The lack of a complete history, though in the distant past, still has an emotional impact on him.

* * * * *

"When relationships sour, from the man's point of view, it's not always a case of falling out of love with the woman. Sometimes a man falls out of love with himself first—if, in fact, he ever loved himself to begin with. Does this happen to women too? I'm sure, but I think it happens more often to men. It also seems to me women are not as tough on themselves as men are. In general, women are more forgiving of their mistakes. For men, the ability to love and forgive themselves starts with their mothers. A mother has to really support and love you if your emotions are ever to 'connect' and 'be whole.' You may look to your father as your role model for career and general male behavior, but it's your relationship with your mother that is your lifeline to emotional happiness. How you get along with her and how much you trust each other are indicators of how you'll deal with women in your adult life.

"In an episode of *Sex in the City*, Sarah Jessica Parker's character, Carrie, is flirting with this cute guy at a singles' bar, when he suddenly turns to her and says, as a compliment, 'You know, you remind me of my mother.' A look of horror crosses her face and she ducks away. The message is, hey, girls, be careful of any guy who is crazy about his mother because you'll end up competing with her for his affection. But that's a myth. Most men I know who have or had great relationships with their mothers end up with healthy relationships with their adult partners. The reverse is also often true. Unhappy with Mom, unhappy with your partner.

"Maybe my childhood story is extreme, but it raises the same issues that a lot of my male friends face but don't like to talk about. They have a number of negative feelings about themselves, and almost all can be traced to their childhoods, and in many cases to specific memories about their mothers. For me it was a phrase I overheard my mother use about me. I was around five years old when I heard it for the first (but not last) time. My mom was on the phone to a friend, talking about my 'bad behavior,' when she said, 'You know, Billy is adopted, and we don't have much information about where he came from or who his real parents were, and you just never know what you're going to get.' That last line—'you never know what you're going to get'—has haunted me ever since, infected me with self-doubt and an insecurity that makes me crave attention, respect and approval, especially from women. And if I don't get those things, I'm not going to be in that relationship for very long.

"I know I'm not bad looking, and I can be one of the most empathetic, charming and articulate men in the world, but underneath that veneer I'm a quivering mass of misfiring synapses and neurons. When it comes to relationships, I live in a state of low-grade anxiety over the need to be loved. Yet, when I get intimacy from a woman, I tend to run away from it because I start to doubt my partner's motives and sincerity. I think, how can she possible fall for someone like me? What's wrong with her? Can't she see what a mess I am inside? She must want something from me, or something's wrong with her, or she's so clueless... Why should I stay in this relationship? I know some women who have similar issues of self-doubt, even self-loathing, and they too tend to always be in flight.

"The family with whom I was ultimately placed was a mixture of African-American (still called 'colored' in those days) on my mother's side, and Hispanic-Indian on my father's. Quite the melting pot. They had no children of their own because my adoptive mother, Esther, couldn't conceive. Esther would turn out to be from the Joan Crawford School of Mothering, which is to say she was beautiful, narcissistic, controlling, emotionally needy, and quick to anger. She wanted to be the perfect mother. It was she who insisted on the second birth certificate just to make everything look 'legitimate.' While she would later tell me different versions of my origins, her most common story was that she was really my biological mother who had been forced by financial circumstances to put me in the orphanage, but that two-and-a-half years later she had come back to do the right thing and claim me. I don't think she was trying to spare me from some bitter truth so much as make herself look heroic. Even when I saw through this lie, and eventually found and met my birth mother, I never bothered to challenge Esther because it would only have made her furious. Esther has never liked being caught in a lie. And I'm not one who loves conflict, even though I've created quite a bit of it in my lifetime.

"Until I was eight or nine, Esther always picked out my clothes and dressed me. She loved to show me off to her many women friends. Even if my skin was lighter than that of the kids next door, and I was often looked at strangely, Esther was determined that I fit in. Fitting in was critical for her. Our house was the sharpest in the neighborhood, and we all dressed fashionably. Every spare penny we had went into appearances. If this sounds like the stereotypical white culture conformist Fifties America, the reality was we were living in an all African-American middle-class suburb, one of the first post-World War Two communities of black attorneys, doctors, and accountants in America. Make no mistake: this was no bastion of black brotherhood or pride. These were African-Americans who wanted to be mainstream upper-middle-class whites. Like most everyone else in our community, my mother gravitated toward material possessions and status symbols, a habit I picked up as an adult.

"My adoptive father, Jorge, was half Hispanic, half Aztec Indian, and didn't blend into the neighborhood color register any more than I did, but Esther's sense of denial was strong. She fantasized that somehow Jorge was special, the man of her dreams, though to me there was nothing exceptional about him. Jorge was good looking, and sometimes a charmer, but I think he looked down on me as an adopted child, as if this was all Esther's idea (and it largely was). I don't recall many times that we played together. What I do recall are the behind-closed-door fights with Esther. Inevitably they were over money, and even at a young age I concluded that money must be the most important thing in the world, the thing that makes you happy if you have it, miserable if you don't. Money would impress girls, I also deduced, so in my teenage years I was a big spender on clothes and a flashy car. I had no role model for saving or investing. Jorge was often traveling here and there on business, chasing different pipe dreams, most of which were failures.

"I realize, looking back, that besides needing a child to complete her ideal family, Esther also coveted a male companion, someone to fill the void that her physically and emotionally distant husband didn't have time for. That companion became me. By the time I was four or five, I had learned two clear lessons from Esther. One, it was never wise to disobey her. Punishment was usually a whipping with a rubber electrical cord. There was also a veiled threat that I could be sent back to the orphanage at any time, though she usually backed away from this because I don't think she could have survived without me. The male companion issue, even if I was just a kid, was part of her identity. The other lesson I learned was how to be cute, charming, polite, informed and ingratiating with all of Esther's women friends. This got me attention, even adoration, and I grew up with an easy charm and comfort with women, at least on the surface, which is characteristic of my interaction with most women today.

"While popular with her friends, I was often a disappointment to Esther and her lofty expectations. Especially when she kept uttering that line, 'you never know what you're going to get.' I wanted to prove her wrong. But if I got a 'B' in math, she asked why wasn't it an 'A.' If she made me clean the dishes every night, she expected me to vacuum the house as well. Esther was a lonely, vain, frustrated woman. Yet she was so good at making me feel guilty that from an early age I came away thinking that when something went wrong in our relationship, it had to be my fault.

"In grade school I enjoyed academics but my social environment was lacking. Esther took me out of our all-black suburb and placed me in a Catholic school because it was reputed to offer the best education. I was one of a handful of non-white students who bore the brunt of the nuns' displeasure (including the frequent rap on the hand with a ruler) as well as getting my ass kicked in the schoolyard for being colored. After a few years of hard-fought tolerance, Esther had had enough. She accused the nuns of racism, pulled me out of the school, and enrolled me in an all-colored school several miles away. There I proceeded to get my ass kicked for being the only white kid.

"Athletics was one of my gifts that allowed me some peer acceptance in grade school (and later in high school and college). However, never underestimate the power of bigotry and racism. By junior high I had developed a strong affinity for any persons who are oppressed or discriminated against. My role models—among them John and Bobby Kennedy, Martin Luther King, Gloria Steinem and Franklin Roosevelt—became people willing to challenge the system and effect social or political justice.

"In the late Fifties, Esther and I moved to California while Jorge stayed in Texas to pursue yet another entrepreneurial idea. To Esther, California was the land of opportunity and represented a new life. Starting over and erasing the past was one of my adoptive mother's life themes. (Eventually it became one of mine, at least with women.) I was now around twelve and this time placed in a more racially integrated school, but still managed to get my butt kicked regularly, just in a more democratic way. I was sensitive and high strung and easily offended, particularly when I was ignored. All my life I've reacted negatively when I feel discounted or marginalized. My reaction is never violent; rather I turn my back on the offender and am very slow to forgive.

"Yet I can also be intuitive, sensitive and empathetic—what a therapist might refer to as my 'feminine side,' a term I have trouble with because it implies that that those emotions largely belong to women. Whether you're straight or gay, I believe that men are just as emotional as women, and while lots of women complain about emotional deprivation in men, they usually do little to help men bring out their feelings. But those feelings are there in most men I know, maybe hidden (for a variety of reasons)—but they do exist. Once I got into high school and developed some independence from Esther and gained some maturity, I had no trouble making and keeping friends, both men and women.

"After I finished my secondary education, I enrolled at UCLA. I was a good student, and in my free time I continued to seek new friendships. I also developed a pattern of exploiting social opportunities. I had this 'me-against-the-world' perspective that is typical of an only child, especially an adopted only child, which is really an attitude of secret entitlement. For example, using my charm, I would convince someone to help me with a

95

difficult class in my non-major, or set me up on a date. Why? Just because I thought I deserved it! But I could also flip the coin and do favors for others, little and big, such as lend friends money, cook them dinner, or give them unexpected gifts. I became quite conscious of my need to please people, to be liked, and to have as many friends as possible. I also like to have friends who are not connected to each other, only to me, so if one of the friendships sours the others won't be contaminated. Being excluded from any group is one of my other deep fears. It doesn't take a therapist to tell me I'm a textbook case of abandonment issues, yet over the years I've gone to a variety of therapists to hear exactly that message, over and over, to wallow in it.

"On the positive side, I usually respond to anyone who is kind, sensitive, intelligent or funny. I genuinely want to be his or her friend, almost instantly. I especially gravitate to women who exhibit those qualities. When a friendship or a relationship with a woman goes south, I'm in trouble emotionally. I love hard and I suffer hard. I look for a safety net in times of crisis: a friend to confide in, a challenging job assignment to keep me busy, or another woman to tell me that I'm okay. I like a friend to tell me that when something goes wrong it's not my fault. When the safety net is not there, I fall into despair. There is an engine of self-preservation in me that drives me relentlessly away from myself and loneliness. I always need other people to make me feel good. I can't stand being alone: that's when all the demons of your childhood come out to play.

"I realize that my self-preservation skills could be construed by some people as artful manipulation. To women with whom I've been in relationships, I come across as someone who listens to and acknowledges their struggles. I think most women look for this quality in a man. Empathy sometimes means as much to them as a man's confidence, power or money—all that bullshit you read in men's magazines and which, unfortunately, is basically true. But looking at myself critically, am I only performing? Am I suckering someone in without exposing that insecure, volatile, high-strung, unpredictable being who lives inside me? My pattern is to have a woman fall in love with me before I expose my other self to her. Perhaps I lure them in under false pretenses, but I'm not sure. Aren't they responsible for their own emotions and judgment? I have this debate with myself all the time. What is my real self, anyway? The fact that I crave love, sometimes desperately, and go 'crazy' when I feel abandoned; yes, that's real, but I am also an empathetic, caring, funny, sensitive person. That's real too.

"The person I'm closest to in the world is my daughter, Liza. She's the product of my second marriage to a talented artist who is Caucasian. Liza is my only child, and obviously I empathize with that station in life. Liza is beautiful and smart, doing well at a prestigious East Coast college, and while we sometimes argue, it is rarely over money. I have not reenacted the roles of Esther and Jorge. If anything, I have gone out of my way to always be there for Liza. I admit to loving her unconditionally. That bond may be the most critical in my life if for no other reason than it is so difficult for me to experience trust with anyone else. I would make any sacrifice in the world for my daughter. Coming up with $40,000 a year in tuition, for example, has sometimes meant, in a lean year, selling some of my art collection as well as forgoing a lot of comforts. But I would do it again in a heartbeat. Liza is also lucky in that her mother is equally nurturing and supportive.

"Speaking of mothers, I should add that I didn't make contact with my birth mother until I was in my forties. Her name was Linda and it wasn't easy tracking her down.

When I spoke to this stranger for the first time, I said, 'This may be very difficult for you to hear and most difficult for me to say, but does July 16, 1946 mean anything to you?' After a very long silence she said, 'Well, not really.' And then she said goodbye and hung up. Linda wasn't rude or dismissive. If I heard anything in her voice it was shock. I sat down and wrote her a three-page letter, giving my life history and adding that I was only looking for biological and historical information I could share with my daughter. Of course I wanted much more. I wanted to know why I'd been given up for adoption.

"Linda called me after she received my letter and gave me the true story. I broke down and sobbed and so did she. She admitted to being my birth mother and said she had never wanted to give me away, but her father had insisted. My father, the Italian Jew with whom she'd had an affair, had disappeared from her life, and Linda already had another child to care for. Keeping me just wasn't feasible. To this day Linda and I are in contact by phone, and I've had many visits with her, my brother, and the three daughters she raised with her second husband. They are all kind, wonderful people. I often wonder what my life would have been like if I'd been raised with them.

"The other disappointing thing for me is while I felt a great weight lift from my shoulders after talking to Linda, my abandonment issues didn't go away. I think maybe we all carry inside us an emotional fingerprint, formed in the first years of our life and like any fingerprint, it is both unique and impossible to alter—not by self-realization, not by new facts, not by years of therapy. It's our emotional identity, like it or not. Speaking of therapy, I've been told by more than one therapist that I'm obsessive-compulsive because of my need for control, afraid of both failure (rejection) and success (I don't deserve it!), and subject to severe mood swings. I can't deny any of it. When I get down on myself I'm a mess for days at a time. When I'm feeling up, I produce my most creative work, and am most connected to the woman I'm with. Because I'm a designer, I also have almost a fixation on beauty and style. How I dress, what kind of car I drive, how I furnish my office, the work I do for my clients—I need everything to be extremely tasteful. This sometimes leads to major overspending, a legacy from childhood and those assumptions that money is the root of all happiness. Whether my high aesthetic standards mean more obsessive-compulsive control or just the need to validate my taste and feel good about myself, I often feel trapped.

"No doubt playing Russian roulette with money is one more mode of self-destruction. Another is that in my relationships I tend to pick quarrels, needlessly, even though I normally don't like conflict. I think I pick fights just to test my partner, to see how much she'll put up with, how much she loves me. Or maybe I want to push a woman away because of that old cliché about being afraid of too much intimacy. Too much intimacy means I'm very invested emotionally, perhaps over-invested, and if something goes wrong, the rejection will be way too painful. I've always been looking to be saved from myself, preferably by a woman—no doubt by an idealized version of my mother, the one I desperately wanted but never got in Esther, or the imaginary 'what-if' one of Linda.

"I've been married three times, and never for more than ten years each time. All three women were different in background and personality; what they had in common, besides being sensitive, funny, usually athletic, and professionally talented, was that in the beginning of the relationship they had a much stronger interest in me than I had in them. That's my *modus operandi* with women. I have to feel secure before I get really interested in someone. Once I have my confidence, I assess how physically and emotionally attracted I am to that woman, and the compatibility of our interests. The passion of the chase, finding out what the woman is all about, both emotionally and intellectually, is extremely important to me. Whatever woman I'm after, I want her to think of me as the most interesting, romantic, charming man she has ever encountered. When I have sex with a woman it's never casual. For me, sex confirms intellectually and emotionally that this particular woman is the right one for me. Depending how connected we feel, it's sometimes further evidence of how much she loves me. I like to keep alive the discovery and learning process between myself and the woman as long as possible. A relationship without excitement is ultimately one reason I fall out of love.

"There are other reasons I fall out of love, to be sure. One is that I get so down on myself that I think of that line, 'I'm the piece of shit that the world revolves around,' or Esther's famous quip 'you never know what you're going to get.' And when I give up on myself I give up on my partner too. I become cynical about how anyone can really love someone like me. I know a lot of men who are prone to self-loathing. For whatever reason, they think they're not good enough. Was it their fathers that set that expectation level so high? Or their mothers for never giving them enough love? The sad thing for me is that I've been married to some wonderful women. In each of my marriages, I gave up on the relationship around year eight, then it took me another two years to wind things down and formally leave. All three marriages fell apart for the same reason and in the same way. Our arguments started out around money, but the issue soon became control and, ultimately, trust. Because trust comes so hard for me, I would find myself slowly disengaging from each of my wives after every significant argument. I rarely verbalized my unhappiness—I didn't know how, not in those early years—but I would keep score, subconsciously, each time

I lost a battle.

"If possible, I like to maintain friendships with my ex-wives and old girlfriends because I don't want to hurt anyone beyond the damage that's inevitable with any breakup. I also have that need to be connected and still loved. Our recent blow-up notwithstanding, I'm now in the fourth serious relationship of my life. Alexandra is in her early forties, and recently divorced from her attorney husband. My hope with Alex, who I love more than any woman I've ever been with (and I hope this is not my addiction talking) is to change from my control mode to an open, trusting way of being. Alex understands and accepts my history, including my hang-ups with Esther, my definitions of success and failure, and why my validation needs are so strong. I know that being a conscientious and loving mom to her two young children is the most important thing in her life. How she succeeds or fails as a mother defines her as person, at least in her eyes. I think she often tries too hard and spoils the kids, but if I ever say that—if I even hint at it—Alex puts up a wall.

"One of our problems is that Alex is not as strong a communicator as I am. Maybe I should say not as needy. In the history of my relationships, I have gone from self-conscious reticence to almost compulsive confession. Words comfort me because they convey emotion. I have to be in touch with anyone I feel close to. So when Alex turns silent I go a little crazy, especially since I've told her how I crave communication. I can send her an email, or leave her a phone message, then wait days for a response. The interlude fills me with doubts—did I offend her somehow? Is she seeing someone else? Is there something she doesn't like about me? Maybe I've gotten too old, or I don't have enough money, or I'm losing my looks. In our year-long relationship we've had three serious breakups. The second occurred for no clear reason (to me) other than that she said she needed some time alone. Okay, fine, take time off, but just tell me why. I always need a why.

"In calmer moments, I count my blessings. I've survived a lot. I have good friends. And when I love, I love with a big heart."

Summary and Interpretation

- A lot of men and women, like Bill, jump from partner to partner because they're constantly seeking validation, or they fear rejection. Because of their childhoods, control is more familiar to them than love and trust. But this kind of "relationship-jumping" ultimately leads to getting locked into sad and unfulfilling partnerships. Always needing someone to make them feel good about themselves, many men never get over the fear of being alone. In a healthy adolescent male, having different girlfriends as he grows up is a form of self-exploration. But for others, relationship-jumping is a way to avoid the "loser" label, and is often accompanied by a strong attraction to athletics, steroids, sex, clothes, cars—anything that resembles a flashy, beautifully wrapped package with a gorgeous ribbon: anything to attract a girl. What many men fail to ponder—long after they leave adolescence—is what happens *after* the attraction process. Do they even know what's inside the package? Do they think no one will ever want to open it up and take a look? Some men, fearful of intimacy, will just pile on the wrapping paper and ribbons, hoping that will be enough to attract and keep a woman. Bill, however, knows there is something deeper in him. He just wants to find it and express it. He wants to find the right woman to validate that depth. But until he's strong enough to validate and love himself, he'll never get over his fear of loneliness or stop labeling himself a loser.

- Popular culture focuses on appearance and instant gratification. Looking cool, thin and young, or being rich or beautiful, or just being *important*, have become the perceived criteria for self-esteem and happiness. While Bill knows intellectually that these are shallow benchmarks, he succumbs to them anyway because they were the values of his mother. For most of us, perhaps real self-discovery gets delayed until a serious crisis—and pain—enters our lives. Until there's emotional pain that can't be ignored, we are adept at avoidance and denial. But even finally admitting to a crisis, our first attempts at a solution are often on the surface. For example, many women, if fearful their partners are falling out of love with them, will start going to the gym, go on a diet, pay for cosmetic surgery, throw out their old wardrobes, redo their hair, or buy a pile of relationship books. They think that men become dissatisfied with them because they have lost their physical appeal, so they respond to a crisis with external solutions. This idea is reinforced by a culture that not only lauds women who look thin and sexy, but stereotypes men as a gender that is only stimulated by a woman's appearance. A good-looking wife or girlfriend is no doubt an asset for many men, but it's not the cornerstone of a sustained relationship. Men are looking, just as women are, to be understood and accepted, to express their emotional needs, and to feel comfortable with themselves and their partners. Perhaps if they acknowledged the importance of a man's emotions to him, women wouldn't be at such a loss about what to do when their relationships run into trouble.

• The strong need for men to have a male role model can't be underestimated. Their self-worth is partly based on the hero they choose—simply through the process of empathy and identification. This starts in boys as early as their second or third year. Spiderman, Superman, The Hulk and GI Joe will never die. The hero and his values are a source of power, instruction and liberation for boys. (Girls, on the other hand, mostly devote their play time to activities that involve nurturing, protecting and taking care of others—such as brushing a doll's hair, or playing nurse, or planning dinner for the family. Nurturing and protecting are often their way of being in charge and having power.) For a boy, besides comic book characters, the hero role is also filled by fathers, uncles or older brothers. If family members are abusive or emotionally absent, the search for a hero can be haphazard, without clear, thought-out criteria. Politicians, celebrities and sports stars often fill the void, or a man sometimes tries to be his own hero, usually with the unfortunate results that accompany expectations set too high. While he admires certain historical figures, one of Bill's major issues is lack of a strong, nurturing male role model. As a substitute, he invests his trust and intimacy in his male friends, his daughter, or the woman with whom he is intimate at the moment. A lot of his abandonment issues might have been abated if he'd had the benefit of a stronger father and a less controlling mother.

- Bill may be an extreme example of someone facing obstacles in finding his roots, but a lot of men never have the opportunity to find out who they are. Consumed by male identity issues, denied the nurturing that girls generally receive, processing the conflicting expectations and messages from their culture, or just caught up in a hyper-masculine environment of competition, they don't have the time to delve into the male matrix. The urge or even need to turn to sports, computers or cars for an emotional outlet is somewhat obvious. Besides a lack of ambiguity, these pursuits are either solitary or done with other men. Rather than interpreting these "male" activities as purely adolescent in nature, they should be seen as a substitute for the nurturing a man never received as a child. They're also an escape from relationships that can be fraught with complex demands and messages that leave men feeling controlled. The importance of having their own world,

WHY MEN FALL OUT OF LOVE

independent of women (just as women have long had one that is independent of men), a world where a man is indisputably in his element, was what Ernest Hemingway was trying to say in many of his novels over half a century ago.

- Men need permission to fail, from their caregivers, their peers, their adult partners, and from themselves. While definitions of failure are highly personal, for most men the concept of success becomes incorporated into their definitions of masculinity and thus they are constantly being threatened by some kind of failure. A man must be successful at *something*, and the more successes he has, the more remarkable a man he thinks he is. For many, like Bill, the deep-seated anger they end up wrestling with in middle age starts in late childhood when they are first saddled with someone else's expectations. If you don't make money, if you can't find a profession that you're good at, if you can't win a woman's affection and loy-alty—something is wrong with you. Women grapple with the same burden of having to prove themselves, whether it's career, motherhood, looking beautiful, or being helpful and nurturing. For a couple, it's sometimes hard—if each has his or her own definition of success and failure—to understand and empathize with the other. A husband may wonder, for example, why his wife is obsessed with the way she dresses every day, while she may question why he's always worried about money. If Bill and Alexandra don't communicate about their childhood issues, there's little chance of each understanding the other's definitions of success and failure. Each needs to reassure the other that as long as they give their best effort, failure is not only okay, it is a vehicle for self-discovery. Masculinity, instead of excluding failure, needs to embrace it as one of the cornerstones of growth.

- The difficult road to self-forgiveness, as Bill experiences,

105

turns a lot of men into miserable partners for their women. They can't stop beating themselves up, or they become passive-aggressive entities who are not happy in their relationships. Like Bill, because of the messages they got from their caregivers, they simply feel they're never "good enough." A lot of the men I spoke to said they feel confused, or just overwhelmed, by the multiple roles they're supposed to play—financial provider, husband, lover, wise father, overall problem solver, weekend do-it-yourselfer, compassionate friend, fighter and soldier—and the idea that they should be good at all of them. Yet they are afraid to complain because they'll be labeled wimps. They are especially perplexed by the myth that if you're a man you can do almost anything because men have always had it "easier" than women. One man interviewed for this book talked about the first time he felt that his life was going to be harder than his sister's. He was about nine years old when his father, a Vietnam vet, told him that the government could re-establish the draft whenever it wanted and he could be called upon to die for his country. He felt heroic and fearful at the same time. If there is danger in the world, a man learns early on that he—not a woman—is the one expected to sacrifice himself to protect others.

- Because they are asked to play so many roles, a lot of men feel they rarely measure up to expectations. So how can they feel better about themselves? First, they would be a lot happier—and a lot less needy—if they stopped trying so hard to prove themselves. Second, if they verbalized to their partners the pressures they feel and then did something about it, like delegating tasks or simply cutting back on their roles, their stress would abate. Third, if they recognized that our culture is riddled with fear-based behaviors and that this is partly attributed to men who run from failure—and subliminally pass the message onto their sons that it's okay to run—they might begin to re-educate themselves and become healthier role models.

- Bill talks about liking to be connected to his ex-girlfriends and wives. "Staying in touch" is common to a lot of men with whom I spoke. The attitude reflects many male insecurities: the denial that they were ever truly abandoned; the need to fill their emotional tank with a reserve memory or two in case their current relationship runs aground; the fantasy that even though a relationship is dead and buried from the woman's point of view, a man, with his special powers (superhero identification), can revive that relationship if he really needs to. The extent that a man fantasizes about his powers and abilities is often in direct proportion to the secret fears of his own impotence.

- Bill also talks about the process of emotionally disengaging from each of his wives, and falling out of love with them, when he feels they are no longer on his side. Perhaps he wouldn't feel so betrayed or abandoned if he didn't have such unrealistic expectations of what they can do for him. He needs to find happiness outside the world of relationships. Again, men—perhaps because they think they're so powerful, or they're so needy—want to make over women to meet their needs. Such expectations only lead to judgment and disappointment, and to a man falling out of love.

Chapter Seven

Tom's Story

A man never tells you anything until you contradict him.

—*George Bernard Shaw*

Say hello to Tom, a retired businessman in his late fifties with a thirty-plus year marriage and two grown children. He looks youthful—his hair is still not gray—and has a quick smile and penetrating blue eyes. Mindful of his health, he has always popped vitamins and worked out religiously. Tom considers himself empathetic and likes to do people favors. Until recently, he's always been driven to succeed—his admitted definition of masculinity—and compares his work ethic to that of his deceased father, a successful medical doctor. Tom prides himself on a close and loving relationship with his two grown children, a bond he never had with his emotionally absent father. The relationship with his wife, Sarah, a tall, striking brunette with emerald green eyes and a killer smile, is more tenuous. She, too, is driven to succeed. This is a common denominator that Tom first believed was a strong link between them. Over the years, though, it became a wedge in their relationship. Looking at himself critically, Tom has identified a series of co-dependencies with Sarah, among them the pursuit of money, that also once moored their relationship but ultimately came to shake it to its foundations.

Between love and money, Tom thinks, it's a toss-up which one people hold in higher esteem. In movies, books and talk shows, kudos go to love, especially romantic love, but in private he's not sure that's how most people feel. Romantic love is wonderful, he says, but it mostly affects adolescents and begins to fade by the time we're in our mid-to-late thirties, at least if we're with the same person. On the other hand, he knows, money lasts a lifetime. It buys a membership at the country club, a trip to Paris, a painting by the artist you love, not to mention comfort, opportunity, freedom, and peace of mind: a happiness that is safe from the violent swings of romantic love. Money is what kept Tom's parents' marriage together and, to an extent, his as well. Seeing himself as a romantic person, part of him is ashamed to admit his dependency on money but, when you grow up in an atmosphere of fear and insecurity, as Tom did, all too often money is the god you fall back on.

* * * * *

"I grew up in the San Fernando Valley in Southern California in the Fifties in an upper-middle-class WASP family. My father was a successful medical doctor, and my mother was a housewife. She was a cold, beautiful woman whose need for attention shadowed her, and overshadowed the rest of us, all her life. I have a brother who is three years older than I, and while our temperaments, relationships and values vary greatly, our impressions of our parents are pretty much the same.

"My dad was a sweet, caring man with a subtle sense of humor. He had many male friends and was particularly loved by his obstetrics patients for his bedside manner. By blood he was a quarter Cherokee and at home displayed that particular Indian penchant for quiet self-absorption. He was warm and aloof at the same time. He never said anything about how he felt. Except for the last day of his life, I never got to know him much beyond his easy charm, intelligence, and strict work ethic. He never once raised his voice. Anger just wasn't an emotion for him. My mother could yell at him on occasion, and certainly a lot at my brother and me, but Dad would just walk away rather than confront her. He didn't confront anyone, ever. He grew up dirt poor before the Great Depression and put himself through Stanford and then USC medical school, was a captain in the Navy, and was nearly killed by a Japanese sniper on Okinawa in World War Two. Just before the war, he met and married my mother while she was finishing nursing school.

"I think my father had a remarkable bio but, typical of his generation, he rarely talked about his past. From letters found after his death, I learned that his half-Cherokee father, a barber, died from alcoholism in his forties. His mother, it appears, was cold, demanding and judgmental. She died when I was around three so I have no memory of her, but according to my brother, she and my mother never got along. Their temperaments were too much alike. Dad, a devoted enemy of conflict all his life, was too smart or too fearful to take sides.

"My father had an office in our house and always locked it when he was away. When home, he spent hours there logging into ledgers every check he deposited or paid out. It didn't matter that he had monthly bank statements; there was just something about money and scrupulously keeping track of it that reflected his fear of poverty. Even after he was a successful doctor, he would return empty Coke bottles to the market in order to get the two-cent refund. But he wasn't necessarily frugal. He could spend whimsically and to excess. I remember him going to a men's store one afternoon and coming home with a dozen dress shirts and six pairs of shoes. He also had a six-times-a-year habit of running off to Las Vegas for long weekends, either alone or with his male friends. My guess is he sometimes lost significant amounts of money, because my mother's screaming fits often came after his return from Vegas.

"Despite all of his easy and many friendships, Dad was a loner at heart. While we had numerous annual family vacations, usually cross-country driving trips to one national park or another, the emotional dynamic was no different than it was at home—four people coexisting quietly without any real emotional connection. We were definitely not a physical family. Hugs and kisses were rare. No one ever said 'I love you.' Maybe we were all loners. It was as if it was our duty to get along but no one necessarily liked it.

"My mother's attitude about raising children was largely Victorian. Until we were seven or eight, when my brother and I misbehaved we were spanked with a coat hanger or our mouths were washed out with soap (for saying 'dirty words') or we were sent to our rooms without dinner. When we did have a regular dinner, we had to clean our plates because 'kids were starving in India.' Where my father was warm but distant, my mother was intense and purposeful. She loved the role of being the doctor's wife. That social status was the pinnacle of her rise out of Depression-era poverty. I never felt she was comfortable in her own skin, however. Introspection was just not her strong suit, yet she was quick to judge others. As a kid I was, in her eyes, lazy, irresponsible and unfocused. A lot of that was true. Besides never doing my chores well, I frequently got into trouble with neighbors, and was the class clown throughout grade school. Her primary duty in life, my mother later told a friend, was to whip me and my brother into shape. I think this was her definition of love.

"As I got older—eleven or twelve—my mother grew more impatient with me, and with her own life. I'm sure the two were related. Getting older and starting to lose her beauty, I think she took out some of her unhappiness on my brother and me. When I entered junior high she told me it was time I became 'a proper young man' and that she wouldn't tolerate any more misbehavior. The problem was, I never knew the definition of acceptable let alone exemplary behavior. My mother didn't give guidelines, just criticism. She definitely didn't give compliments or praise. Maybe it was a legacy from her mother—the idea that children, or certainly boys, didn't need to be praised because if you coddled or indulged them in any way they became spoiled. Yet I longed for her approval. My dad made his impact on me—he was my role model for achievement—but it was love and nurturing that I wanted from my mother.

"When I was fourteen, my mother contracted tuberculosis and spent almost two years in isolation in her bedroom. She took what seemed like a hundred horse pills a day. During the two summers of her convalescence my brother and I were sent away so we wouldn't disturb her rest. I lived with a family with six kids on a farm in Oregon. I enjoyed the rural life because it was so different from what I knew. But what I remember most were the many letters I wrote to my mother, which I found after her death. She had saved them without ever telling me. My letters were all incredibly sweet, anxious, lonely and full of concern for her. Looking back, I see them as love letters. I was afraid for all the pain she was in. I was afraid I would never see her again. Once in a while I got a letter back from her, reporting that she was doing as well as she could but no one had any idea how much she was suffering. I didn't understand the source of my anxiety at the time, but it was the same mentality, almost obsession, that would follow me my whole life. I kept thinking that if I told my mother how much I loved her, or did well in school, or my career—if I worked even harder and showed her how successful I could be—one day that compliment or big understanding hug would come my way.

"Throughout high school I didn't have a great social life because I had this stupid, sometimes paralyzing self-consciousness. The fear of failure was like a cloud over my head. I put pressure on myself to not make mistakes. Migraine headaches were a frequent event, and I began brushing my teeth so furiously at night that I eroded the gum line on my molars. I dated sporadically but was guarded about my emotions. Part of the problem was that I didn't have a role model when it came to intimacy. Mostly I was consumed with the future—college, career, how much money I needed to make—and soon became the classic overachiever: foreign exchange student, student body treasurer, honor society president. I was even afraid of getting sick because I thought illness was a kind of failure. If I stayed healthy, or gutted it out when I did get sick, I reasoned that someone would praise me for never missing school. When I finally graduated, I was the only one in my class who never missed a single day for six years. Except for my brother, who shook my hand perfunctorily, no one seemed to notice.

"Even when you're sixteen or seventeen, you may not really know what the rest of the world is like, not for sure. But you know your family's values, and you take them as the definition of normalcy. Dad kept up his familiar pursuits, which meant golf with his male friends, occasional weekends in Vegas, woodworking and photography in his spare time—the things that largely excluded Mom. Their universes were so separate that I'm sure they thought about divorce. Besides the social pressure to stay together, I think one of their bonds was money. Dad earned it and spent his share on all the material things he never had while growing up. Mom spent her portion on clothes, cosmetics, and parties. At the dinner table, our conversations were never about how anyone felt, except for my mother who, with menopause, began to complain about one physical ailment after another. Unlike the men in the family, for whom complaining or whining was considered a weakness, my mother had *carte blanche* to express her feelings. Half the time you would think the world was coming to an end. You would also think that a doctor-husband would notice, but Dad showed no special interest. I suspect he had fallen out of love with her, but I never asked or wanted to know because I didn't want something else to worry about. So many times Dad had to run off to the hospital to deliver a baby, leaving my mother stranded at the dinner table or just as they were leaving to attend a party. That made her crazy. I can see why she felt abandoned.

"I went to Stanford, just like my father (and brother), and graduated with a degree in English. Mostly I studied, got good grades, had a few inconsequential dates, and drifted home every summer for the mandatory manual labor job. I remember that my parents acted increasingly strange during this period. A lot of their friends were getting divorces or having mid-life crises, but my parents didn't talk about any of it. I know now, looking back, that social structure and stability were important to anyone who grew up in the Depression, so perhaps there was a lot of fear in both of them about breaking up.

"In my senior year I applied to graduate school near Chicago, in no small part to get far away from home. I chose an MBA program because I had no desire to go to law or medical school, yet I wanted the security of making a good living. My most significant accomplishment in graduate school was that I lost my virginity. This was during the late Sixties, the cradle of the sexual revolution. I was the poster child for late bloomers. Jo was a sweet, smart, cute girl from Missouri. Her sexual experiences were also limited but definitely not like mine, not zero. Once we became emotionally involved, and we began to make love, it was very awkward for me. I was afraid of being criticized by Jo. I had no idea about technique, or what brings a woman pleasure. Essentially, I thought, a guy just comes, and a woman does too. I didn't understand anything about correlating sex with intimacy and trust. But after a while I became more comfortable with myself, and more confident in my skills if not my deeper emotions. The same went for Jo. Ultimately sex meant liberation for us. On weekends we also closed down quite a few bars on Rush Street. For the first time in my life, I was really having fun. But after going together for about six months, we broke up. Looking back now, I just didn't know how to relate to a woman. Also, my anxiety over just about everything, particularly the war in Vietnam and the prospect of getting drafted, didn't help. But I never told Jo. To reveal doubts about myself was an internal taboo. I thought it was better just to get the hell out of the relationship.

"The strange thing about our breakup was that while it was initiated by me, I took it much harder than Jo. I realize now that if you have abandonment issues, it doesn't matter who does the rejecting—you still suffer. Sometimes you reject your partner before she rejects you, to avoid that pain, but you only end up feeling guilty and inadequate. Jo seemed to bounce back and find another boyfriend. I remained upset and not a little depressed for almost a year.

"By the time I finished graduate school, my need to be successful—and my corresponding fear of disappointing people —were ingrained in my behavior. While I appeared confident and projected the image of success, my self-esteem fluctuated on a daily basis. I constantly looked for approval from almost everyone I ran into—the waitress in the coffee shop, the cab driver, the dry cleaner—and would do so for the next twenty-five years. Then, later, as the tension in my marriage with Sarah began to grow, I started to understand where my fears and unhappiness really came from.

"I was drafted into the Army shortly after receiving my MBA, and ended up at Fort Ord in Monterey, California. While I had been dreading this for a couple of years, the reality was somewhat of a relief. I had been drafted, against my will, so whatever happened to me now wasn't my fault. I couldn't be judged. Because I'd been an English major, after finishing basic training I ended up as editor-in-chief of the Fort Ord newspaper. It kept me busy, and my thoughts away from the possibility of being sent to Nam and ending up in a combat zone.

"When I went home on Christmas leave that year, Dad seemed more tired than usual. But he was still his sweet self and, incredibly, the night I had to go back to Fort Ord, he asked me about the Army in detail. He also talked about his military experience, fighting the Japanese, all the death and destruction he knew, how afraid he'd been, and how guilty he'd felt to survive. For those few hours I think I got to know him better than I had in the previous 22 years. I kissed him on the cheek goodbye, wishing I could have stayed and talked more. I flew back to Fort Ord that night, then got a call at two in the morning from a friend of the family. My father had died in his sleep, apparently of a heart attack.

"I tried not to cry on the flight home, but at one point I broke down and sobbed. I kept telling myself to suck it up, that I was 23 years old and needed to be tough, but for the first time in my life I had absolutely no self-control. I felt this incredible hole in me and didn't know how to plug it. When I got home, my mother, in spite of being sedated by a doctor, was beside herself. Besides missing my father, I think she never imagined this kind of thing happening to her, and now that it had happened, she didn't know what to do. She was never the same again. She didn't remarry, despite many suitors. She became isolated, and somewhat bitter about no longer being accorded the status of a doctor's wife. Yet more than ever she needed to be the center of attention.

"Every weekend she would insist that my brother, who lived nearby, do her grocery shopping or fix something around the house or take her to dinner. Clearly, he was taking the place of Dad. Mom must have felt he was an improvement because my brother was giving her the attention that my father never had. This went on for years. I didn't know why my brother, by then a successful attorney and married, put up with this. (Today I do know. He was looking for that approval and love from her, just like I was in my way.) Part of me also wanted to be the dutiful son, but in the back of my mind I was thinking of my own needs, and about all the anger that I felt toward my mother. Why did everything have to revolve around her? But conditioned not to complain, I just pushed my anger deeper inside me.

"By sheer luck, I was never levied to Nam, and less than a year later I was honorably discharged from the Army. In a speed record that I was barely conscious of at the time, three months later I was married. In graduate school, a year after my breakup with Jo, I had met a sorority girl and drama major. Sarah was a tall, svelte brunette with high cheek bones and dazzling eyes. Intellectually we were extremely compatible, and our dates were mostly to museums and art films; we could talk for hours on almost any subject. For the first time, I felt genuinely comfortable around a woman. Sarah also had a big personality—she had more energy than anyone I'd known—that brought me out of my emotional shell. The eternal optimist, she was never down, never in a bad mood. She was also Jewish, from a prominent Connecticut family, and that too had an exotic appeal for me. I wanted to be involved with someone who was as different from me as possible.

"We kept in contact after I was drafted, and got back together once I was out of the Army. As I tried to adjust to the world, to find a job and a place to live, Sarah was the only one who seemed to embrace and accept me. She was my sanctuary. I was terrified of losing her. I also had strong feelings for her, stronger than I'd had for anyone else. So I proposed marriage, and she accepted. She said she knew it was her fate to marry a blond, handsome man from the West Coast. I know we both had deeper, more complex feelings, but neither of us really talked about them. I think, looking back, neither Sarah nor I considered ourselves emotional people. It was clear from our dating that we had a lot of similar goals and interests, and we both perceived those as one of our strongest bonds.

"I had only met Sarah's parents once, when they visited her in L.A., but suddenly I was living in a spare bedroom in their house and getting to know them well. Sarah's mother was gorgeous—a former Ford model—and a talented Vassar graduate who was full of personality, humor and warmth. She was the perfect mom. I had no idea at the time what impact this had on Sarah. My fiancée was pretty—very pretty—but she lacked the poise and classic beauty of her mother. Sarah's dad was from a wealthy family, a graduate of a prestigious college, and a successful stock broker in Manhattan. He was on the formal side, a judgmental man I was always careful to step lightly around for fear he wouldn't like me. Sarah seemed close to both her parents. I interpreted these as loving, caring relationships. There was no sullen anger, no self-pity, no lack of communication, no hidden agendas that I could spot. They were all interested in me, and for

118

once I could talk about my feelings with them. It felt great. This family had it all together. I thanked God it was so different from mine.

"About six months after Sarah and I were married, we got into our first serious argument. I don't remember the subject, but I started it. We were outside a restaurant, and people overheard us. Sarah was shaken. Ironically, for someone who had plenty of insecurities and who had a father who never fought, I could hold my own in a confrontation. Part of this was anger at my mother, I'm sure, getting misdirected at Sarah. It was also my misguided concept of masculinity: rather than surrender, a real man fights to the bitter end. Where I picked up that attitude, I'm not sure, because it was just the opposite of my father. 'Tom,' she said, 'I can't stand to fight with you.' She told me that her parents didn't even raise their voices, let alone get into arguments, and she didn't want to either.

"I soon learned that Sarah liked keeping anything that was unpleasant, like our argument, a secret. The rule was that you always 'put on a face.' If your dog had just died or you'd been in a major car accident, if someone asked how you were, you piped up, 'wonderful, thank you, how about you?' Sarah admitted her mother had raised her this way. I was confused by this message. After escaping my repressed family, and being encouraged by Sarah's parents to talk about my feelings, my inclination was to be more truthful, more emotional, even if it meant blowing up sometimes. But Sarah had received a different message. At the end of the day, her persuasive gifts won me over. I promised I would try not to get into arguments with her. I wanted her to be happy. I didn't know it at the time, but this seemingly harmless capitulation marked the moment I went back to burying my emotions in general.

"I believe this was also the start of our first co-dependency. I relied on Sarah's judgment in all things social, which allowed me into her Connecticut family and its privileged world. And Sarah felt secure because I was a smart, good-looking, successful young man who she was proud to marry. We gave each other validation. Was she in love with me? I think her emotions were just as jumbled as mine. We needed each other emotionally, for sure, and there was definitely love and tenderness, but I think 'being in love,' the absolute merging of souls, the Hollywood version of head-over-heels obsession, eluded us. Without either of us knowing it, ours was also a partnership with responsibilities and duties.

"A year after we were married, Sarah's mother called out of the blue. She told Sarah that she had just packed her suitcase and had left the house, and would be seeing a divorce attorney in the morning. Sarah and I were in shock. This couldn't be happening, not to her family. Sarah tried to talk her mom out of her 'drama,' but with no luck. Even today, more than thirty years later, Sarah has difficulty acknowledging the full impact of her parents' divorce. The perfect family—the couple who never argued, the couple who wanted me to talk about my feelings but didn't take their own advice—wasn't so perfect after all.

"The next day we drove to Connecticut to keep Sarah's father company. He was as mystified as we were about the reasons for his wife leaving. I felt sorry for him but it was hard to know how to help, except to be sympathetic. His wife had never given him a hint that she was unhappy, and he'd done nothing to make her so, he said. A week passed before Sarah's mom admitted to us that she was in love with another man. She was not one to divulge details—her life, I began to see, laid a heavy premium on appearances and secrets—but we pieced the puzzle together. She'd been having an affair with this man for at least fifteen years (and would soon marry him) because she had lost respect for Sarah's Dad, and fallen out of love with him a long time ago. I wondered how Sarah's dad could have been so clueless for so long. Was it denial? Was he just not observant? Or had Sarah's mom just wanted to live a secret life?

"Sarah was deeply hurt, yet it was against her upbringing to admit that life was anything less than rosy. Her self-definition was to be just as perfect as her mom. The ultimate effect of the divorce was to make Sarah want to be even more perfect. Whether this was to make up for her mom's 'mistake', or if it was some kind of competition with her mother, or something else, I had no idea. But Sarah would suddenly go out of her way to be liked—not unlike my own behavior, or my mother's—by virtually everybody.

"Sarah, it would turn out, was even more insecure than I was. Shortly after her parents' divorce, we were supposed to meet at a club for dinner. Sarah showed up two-and-a-half hours late. She couldn't understand why I was upset. She explained she was having a drink with an old friend of her father's, and having arrived late, she didn't want to be thought rude by leaving too soon. This became one of her patterns throughout our marriage. Sarah had to be seen by the whole world as perfect.

"But the more Sarah was there for everyone else—helping them solve their problems or offering advice or just being social—the less time I felt she had for me. Whenever I grew upset about her pattern of neglect, she would assuage me with some excuse and swear that it would never happen again. 'Tom, you know there's no one in my life more important than you.' Every time I would believe her. She also reminded me of how much she hated fighting, and that I had promised her not to get into arguments.

"Yet Sarah's behavior continued, and that became another of our patterns. She would get me upset—I would let her get me upset—and then she would make me feel better by fixing me a special dinner, or making love, or buying me a small present. And I liked it. I liked being taken care of. Sarah could be warm and intimate. Our lovemaking was terrific. I remember holding her afterwards in my arms—there was no better feeling in the world.

"I know now that I shouldn't have focused so much on Sarah's shortcomings. I wasn't taking responsibility for dealing with my own emotions and problems. All the anger I felt toward my mother (and sometimes even my father for his benign neglect), and especially with myself for living a repressed life—I didn't deal with any of it. To a large extent I let Sarah control my emotions. I let her heal me rather than learn to heal myself. And my irresponsibility allowed Sarah, by repeatedly coming to my rescue, to feel more secure in an unhealthy way. Maybe Sarah's deepest fear was that I would divorce her, so on some level she did everything in her power not to let that happen. This co-dependency grew deeper over the next thirty years without either of us really being aware of it.

"In our first years of marriage I worked hard, and not only at my public relations job. I would rise at four every morning to work on a novel. Even if I had a master's degree in business, I had learned about writing at Stanford and wanted to try my hand at fiction. I was disciplined and determined to be successful at whatever I tried. In the ambition department, however, Sarah was right behind me. This was the Seventies and women were suddenly flooding the workplace. Sarah decided to go to law school and was accepted at NYU. She studied incredibly hard, yet managed to keep our social lives intact. A drama major, she had an obvious talent for theatrics, so when in her third year she announced that she was going into criminal law because she liked the idea of arguing before a jury, I knew she'd be a natural.

"While there was one private side of Sarah—the sweetness and innocence of a child (the side I loved the most), there were two public personas. One was cheery, generous, empathetic and loyal. Sarah could make anybody think she was their new best friend. Like her mother, she could turn on her personality like a 1000 watt bulb. Winning new friends, or just making a strong first impression, was a way for her to get validation. This is not to say she was a phony. Sarah really did like most people. It was just that once they were out of her life, she more or less forgot them. I was keeping in touch with buddies from college and high school; Sarah rarely gave any of her old friends a call, or brought their names up in conversation.

"Sarah's second persona was more complicated. This was someone who acted supremely confident, feeding off the power of the Women's Movement, challenging anyone in her law class and later her firm with her ideas and ambition. This Sarah could be highly competitive, controlling, and secretive. Even though she didn't like to fight with me, she would willingly take on someone at work. She was not one to back down. She was clever at disguising this side of her—maybe she wasn't even aware of it—because her other persona was so dominant. With her charm and an infectious ability to please or persuade, Sarah could usually get people to do what she wanted. But if charm didn't work, she could go in the other direction, pressuring people with criticism. She was always a step or two ahead of everyone else.

"When she started as an associate at a prestigious Manhattan criminal law firm, she worked even harder than she had at law school. I began to see that her work ethic and drive for success were even stronger than mine. Yet if you paid Sarah a compliment, she would brush it off. If someone remarked, 'Sarah, what a great dress that is,' she would say, 'thank you, but my hair is a mess.' Or, 'Sarah, what a terrific job you did preparing that brief,' she would answer, 'it was okay, but the next one will be better.' She had made herself the center of attention, yet too much scrutiny or praise made her uncomfortable. This has been a habit most of her life. To me it reveals Sarah's core insecurity. She must have figured out while growing up that playing the role of the perfect daughter in the perfect family was wrong. Yet she didn't know what to do about it, except not to tell anyone and keep playing the role.

"After seven years in Manhattan, Sarah told me one weekend that she was tired of New York and wanted to move west. I was mystified until she revealed that she was having a major disagreement with her boss (with whom she'd often been in conflict), and that New York had begun to feel claustrophobic to her. Then, with a huge smile, she also told me she was pregnant. I couldn't believe it. We'd been trying to have a child for a couple of years. Being a father—a good and caring father—was extremely important to me. We were both deliriously happy. When I thought about it, I didn't mind the idea of a move. I had now published a couple of novels and had quit my public relations job. Two of my books had become minor best sellers, both had been reviewed in the Sunday *New York Times* book section, and one would eventually make us over $100,000. I saw a career ahead of me.

"After an exploratory visit to Phoenix and a job offer from a law firm there, Sarah couldn't wait to move. I wasn't as sure. Phoenix was another metropolis, I argued. We could go anywhere—why not somewhere near the ocean? We debated about it for a couple of weeks. In the end I went along with Sarah's wish. Looking back, I wish I hadn't agreed so quickly. I had fallen under Sarah's persuasive spell like most everyone else. This was to become another pattern in our relationship that started out benignly but ended explosively. Too often I would do what Sarah wanted rather than express my own will. None of my behavior in those days makes me proud, but it was conditioned behavior from my childhood: accepting familial authority, especially maternal authority.

"For Sarah, leaving New York fulfilled another emotional mandate. Both her parents were now remarried and she continually remarked how weird it felt to visit them in different households. I think the little girl in her still fantasized about her fairytale past. Because that was now all but wiped out, there was only one solution—get away from it all.

"We bought a house in Scottsdale, basking in the warm weather, and once our son Robert was born, Sarah wasted no time going to work at her new firm. She put in long, exhausting hours, and I did most of the childcare while also writing my next novel. Neither Sarah nor I complained about our new lifestyle, as taxing as it was at times. Sarah's assertive personality, incredible work ethic, and natural leadership abilities prevailed at her firm. Within three years she was billing almost twice the hours she'd billed in New York. We also had our second child, a beautiful daughter we named Alice. This didn't slow Sarah down. Because she insisted on nursing, Sarah went to her office every morning carrying Alice in a bassinet.

"I wasn't jealous of Sarah's success. I was proud of her. I was a believer in the Women's Movement because I thought all efforts at pushing gender equality were positive. Besides, my wife earning a good salary took pressure off me. While I had published my third and fourth novels without difficulty, I was suddenly struggling on my fifth. After getting a dozen rejection letters, my agent diplomatically suggested I start another book.

"As she grew more successful in her law practice, Sarah's old patterns of lateness and broken promises resurfaced. 'Sorry, I was busy with a client,' became such a common excuse for Sarah showing up late for dinner that I just accepted it. My self-esteem was not exactly flourishing, though I pretended to Sarah that I was just fine. I pretended to myself as well because, frankly, the truth was way too painful. My fifth novel never got published, and my sixth was in a third rewrite. Because I was in professional turmoil, I felt I had to carry my share of the load by at least taking care of the kids and the house.

"Another pattern also surfaced at this time. Sarah was becoming embroiled in a growing disagreement with senior partners over how the firm was distributing its case load. Because Sarah did not get along well with authority figures, I could see it coming: one night she told me she would be leaving her firm and starting her own. Then she dropped a bombshell: she wanted me to join her. My MBA and experience in finance would come in handy. We would be a team. This would be 'our' company. She asked—she pleaded—that I really think about it. I wouldn't have to do that much, she said; just keep the office running. We'd only have to hire a couple more attorneys to make the venture profitable. I looked at our financial needs with two young children to raise. It seemed like the perfect solution. We could use every extra dollar, to be sure, but money was also important to me psychologically, just as it had been to my parents. But it wasn't everything, I knew. Sarah and I made a pact. Once we made a certain amount of money, I could leave our new venture and go back to writing full time.

"My pattern of accepting Sarah's ideas had already started

with the move to Phoenix. Really, it had started with our first argument outside the restaurant. I would capitulate to Sarah many more times in the future: to grow our law firm despite her promise to keep it small, to take on more overhead, to put in more hours. Years later, long after we had reached our financial benchmark and I was free to leave, I continued to stay on. I am honestly not sure why. Did money—and the power and respect that came with it—become more important to me as I got older? Did I lack the confidence and the will and emotion to go back to writing? Struggling with the fifth and sixth books definitely felt like failure to me, and I didn't know to deal with failure. There had been no real precedent, and no role models. If you come from a family where love and approval were tied to being successful, failure becomes a real problem. In order to feel successful, wasn't it just easier to stay the course with the law firm? When we hit our financial benchmark, Sarah didn't exactly insist that I leave; she reminded me of my option to leave, but it was clear she preferred that I stay.

"Anyone reading this story can probably guess its climax. Sarah was unstoppable in her pursuit of excellence and approbation. In the next fifteen years, the firm expanded to twenty partners and twenty-five associates. I went from working three-to-four hours a day to ten-to-twelve. I never matched Sarah's tireless energy, not at work, but I became the primary caregiver for Robert and Alice. Even though we had live-in help, out of guilt I would dash from the office to take the kids to soccer or ballet, then out to dinner, then back to the house to help with homework, then once more to the office for details that needed attention before morning. Sarah, busy with her cases, was often nowhere in sight.

"Life became so crazed that I forgot how to think, how to breathe, how to do anything but to be on call 24/7 for either our firm or for Robert and Alice. I was in adrenaline mode. How else did one get by? I don't want to say that Sarah was deliberately neglectful. She was doing her best to make a handsome living for the family, and when she was home she was a conscientious mom. No birthday was unmemorable. For holidays she pulled out all the stops. But as much as Sarah adored Robert and Alice and they loved her, their memories of growing up are mostly with me.

"There was virtually no time for me to write anymore. Still, I would try, rising at four in the morning again, and every now and then I published a book. But I no longer had the focus or energy to write the significant novel of which I thought I was capable. And there was a second, even stronger frustration building in me. While Sarah enjoyed the public limelight, I was buried in the office, solving myriad behind-the-scenes problems. Whenever Sarah saw how overburdened I was, she would promise extra help and that soon I could get back to my writing full time. Her speeches cheered me.

"Down deep, however, the validation issue began to trouble me. While Sarah had become a marquee name in Phoenix law circles, most people hardly knew my role. The attorneys in our office appreciated me, but Sarah had the habit of jumping in and solving administrative problems that were supposed to be my responsibility. Whenever I confronted her, she would say, 'Tom, I'm only trying to help.' But I felt it was as if she wanted to take credit for everything. She wanted to prove to the world she was Superwoman, yet she seemed to have no idea how this was making me feel.

"Part of the problem was that we were both perfectionists. We were competing against each other without fully acknowledging it. I wanted credit for things just as much as Sarah did. We would tell ourselves we were being supportive of each other, but it was an unhealthy competition that, looking back, obviously had a lot to do with control. My one undisputed power in the company were the finances. Sarah cared about money because it was basically a yardstick of her success, but little more. She didn't want to read a profit-and-loss statement or balance sheet. All that was left to me, including investing our savings, which I did successfully. Like my father who had poured over his ledgers in his study, combing through every financial statement and watching over our every investment made me feel secure.

"After too many drinks at a party one night, I commented to one of Sarah's female friends that I sometimes felt overlooked and overshadowed by my wife at work. I was just trying to be honest and to let some of my frustration out. The woman cocked her head at me and said I had way too big an ego. I was being unsupportive of Sarah who, after all, had started the law firm from scratch and was largely responsible for its huge success and the lavish lifestyle we were now living. I had a typical male ego, insecure and competitive, afraid to give women their due, she said.

"When I repeated the conversation to Sarah the next morning, she pretended that none of it mattered, and changed the subject to a vacation in Mexico we were planning. I looked away. I had begun to feel I was no different than a client in Sarah's eyes. I was someone who had to be stroked and mollified at the right time before she went on to solving the next crisis. If I started an argument, Sarah only reminded me that arguing was unproductive, that it reminded her of the pain of her parents' divorce. There was nothing I could say that Sarah didn't have an answer for. I began to feel invisible. Clients would phone all evening and Sarah unfailingly took their calls.

Memories swept over me of my childhood dinners and the patients who called my father, and how angry my mother would get.

"Somewhere around this time, Sarah and I stopped looking into each other's eyes. Sex became a once-a-month event at best. And because I didn't vocalize my unhappiness, Sarah, the eternal optimist, assumed everything, while stressful, would ultimately right itself.

"By the time I turned 57, I began visibly to unravel. I became sloppy in helping employees and attorneys. I often didn't return phone calls or e-mails. My energy and love for my work was no longer there. My energy for anything was no longer there. I had the feeling that if I disappeared tomorrow, no one would miss me. I was miserable, and the source of my misery, I decided, was Sarah. One weekend I finally told her, calmly, how I felt and why. I said my problem was perhaps one that she could not solve this time. She masqueraded to the world as Ms. Perfect, but in reality she was as insecure as I was. She had lured me into her world with false promises, I added, and while I was not blameless—I had gone along with the program—I thought that she didn't really care about my happiness. I was tired of being a 'we.' I wanted to be an 'I' again, or perhaps the 'I' that I'd never been. The loneliness and the desire to be one with someone that had pushed me into my relationship with Sarah were now the same forces pulling us apart. I think this happens to a lot of men with lost childhoods, ones where they never had a voice. Sarah burst into tears and then grew angry, as if she had been holding something in for a long time. She attacked me for being emotionally disengaged, indifferent to her accomplishments, and for criticizing her as her father had done. Then she accused me of wanting to divorce her, to cause her more pain.

"I didn't want a divorce necessarily—I was too confused to think clearly—but a separation was definitely called for. Sarah reluctantly agreed, and I moved into the guest house on our property. About this time my mother, still in California, was diagnosed with dementia. My brother and I put her in the best assisted-care home we could find. In her moments of clarity she let us know how unhappy she was, and asked angrily how we could do this to her. Sarah tried to be supportive of what I was going through but I kept doubting her sincerity. I felt it was more of her general efforts to make me or anyone else feel good. My old abandonment issues resurfaced. Fair or not, linking Sarah with my mother in my mind was unavoidable—two strong women who could manipulate me. I slept two or three hours a night, took to eating most of my meals alone, and jumped in my car and made midnight drives to nowhere.

"That summer my mother was rushed to the hospital with kidney failure. My brother and I were at her side in less than 24 hours. While she was still conscious, she kept looking at us but didn't say much. I told her that I loved her, even if I didn't feel it, but she didn't offer any 'I love you too,' nor that elusive compliment or hug I'd always longed for. As I watched her die, I couldn't believe it was happening this way. I took her hand, met her stoical gaze, and then she was gone.

"After her funeral, I thought that her death would finally release me from the pain of the past. Instead, I felt more angry, hurt and alone than ever. I went back to my habit of taking midnight drives and hanging out with friends. I didn't care about eating or taking care of myself. I lived moment to moment. I knew I was having a breakdown, but it wasn't an entirely negative thing. As I grew disengaged not just from Sarah but our series of co-dependencies, I felt a burst of powerful new emotions. I could be sitting and reading a book, then suddenly have a new insight into my life or be overwhelmed by childhood memories, and the next thing I knew I was in tears. I was awash in emotions that I hadn't felt in decades. After thirty years of marriage, I wanted less to do with Sarah and more to do with my friends. The trust and intimacy I had been unable to access in myself as a teenager now came welling up. As a teenager I had felt awkward and insecure around girls; now I sought out women not so much for approval but just for their company. I wanted to be relaxed and open.

"With Alice and Robert, Sarah liked to tell them that everything was fine, but I was more forthright with the kids, who were now in their twenties. To work with your spouse day in and day out for nearly thirty years, come home together, wake up together, and still have a romance-based, loving relationship, I told them, was not an easy thing. I also tried to explain my childhood issues, and then the series of co-dependencies that bonded Sarah and me. I don't know if they understood. There was a huge amount of disappointment and sadness in their eyes, but there was also acceptance.

"Sarah and I agreed to try a marriage counselor. By now the whole office knew of the friction in our relationship. Tongues wagged. There was so much new gossip every day that I didn't want anything to do with the firm. With the help of the marriage counselor, Sarah and I both raised good points, but ultimately little seemed to get resolved. I then went into several months of private therapy. When I suggested to Sarah that she and I had similar issues with validation and perfection, she refused to understand. The more I delved into my emotions, and the more I admitted to myself the destructive patterns of my life, the more unsettled Sarah grew. She blamed me for not only hurting her personally but jeopardizing all the success we'd achieved together. I asked Sarah how well she knew herself, and did she know how hard it was for two people to live and work together who were both relentless overachievers?

"To her credit, Sarah slowly came around: to understanding my point of view just as I came to understand hers; to going into therapy to deal with her own issues; and to stop obsessing about success and being liked by the world. Around the office she held her head high. She came to learn what I had already accepted: that people who gossiped and judged you were the most insecure people of all. After another year of living with the demands of her career, and simultaneously accepting how her personal world was changing, she decided to retire. I have since become involved in other business ventures while Sarah is still considering her options. Being free has been a huge adjustment for her, but a healthy one. We now hold nothing back from one another, and have given each other the freedom and trust we should have bestowed decades ago.

"What I have learned from this journey? When you get overwhelmed by your emotions, especially by your childhood and adolescence, it is extremely hard to have clarity on anything. You keep waiting for the issues to resolve themselves, but they rarely do. You have to be the agent of change. Looking back on our turbulence, I think neither Sarah nor I had strong identities, despite what our clients, friends, children, and peers thought. We had strong personalities but not clear identities. A personality is something that other people relate to. An identity is something you relate to. Our lives were based on achievement and not on understanding who we really were or whether we even liked ourselves. I think the sad fact for many men and women is that in the middle-age years they stop growing, questioning, exploring and challenging themselves. They settle, rest, and compromise. They also turn toward a pursuit of the false gods with which they were raised. Just because you reject those idols intellectually doesn't mean you escape them emotionally. If you grew up aware that your parents believed that money, material acquisitions and social status were worth pursuing, the emotional connotations you place on those goals just don't go away. And if you fail to achieve them, the affliction of failure weighs on every part of your life.

"I sometimes think about my dad, what quiet strength he had without needing anyone to tell him he was great. His life was his validation. While he had his hang-ups and weaknesses, he also had his own universe of hobbies, friends, golf, and trips to Vegas. A male universe, a world without women. Looking back now, I think that was pretty significant. Perhaps there was a definition of masculinity, self-esteem and independence for me all along. But like my dad's personality, it was just so quiet and subtle I never picked up on it."

Summary and Interpretation

- Tom, like many men, suddenly wakes up in middle age to realize he's not happy, that his life feels like a fraud, and that he has little respect for himself. Memories and emotions from childhood come welling up in a tidal wave of anger and frustration. A psychologist would add that Tom, like a lot of men, carries around a significant amount of guilt for not measuring up to his caregivers' expectations (in Tom's case, his mother) and re-experiences those feelings of guilt whenever he disappoints Sarah. He's one of those emotional time bombs that, when it goes off, scatters the fragments of his life in all directions. It's not clear whether Tom actually fell out of love with Sarah or if he simply fell into a deep relationship crisis. He's in a car with no brakes, careening down a foreign slope. But just when he's the most out of control, he has unexpected insights and moments of clarity that bring him some calm. He realizes that giving up his definition of masculinity—the idea that a man always has to be responsible and hard working, that he has to succeed—is a necessary transition to getting away from his guilt and anger.

- The label of "mid-life crisis" seems to get pinned more on men than on women. This is certainly not because women don't have crises, but perhaps they are more aware of the changes in their emotions, hormones and bodies as they approach and go through menopause. Because of this self-awareness as well as the socialization process, women may be better prepared to confront a crisis because they see it coming. Men, on the other hand, too often are unwilling to deal with their childhood issues, buried emotions, and partnership problems until a crisis hits them over the head. Often several crises come at once, as they did for Tom: careers peak, virility wanes, they are no longer needed as fathers, and they lose respect for themselves because they fear they have lost the respect of others.

- The goals of money, success and control as raised in Tom's story represent other components of his masculinity. Focusing on externals, such as material comforts, allows Tom to hide from his deeper emotions. For a lot of men, when money and acquisitions become their accepted yardstick for success, and they see other men, including their role models, subscribe to the same values, it's easy to believe they're doing the right thing. Conformity is a strong lure for anyone who lives with a lot of fear. Fear also becomes the foundation of a false masculinity—a masculinity that is as much about things men shouldn't do as things they should. *Don't show your weaknesses; don't surrender; don't trust your competition; don't compromise unless you have to; don't feel sorry for yourself; don't let anyone too close because they might want something from you; don't let anyone see you sweat; don't admit your pain...* For a man, there are more "thou shall not's" than there are in the Ten Commandments.

- Like other men in this book, Tom's life is an illustration of the influence of his mother on his emotional development and self-esteem. Sometimes one or two seemingly innocent moments can impact a life forever, such as Tom's mother telling him, at age 13, it was time to become "a proper young man." At the age when other adolescents are just beginning to explore who they are and have fun, Tom shuts down. It's almost as if a domineering mother "owns" her son until he enters adolescence and, in Tom's case, emotionally dominates him for years afterwards. As an adult, still shut down, Tom faces the same need for validation his unhappy mother faced, and has the same difficulty that his mother had in expressing that need to Sarah.

- When Tom eventually begins to self-destruct, at first he seeks validation the old fashioned way—though the traditional masculine outlets of work, money and achievement. When that doesn't fill the void, only then does he look into himself for a solution. For a lot of men like Tom, admitting their lack of self-love is the first step to healing. The second step is to acknowledge that seeking validation from others is a losing game. The third step is to shed the fear of failure. Once that is accomplished, the fourth step becomes possible: to be completely open to, and trusting of, yourself and your partner.

- Women are understandably sensitive to mother-bashing. After all, being a mother is a major definition of being a woman. What comes from their womb, women feel, rightfully, is their responsibility, and many don't want men telling them how to raise their children. It's when that sense of responsibility somehow gets translated into domination, control and ownership that the relationship becomes distorted and the child begins to feel resentment. However, anger towards one's mother is almost always suppressed. Men know it's taboo to openly attack one's mother or motherhood in general. (Women have less restrictions in criticizing their mothers, as men do their fathers.) While there are no official statistics that I'm aware of, retailers report that Mother's Day cards outsell Father's Day cards by a significant margin, and the majority of buyers are men. Whether from guilt, duty or genuine love, men are reluctant *not* to honor their mothers.

• But many men, if they're being truthful, will admit to feeling failed by their mothers. To use corporal punishment on boys, to refrain from nurturing them, to urge at an early age that they "become men," to teach them that success and achievement are the quintessential male values—this gives a boy the hidden message that love is conditional. *If you do what I tell you, I'll be so proud of you.* Out of frustration with her own life, a mother like Tom's is sometimes determined to mold her son into the kind of man she'd like her partner to be. This may be subconscious behavior, but it is likely to turn the child into an adult who feels burdened by expectations. He may feel, as Tom does, that he can simply never be good enough. In the back of his mind is his mother's voice, telling him what he needs to do to be loved. To disguise his fear of inadequacy, he makes himself as charming and sympathetic as possible, and he overachieves in spades. Any man who has been raised by a domineering mother might, in the beginning, be attracted to a strong, willful partner, but in the end he may pull away from her, and harbor a distrust of women in general. In Tom's case, his resentment toward his sick mother, who never showed him the affection and acceptance he craved, paralleled his growing disengagement from Sarah.

- Several men interviewed for this book (but who chose not to write their stories) talked about their devotion to their mothers. In their homes, they admitted, were an abundance of photos of their parents or, in particular, photos of them with their mothers. However, the more details they revealed about their lives, the more their mother-worship seemed like an escape from an unhappy marriage, problems with their children, a job they hated, or a lack of friends. Seeking a connection to a time in their lives when they felt safe and secure, these men, usually overprotected by their caregivers, may never have had the opportunity to learn to problem-solve, trust their judgment, set boundaries, or relate to other adults, including their adult partners.

- It's important to make the distinction between men who had healthy, nurturing and supportive relationships with their mothers—and who make sensitive, empathetic lovers and husbands—and those who were suffocated and controlled, even in the name of love. A lot of parents, because they were emotionally neglected as children, try to "make up" for that neglect by being overly indulgent with their own children. In the end, they only rob their sons and daughters of confidence, independence and emotional maturity.

- The cliché that men are not communicative, especially about their emotions, is challenged in Tom's story. When Tom figures out his emotions, he can't stop talking. Part of his frustration in not getting along with Sarah is centered on Sarah's inability or unwillingness to listen to him, and to be forthright about *her* feelings. Perhaps too many women believe that men don't care about their own emotions and thus they see no need to care either. But, in fact, men ultimately disengage from their partners when their feelings are continually discounted or marginalized, and particularly when they feel rejected.

- Tom sets the stage for losing self-respect by his complicity to live under Sarah's dominant shadow and by his failure to assert his own feelings. Relationships in which men or women let themselves be controlled by their partners because the basic lifestyle is "comfortable" have a high likelihood of imploding. Also, the masculine sense of sacrifice—in this case nobly living with his unhappiness—is another of Tom's weaknesses.

- For Tom, there were many reasons for failing in his relationship with Sarah: a lack of self-love in both of them; getting lost in work; getting addicted to power, money and control; and confusing their co-dependencies with intimacy. Tom recognized what was happening before Sarah did. Yet, not fully accepting the lessons he learned, or unwilling to admit failure, he was slow to communicate with Sarah.

- As Tom recognizes, a man's need to be whole, to be healed, and to be one with another soul is a galvanizing force and can be defined as one way of falling in love. But when the bonds begin to dissolve, and the intimacy and unification he was once seeking slip away, he will tear away from his partner, often in an attempt to find a happiness he never had in his childhood.

- In judging the attractiveness of a man, most women rank self-esteem and confidence as "must have" qualities. Tom admits, however, that his confidence is not what it appears to be. Like strutting peacocks, dazzling their audience with brilliant colors, men often make a show of confidence because they know that's what women desire or even expect. This is not dissimilar to adolescent males condoning lies and deception to get a girl into bed. It's linear male logic: to get what you want, just tell them what they want to hear, show them what they want to see. Burdened by

139

the mandate to succeed, it's very difficult for men not to play the role of impostor to some degree. Even after a man has won over a woman, without a continued display of confidence he fears his partner won't respect him. Worse, a lack of confidence in one area is the harbinger of failure in others. Tom was brought up to believe that if you fail, nobody is going to love you. That's why in high school he was desperately seeking validation from his peers when he couldn't get it from his parents.

- One of the more destructive assumptions of masculinity is that men need to lead and make the tough decisions because this makes them feel in control. Many women, holding the real control in a relationship, allow their partners to feel they're in charge because it makes the relationship run more smoothly. This was certainly the case with Tom and Sarah. While being a leader is supposed to be "men's work," it's really just another prison cell. Because they often don't like to lead or compete in areas where they aren't competent, men are often afraid of trying to new things. The old joke about men refusing to ask for directions has a serious underpinning: admitting they are lost is like admitting they have no power, no confidence, no ability. Even in areas where they are competent, most prefer a routine where the rules for success and failure are clearly defined. This also applies to relationships where the roles of each partner are agreed upon: who washes the cars, who makes the beds, who does the dishes, who pays the bills, who drives the kids to school. These are terribly important from a male point of view. All tasks need to be defined, assignable and consistent. Logic and order must rule the day. If he does his job and does it well, a man thinks, he escapes blame and judgment, and wins praise. When his partner tampers with the rules and routine of the relationship, a man will either fight back or begin to disengage emotionally. Falling out of love is gradual.

- Why are so many men more determined to meet their definition of masculinity than to put the same attention and effort into a successful relationship? The answer might be that "being a man" (depending on how one defines it) is less complicated than developing a lasting, intimate relationship. This is the double-edged sword of masculinity. While some of its manifestations are an immense and confusing burden—full of conflicts, hidden messages and stress points—other definitions can be life saving. Compared to building and sustaining a relationship, the emotional dividends from masculinity are more dependable and immediate. Getting involved with sports, cars or computers, for example, or any pursuit that has a clearly defined goal and doesn't involve ambiguity, has great appeal to men. Some definitions of masculinity are so simple and straightforward. Whether it's scoring a touchdown or fighting in Iraq or just going to work every day, men see themselves as performing their sacred duty. In their eyes, they are behaving heroically and often sacrificing themselves for others. They don't understand why their partner gets upset when they work a sixty-hour week and come home tired and irritated. They expect acknowledgement and praise, not criticism. Criticizing or belittling men for their passions, or what they perceive as their duty, can quickly create a wedge in a relationship and a reason for men to fall out love.

141

Chapter Eight

George's Story

Misery and shame are nearly allied.

—*Samuel Johnson*

The most likely place to find George in his free time is riding his motorcycle. Thirty years old, single, a self-employed writer, musician and filmmaker, he has "don't fence me in" written all over him. He wears his hair long, favors a leather jacket, and is more comfortable in work boots and jeans than anything fancy. His face is long and expressive, and his skin is pale. His life is driven by a strong intellectual curiosity about politics, the arts and social values; the struggle to grow comfortable with his emotions; and an effort to balance his life between loving someone and seeking a Thoreau-like independence.

An only child, George was born and raised in an isolated town in northern Wisconsin. There was a small population of Ojibwa Indians nearby but most families were Caucasian and blue-collar. Most fathers worked at the paper mill, the town's largest employer. Definitely a company town, and not a particularly happy one because of periods of high unemployment and the chronic fear of being laid off, George remembers. There was no such thing as high culture, he adds dryly, unless you count hunting and fishing.

George describes his small-town environment as being as soul-crushing as Wisconsin's interminable winters. He doesn't ever romanticize blue collar life. Growing up, it was considered cool by his friends to bash anyone who went to college, and no one was ever caught dead in the library after school. "If you didn't start drinking beer by age 10 you were judged a freak," he says. "I don't like looking back at my childhood—it was tense and volatile—but I do so in order to understand where my life is today. I call myself a free-thinker, a liberal, and anti-authoritarian in every healthy way. Social injustice and poverty make me queasy. I wasn't born until the Seventies, but my attitude and idealism belong to the Sixties."

George was one of the few in his peer group who did make the jump to college. Being different in an environment of overwhelming conformity made him grow up quickly. Self-esteem, he says, didn't come without surviving a period of adolescent depression. Later, a Jack Kerouac-like journey with his girlfriend across the country turned him into a self-described existentialist. The basis of his "male values," he says, is a confluence of childhood lessons and a strong sense of self-preservation.

* * * * *

"My mother was a professional bookkeeper, and even though we needed the money from her work, she committed to staying home with me until I was five. My Mom is funny, witty, sharp as a tack, and in some ways tougher than a Sherman tank. We've always gotten along. Dad worked in a non-management job in the paper mill for thirty years before it was shut down in the orgy of downsizing in the Nineties. When he was forced to retire, he never did get the full pension he was entitled to. Even before that, he was disgruntled and angry for most of his thirty years at the mill. He truly hated his job—yet, paradoxically, he was devoted to it. He couldn't stand being sick or missing a day of work. But whenever he came home he looked miserable. His temper was explosive. Without warning, he would throw chairs, go off on tirades about the people he worked with, or belittle me for the slightest perceived infraction. He was a cruel father even if I don't think he meant to be.

"One of my worst memories took place one weekend when I was passing my father some bricks off the back of our pickup, and he was pounding them into the ground to make a walkway. Each pair of bricks was either horizontal or vertical in relation to the line of the sidewalk and they alternated according to position. I was supposed to be setting the bricks on the tailgate in the correct position so dad could just grab them and automatically put them in place. Apparently I set them up wrong. He glared at me. 'Nine years old and you can't even take a simple direction, can you?'

"I also remember him on weekends, just sitting at the kitchen table, chain smoking, brooding over his coffee, making lists of things to do. I think he liked to keep busy to keep his anger at bay—and to avoid interacting with Mom and me. He was so straight-laced and uptight that he didn't even allow himself the luxury of an occasional beer. He was obsessed with work. He burned the concept of a work ethic into his brain—and mine. He would always work at least 50 hours a week, sometimes 60, and once or twice he put in ninety hours. It was insane, yet if he'd been asked to work even harder he would have said yes. In his thirty years, except for vacations, I believe he missed maybe four or five days because of illness. It was as if his job, which I only later came to understand was the cause of much of his anger, was something he couldn't leave unattended. He couldn't allow himself to fail. As I said, he was tormented by his job, yet it also defined his self-worth.

"I have friends today who, every time they've lost a job,

experience a sense of defeat that affects their relationships with their partners and children. You start to think that if you screw up in this one pivotal way—the role you were born for—you wonder if something is wrong with you. Your confidence and self-esteem are shaken, and inevitably you take it out on other people.

"It was only much later, when his position at the mill was eliminated and Dad spent more time at home, that I really got to know him. I was about sixteen or seventeen by then. He suddenly opened up to me, as if he realized that that was one of the things he owed my mother and me after years of shutting us out. I began to see where his rage had really been directed. He had had a Dickensian childhood. His father turned out to be already married when he married my grandmother—that kind of dysfunction set the tone for the family—and there was never enough money. My dad was the oldest of eight brothers and sisters and to a large extent was responsible for raising them. When the slightest thing went wrong, he was blamed by his parents. He never had a chance to speak up or defend himself, or just to be a kid. That same shame-oriented environment was duplicated at the paper mill, a hyper-masculine, high-stress workplace where you never spoke back to your boss. Also, Dad was so much more capable and intelligent than the work he was assigned. So the rage just built and built and had to come out somewhere. As Anaïs Nin wrote, 'shame is the lie someone told you about yourself.'

"My dad's life taught me that what society expects of men, at least the working class, is far from human. The stoicism, the obedience, the group-think—it's all this pseudo-masculinity. If those concepts are taken too much to heart, they wound you and wound grievously. To this day, because of what happened with my father's life, as well as what I learned on my own, I came to see how undemocratic most democratic institutions can be. I will always have a strong distrust of authority. As symbols go, flags, jails, churches and court houses are scary to me. I'm suspicious of anyone who blindly follows the common wisdom and doesn't think for himself. At my core I guess I'm something of an anarchist. I hope I never age out of it.

"For four years my parents sent me to a Catholic elementary school. Even at that young age, while I could recite the required liturgy in the required robotic voice, I never felt spiritually elevated or that I was part of something bigger than myself. If anything, I felt more alone and isolated. In my view, the Church was just one more institution to be leery of. I'm not hesitant to say that today I'm an outright atheist.

"My mom was to some extent my salvation. And not because she coddled or overindulged me to compensate for my dad's rages. Just the opposite. If I got in fights with kids and came running home, Mom told me to go right back outside and 'take care of it.' That meant go back and kick the crap out of someone. That wasn't easy. I was small for my age, socially awkward, and not especially aggressive. But Mom knew that in my neighborhood, if you back down, you'll always be picked on. I did what she told me. In many ways it was my mother, not my father, who taught me to embrace my masculine side. Mom also had a great sense of humor and I adopted it as my own to get through many family crises.

"Mom also encouraged me to read and learn as much as I could. I remember subscribing to *Discover* magazine when I was in the fourth grade and loving everything about science. This didn't fit with my more sports-oriented, library-hating friends, and by the process of elimination, I suppose, I was soon labeled a geek. I garnered attention by reading the ingredients on the labels of whatever god-awful food we were served in the school cafeteria. It doesn't sound like something to brag about, but being able to read 'partially hydrogenated animal protein' in the fourth grade secured my reputation as a brain.

"My first real role model was Indiana Jones. The Harrison Ford character in the movies was exactly who I wanted to be: strong, quick and deadly, but driven by a quest for knowledge rather than a desire to be rich or famous; basically a geek who no one wanted to tangle with. Later in my life I would take up martial arts and became good enough to make money teaching it.

"When I was around nine, my dad developed an interest in commercial dog-sled racing. Because a kennel wasn't allowed within city limits, we had to move to an even smaller town, twenty minutes away; it might as well have been another planet. When I entered fifth grade there, I was greeted like the outsider I looked like. Already I kept my hair long and my choice of clothes wasn't the usual blue-collar wardrobe. I was rechristened a geek but not a helpless one. In Catholic school I'd learned to defend myself with my fists, so being picked on didn't worry me. My concern was that it was hard to make friends with people I found truly interesting; they tended to snub me. I suppose they couldn't get beyond my appearance, or that I was the new kid in town. This, by the way, seems like one of nature's cruelest tricks: how do you meet people if you're introverted but still need friends? I developed a pattern that I maintain today of having two or three very close friends whom I trust implicitly. Everyone else, while I'm polite to them, I keep at arm's length.

"I was an unmotivated student in junior high and, whether it was cause or effect, adrift emotionally. My dad still scared the hell out of me at this time. We got into ferocious arguments about the Gulf War, drugs, the government—anything I could think to pick a fight about. I found my own temper flaring irrationally. I did the same thing Dad did. He let people walk all over him without saying a word, and suddenly, two or three weeks later, he'd explode at some innocent party. There were moments when I wanted to physically hit my dad because I was so angry with him. But nothing is one-sided. I picked up on some of his positive traits too. While he couldn't express his own feelings, he'd make a point of being there for somebody else when they had a problem. His brothers and sisters often called him for advice, and my mom, as tough as she was, relied on him for nurturing as well. To this day I credit my more sensitive side to my dad, as well as my work ethic.

"I just wish for Dad's sake that he had those 30 years at the mill to live over, to become a more enlightened and happier person. He missed out on so much. Somewhere along the way I think a lot of blue-collar men turn into 'grinders.' The shadow of Calvinism still reaches the width and breadth of America. Today a lot of men (and women too) are the reincarnation of the Organization Man of the Fifties—they work themselves practically to death and leave little time for anything else. God knows why. To prove they're men? To avoid their emotions? To make tons of money? Whatever, it's pretty sad.

"While in high school I discovered that I had something else in common with my father. I suppressed my feelings and desires, often to cater to the needs of others. I liked to be helpful to friends and acquaintances. Maybe that was my way of getting some attention, or making new friends, or maybe it's just my basic nature. But ignoring your own feelings comes with a price. I began to have this tormenting sense down deep that my sexual appetites were on the unorthodox side. I just wasn't aroused like most boys by lurid pictures of the female anatomy, or the prospect of

148

getting laid. When I focused on what did turn me on, it tended to revolve around sadomasochism fantasies. If my tendencies meant I was bisexual, so be it. But I kept my thoughts and feelings secret. This is not something you casually mention in your typical small-town Wisconsin bar. You don't even tell your family. You especially don't tell them. So I tried to persuade myself that I wasn't bi or kinky, as if that would make 'the problem' go away. And to prove I wasn't as weird as I thought I might be, all I had to do was concentrate on girls.

"I lost my virginity at age 16 to a brunette named Emily in a cold, wet ditch after a graduation party. We were both drunk and inept. It was a pretty miserable experience. My more romantic interpretation is that I actually lost my virginity twice. The second time was to a beautiful girl, Gloria, who was athletic and smart and liked to come to me for advice. She knew I stood apart from jocks and the lesser lights in the classroom. One time she actually asked me for advice about sex. I was no expert but I acted like I was, and I could convey enough empathy that I soon won her over. The discussion was also exhilarating and erotic. This might have been the first time I was conscious of falling in love with someone, or coming close to it. I had an incredible crush on Gloria. I was more her confidante than boyfriend but Gloria and I just clicked. And we did have some physical intimacy, which was terrific. Our relationship didn't last more than a few months, yet it was a huge boost to my self-esteem.

"I took up the guitar in high school and was part of a band that got some local gigs. There were drugs, of course, and girls, but I also developed a reputation as a decent musician. Music is still one of the driving forces of my life. It certainly helped me get through high school, though it wasn't quite enough. Suppressing my unhappiness and especially my sexuality, I lapsed into a state of depression around my junior year. It wasn't that I was lost in some deep funk and walked around with my eyes continually cast down; I just couldn't feel anything. It's a hard thing to convey to someone who hasn't suffered from depression. You feel like you're not tied to anything. Life is something you watch but never participate in. You can be talking to a good friend and at the same time watching yourself from somewhere outside of yourself, wondering who the hell you are and what you're really saying.

"I'm sure part of my depression was due to the guilt I carried inside me. As Tori Amos laments in one of her songs, I had enough guilt to start my own religion. Guilt about my sexuality, about not working hard enough, about not living up to my dad's expectations, about not knowing what to do with my life. I knew I was smart, but that didn't seem to get me anywhere or answer any key questions. I tried recreational drugs, conventional sex with women, and more sadomasochism. If I kept some things a secret from the world, I was still open to finding out who I really was.

"I moved to Minneapolis the summer after high school, worked odd jobs, and qualified for enough student loans to enroll in a small state college. This was a major statement of ambition for a kid from a blue-collar family. I skipped most of the liberal arts curriculum and focused on sociology. Coming from a small dot on the map, I desperately wanted to know what other cultures were like. How different am I, and is there anything that passes as a definition of normalcy? I loved my courses and professors—for the first time in my life I was intellectually challenged—but I was still wrestling with my private demons.

"In my sophomore year I met and began living with a woman named Grace. We slept together, experimented with drugs and various modes of sexuality, and traded confidences. In my gut I think I knew there was something 'off' about Grace, but because I'm the kind of person who feeds off intimacy, I confided in her about my bi-sexuality and sado-masochistic tendencies. She was only the second person to whom I'd admitted the truth. The first was another girl I dated and who accepted me without judgment. But Grace turned out to be different. She decided to share my secret with the world at large.

"Overnight I lost just about every friend I thought I had. I became extremely isolated and, given that I was already prone to spending most of my time alone, I now would hide from the outside world for weeks at a time. Insomnia became a chronic problem. I really thought I was losing my mind. I went into therapy, was prescribed an antidepressant, and lost myself as much as possible in academics. The therapy helped in that it gave me insights into myself. From my mom I'd learned how to pick myself up when things got tough. I was still not ready to come out of the closet, but I suddenly was making new friends— intellectual types that I'd never been exposed to before. To this day I'd rather have one scintillating conversation with a stranger than ten dull ones with acquaintances. Having to make small talk while trapped in a car with someone is one of my visions of Hell.

"Then one day at school I met Roni. I didn't know it at that moment, but looking back, my life changed in a heartbeat. I would have to call Roni the love of my life. She was, and remains, stunningly beautiful. Half Korean, half white, she was born in the Midwest but with an other-worldly soul. She has a body that might have been designed by a horny teenage boy, but I was even more attracted to her wit, sensitivity, intelligence and sense of humor. I mean, she could have been a chubby half-Korean with a weird face and I would not have loved her any less. Roni liked to talk about politics, the environment, human rights—and she could do trigonometry too! Even more astounding, she appreciated me for my brains and sensitivity, things I liked in myself. We didn't hold anything back from one another, except in one crucial area. In our five-year relationship she would prove to be my greatest teacher, as I was hers. Not to tip the scales of sentimentality too far, but we covered so much territory emotionally, endured the agony of ironic fates, and wove our lives around each other with such texture that if I were Shakespeare, I would have written Roni a sonnet everyday.

"Falling in love is less of a process than falling out. Falling in love is spontaneous, out of control, compelling, enthralling. It starts with infatuation, which is so powerful the first time you experience it that the emotion stays with you forever. In fact, it haunts you because the second time you fall in love, infatuation doesn't have quite the same grip. And the third time, if there is one, the power is even less. With Roni, I didn't want to be one second, one breath, without her in my presence. We could make each other laugh. We could piss each other off. We could make each other insanely lustful. It was beautiful. For a while I thought my issues and my confusion over my sexuality were over. I was a straight male after all, and I decided not to tell Roni about my past forays. Why should I, I reasoned, if they had no bearing on the present. That decision would turn out to be a devastating mistake.

"When you're first in love, you don't really know who you're in love with. You think you do, but the real discoveries, both positive and negative, only come with time. I think that staying in love for a lifetime—at least in the romantic, early-phase definition, the one where 'spark' rules—is almost impossible. With Roni I never thought about a future, certainly not at first. I was totally absorbed in the moment. When I had to drop out of college because

I could no longer afford the tuition, Roni dropped out with me. We decided, pouring over a map one day, that we would become explorers, travel the country, and be the captains of our destinies. We had had similar childhoods, deprived and fear-based (the Korean culture can be even more repressive than my Catholic blue-collar one) and we now empowered each other to be free.

"For the next five joyous years we traveled here and there, took dead-end jobs, endured some humiliating family visits back home, and learned new things about the world together. We also taught each other about emotions and happiness. We ended up in San Francisco, where I landed a writing job with a newspaper covering the arts and music scene. Even though I had no journalistic experience, I was good at it and, unlike my father, I now had a job that I really loved. Roni didn't have to work because she got a tip from her cousin about a tech start-up, and she sold her stock at the right time. That paid for a year of leisure, reading books, self-exploration, and indulging herself for the first time with a few material acquisitions. We could have been mistaken for a straight, aspiring middle-class couple. And we might have pulled it off, if one night Roni hadn't come out of the closet on me. She said that after a lot of painful soul-searching she knew that she was gay. In her year off from work she'd found the courage to be herself. She gave me some credit for giving her that courage. I should have seen this coming—things Roni had said or hinted at during our years together—but I was totally blown away. I was hurt. I was angry. I never yelled at Roni and my most aggressive moments were those patterns of anger-stewing silences I learned from my father. Of course, all that anger was basically coming from confusion over my own sexual identity.

"When I told Roni that I was bi, only a few days after her revelation to me, it was a catharsis for me on the one hand, but the end of our relationship on the other. The irony, of course, was that if I'd been more honest from the beginning, or if she'd said she was bi as well, and not gay, maybe our relationship would never have unraveled. To this day I regret that I didn't have the courage to be more honest. When you live in fear, nothing goes right.

"Sometimes I wonder if our uncertainty over our sexuality wasn't part of the initial attraction process, something working on a subconscious level. I kind of believe that. But what can bring two people together can in the end tear them apart. Ultimately you can't be in love with someone, or stay in love with them, if your sexual orientations are different. That may seem obvious to some, but it's still one of the 'why's' that I grapple with. Our souls were so entwined—wasn't that enough to keep us in love? I honestly believe that nothing can be deeper than a soul connection, but without a physical connection—when your sexual orientations are pulling you in opposite directions—it's impossible for a romantic relationship to survive. When Roni actually started dating other women I felt hurt and abandoned all over again. My biggest fear was we would become strangers.

"It was an awkward, confusing situation for me. To some degree I'm still in it. Roni and I moved together to another town, and for a while we saw each other at least once a week. Actually, we slept together a couple of times. What was that about? Perhaps I couldn't let go and neither could she. Yet, with time, we began to lead separate lives. To survive emotionally I began to will myself out of love. Some part of you has to die to make room for something else to be born. But it takes a long time to recover. In the middle of the night I'm still capable of memories of Roni that are so powerful that I can't go back to sleep. I suppose, if one will allow for an elastic definition of love, Roni and I are still very much attached. I've never come to love her any less; it's just that the nature of that connection has changed. People have far more dimensions than three, and a couple has way more than six. That's one of the lessons she and I learned from our breakup. And I wouldn't have learned it if we hadn't broken up.

"So Roni changed and I changed. The nature of our love was now built around openness, respect and liberation. We'd always had those qualities, but they grew in importance. Through Roni I became exposed to the post-feminist movement which, as far as I've seen, relies more on self-realization than male-bashing. Another positive was that I stopped being in the closet. I finally learned not to coddle other peoples' insecurities. It's a far worse thing to lie than to present someone with something with which they may not be equipped to cope. You have to be true to yourself. Thank you, Shakespeare!"

Summary and Interpretation

- As a son, George is the end product of a traditional couple: a rigid, responsibility-obsessed, critical father, and an accepting, fair and loving mother. This dynamic does not allow for a genuine male identify to form. Instead, it leads to George heavily identifying with his supportive, comforting and accessible mother. Because his deeper self identifies with his mother, his sexual orientation also comes from her.

- George is open in an abstract way. He can philosophize and intellectualize about who he is and what his emotions mean to him, but on an intimate level there's still guilt and secrecy about being bisexual, homosexual or a sado-masochist. His sexual crisis began in high school when he "couldn't feel anything." The depression was probably protection against his growing awareness of being "dif-ferent." His numbness was his effort to distance himself from it. But perhaps he still fights depression. Despite having come out of the closet, his story doesn't reveal his sexual fantasies or go into the emotional ups and downs of feeling different and out of the mainstream.

- Like many men struggling with strong female identification, George was attracted to a strong, masculine woman in Roni. If one accepts that real gender is often disguised, Roni played the role of the male and George was more of the traditional female, dependent and often clingy. He embodies the sexual confusion, vulnerabilities and defensiveness of many men. George wants or expects—despite the impossible blend of having a close, loving bond with his mother and a negative, distant relationship with his angry father—to emerge as "all male." The difficult dynamic of being raised by two contrasting parents makes George confused, self-punishing (masochistic) and in need of validation. Growing up, he had nowhere to acquire the identification to feel, on a gut level, that he was the man he'd like to be.

- As he grew up, George was confused and out of touch with his feelings about his father. I'm not sure whether he hated him or loved him, or possibly hated him but admired him, or wanted to love him but couldn't because his father's anger pushed him away. He was deeply frustrated by having a father who was so lost, defeated and emotionally disengaged. George is also a manifestation of the internal conflict of every heterosexual male from a traditional family who struggles to "feel like a man"—sexually and otherwise—but internally identifies with his mother because the father is emotionally absent. George comes to understand and accept, even appreciate, what or who his dad is, in part because he longs for identification with a strong father figure. But this intellectualization belies his emotional self which is still angry and hurt.

- There are no statistics on how many men truly hate their

jobs—as George's father did—but just listening to men talk, the number seems significant. The irony, as George pointed out, that a man can detest his job but still be devoted to it is explained either by a definition of masculinity or simply a fear of getting fired. So many men define themselves by what they do and nothing else. When losing their job is paramount to losing their identity, they don't know how to redefine themselves unless it's by getting another job. The most commonly asked question of a stranger at a cocktail party is "and what do you do?" If the next question were "and who else are you?" most men would shrug their shoulders in confusion. But anyone who understands the second question and can answer it intelligently understands himself.

- Like a lot of men, George exhibits a fear of disappointing people, and a strong need to be liked and loved. His primary issue is his sexuality, but in a broader context it is about living up to expectations, not to mention a definition of masculinity. Even when they have a problem in their lives or their relationships—and acknowledge that honesty is called for—men are still slow to look for support. George says he likes to have a couple of close friends but feels no need to confide in anyone else. If he holds nothing back from his friends, he's in better shape than most men, who are too competitive and distrusting to share their problems. The Stephen Spielberg *Band of Brothers* vision where men stand tall as caring comrades in times of adversity is ennobling, but not an everyday occurrence. Perhaps it does show what emotions men are capable of, if daily competition—and living in a fear-based culture—were replaced to some degree with empathy and support.

- Sooner or later, faking confidence is not enough to hide a man's insecurities. Once those insecurities and secrets are exposed to the world—deliberately or unintentionally—a man like George has to deal with his anger, shame and humiliation. Unless his partner is understanding and supportive—Roni, caught up in her own liberation, seemed to have a mixed response to George's news about his bisexuality—a man may begin to pull away from his partner because he feels rejected at this crucial juncture. A lot of men I spoke with said rejection is one thing that pushes them out of a relationship, and out of love. "If a woman doesn't really love me, or if she's not attracted to me anymore," one man said, "I'm going to kill all my emotion for her, even if I had been in love. Some women want you to adore them forever, but that's not going to happen."

- Popular culture—and the billion-dollar industries that revolve around fashion, beauty and romance—perpetuates the myth that something is wrong with us if we can't find our soul mate. As George points out, loneliness is the great bogeyman. We fear it almost more than death. In some ways loneliness is death. But loneliness should not be confused with aloneness, or the validation and self-esteem that come with taking private journeys and personal risks. Being different, being without a partner, can be okay for many people. A lot of women have been liberated from the mindset that to be whole they have to be part of a couple. Most men have not. If you don't have a woman at your side, what kind of man are you? Are you gay? Are you depressed? Do you have self-esteem issues? The sad irony is that men often cover up for their lack of self-esteem by hiding in their relationships. Men could learn from women, especially the current generation, about flexibility, strength, independence, and letting go. It's what George was finally striving for in trying to separate his identity from Roni.

PART FOUR

CONTROL AND PERFECTION

Chapter Nine

Barry's Story

Sixty-three percent of men expect women to make an effort with their appearance, including firm breasts, a toned stomach, and cellulite-free thighs. Ninety-two percent of women expect the same thing of themselves.

—Daily Diet Tracker

While Steven has his argument with Renee in New Mexico and Bill sips his scotch in his Los Angeles pad, in Denver, Barry, 38, walks his dog back to his expensive condo. A successful executive head hunter, Barry is over six feet tall, with dark, floppy hair, a big smile, and purposeful eyes. In some ways he reminds one of a fraternity rat—a fun, prank-loving guy—but there's a seriousness underneath his carefree demeanor. It's Saturday night, he thinks, and what am I doing? I'm walking my dog! He laughs, more annoyed with himself than depressed. Recently divorced, Barry is dating several women, but none of them really interest him. Rather, they interest him at first, but it's only a matter of time before he finds something he doesn't like about them. He knows his standards are high, but why shouldn't they be? After his disastrous first marriage, he's not going to settle for just anyone. The woman in his life needs to be close to perfect, or he's not going to be happy.

Maybe he just should drive to the office tonight, and do some catch-up work before Monday. Imagine, working on a Saturday evening, he thinks, but he doesn't mind. Barry is not an untypical businessman, whose yardstick for self-esteem is money and success, but Barry pushes himself harder than most. He will succeed. He also has a high degree of sensitivity to, almost an intolerance of, criticism. He works his butt off and he resents anyone who will say differently—an echo from his childhood where no accolades came his way, only taunts of being a loser. He has come a long way in his life. He has slowly fashioned a lifestyle that minimizes any chance for failure by carefully controlling his social and work environment. Control is very important to Barry. He simply won't allow anything to interfere with his game plan. He will not compromise his professional goals, any more than he will his high standards for the women he dates.

✳ ✳ ✳ ✳ ✳

Barry thinks of himself as a fairly complex person because he lives with several heavy-duty internal contradictions, and not a small amount of guilt. Growing up, he was the kid chosen last for the baseball team, had no social skills, no friends, and zero self-confidence. What he had in spades was anger. "Getting left out or left behind all the time does that to you," he says. Then he was sent to Catholic school, and that turned out to be a mixed blessing. The discipline and structure were a positive, but emotionally the school felt dehumanizing. Barry was taught that the Virgin Mary was the quintessential mother figure, the role model for all women in all walks of life. The nuns drilled this into his head. "Somewhere along the line," he says, " you develop the notion that not only should you strive for virtue and perfection in your own life, but the woman you're ultimately seeking as your wife has to be perfect too. Someone on a pedestal, someone with all the 'assets.' Not that Britney Spears should ever be confused with the Virgin Mary, but in some ways Britney and other divas take her place today. Men are always looking for the perfect woman, the '10' that Bo Derrick represented a long time ago."

Catholic school, then, was Barry's introduction to the

concept that a woman, his woman, needed to be perfect in looks, temperament, sex, athleticism, wit and brains. Plus she had to love him to death—"just like Mary adored Jesus!" he says.

* * * * *

"The 'perfection dream' holds true for a lot of guys. They want to make over some girl exactly in the image that suits their needs. Maybe this is because as our world grows increasing complex and unpredictable, the idea of control becomes increasing important, and linked to our happiness. Also, men are acquirers by nature, and many guys think of women as another acquisition. (I know this is politically incorrect, and you don't dare say it in public because a feminist will shoot you in the kneecaps, but a lot of men still think this way.) Ultimately, your relationship will be doomed to failure because women, or men, don't want to be made over into anything. When the relationship crashes, you initially blame your partner but in the end you feel responsible. And if you're Catholic, you *never* stop flogging yourself.

"Yet idealism dies hard. Even after my divorce and all the lessons I learned from it, there's a part of me that still is searching for the perfect woman—my perfect woman—as I begin to date again. I go through women quickly, saying goodbye when they disappoint me, but on the other hand, I've been tossed out of some relationships too. Some women think of me as too critical and demanding. I tell them half-seriously that I'm a Virgo, and Virgos are first and foremost hardest on themselves. Does the perfect woman or man exist? Of course not, but that doesn't stop either gender from setting the bar pretty high. Partly I blame the media, especially those reality TV shows. If you check out *Elimidate* or *Blind Date*, you might say, come on, this is just entertainment; it's *supposed* to be about degradation and cruelty. But there's a subtext that is taken seriously by viewers. The subtext is that this is a competitive, judgmental world, and you better be as perfect as possible if you want to find your dream partner. What you do with your looks, how witty you are, how funny, how *appealing*—this is crucial because we live in Judgment City. And if you're not close to perfect, you're more or less thrown in the trash heap. The singles scene is one of the circles of Hell that Dante forgot to include in *The Divine Comedy*: peaks of pleasure alternating with valleys of rejection, pain and despair.

"When you marry the woman of your dreams you never know what's going to happen. You're in love, and you hope you're also compatible and comfortable when that rush of love wears off. I thought my marriage offered me comfort and security. Sometimes the sex was good, sometimes not, but that wasn't as important to me as the feeling of being accepted and wanted. My marriage lasted ten years, eight of which I would call prosperous and generally happy. Then came as unexpected a deterioration as I could imagine. I didn't want my marriage to die, and even today, more than a year after my divorce, I feel the breakup was my fault. Divorce felt like a huge failure to me. I look at my parents—they've been married for almost four decades—and I ask what happened to me.

"Failure is something I've been conscious of most of my life. In fact, it's one of my greatest fears—maybe everyone's ultimate fear, men and women—and a motivator in my professional life. I can't stand to fail at anything. Growing up on the East Coast, I was the oldest of three kids but the one with all the problems. I looked like a dork with Coke-bottle glasses and was awkward socially and physically, a lumbering giant who had few if any real friends. The neighborhood scapegoat, I had no protectors, and no witty comeback of my own. I simply could not think on my feet. Today, I dislike silences and tend to fill them with words rather than to stand there and be judged a dummy. I had learning disabilities too, and not much help in diagnosing or correcting them. Even if they didn't say it, I always thought I was a disappointment to my parents. My life was the perfect storm for low self-esteem, chronic anxiety, and unfocused anger.

"My family did a lot of moving around as I grew up because Dad kept climbing higher on the corporate ladder. He was a loving but absent man, though now, in his retirement, we're close and get along well. Both my parents were incredibly supportive of me during and after my divorce. When I was growing up, however, my mom turned to religion to keep from going crazy with raising three kids. Catholicism gave her a lot of solace. When we became teenagers, she went extreme, even speaking in tongues. She was the quintessential true believer. She thought being devoutly religious would cure her of all the anxiety, frustration and stress of trying to be the devoted wife and mother. In the end, she learned that extremism cures nothing, and she now takes a more centrist position about her life. Both my parents believe that personal growth does not come without some experimentation, risk-taking and pain. They are great role models for my siblings and me.

"Growing up, I was a handful for my parents because I was always in trouble. I may not have understood the impact of peer rejection at the time but I felt it and reacted to it. Both Mom and Dad thought Catholic school would give me the discipline and confidence I sorely needed. In one sense, from first grade through high school, the nuns definitely gave me that gift. In the Church there is the sense of belonging to something bigger than yourself. For a time I even thought about becoming a priest. Catholic schools are run like the military-industrial complex, a bureaucracy where regimentation and procedure are an end in themselves. Rules mean everything. Without rules, there is only chaos. As an adult, I attribute a lot of my professional successes to a basic organization of my life and daily conduct.

"But another side of me, the part that felt unloved and alienated from the world, was a rebel. As I became an adolescent, I was moody, had an unpredictable temper, and was cynical or sarcastic about everything. I didn't know how to handle conflict and confrontation. I was as undeveloped emotionally as I was physically. Because I was in an environment where confrontation was not tolerated, I hung with the out-of-orbit clique. It was easy to slip from unfocused anger and discontent into drugs. I was messed up a lot of the time.

"My views about the nuns gradually grew darker. There is a long-term effect on your psyche from an educational system run largely by women, a system that is unforgiving of anyone who breaks the rules. And I was always looking for ways to undermine the system. If I could buy a piece of candy on the outside for a nickel, I would smuggle it into school and sell it for a dime, because the school store charged you fifteen cents. That's how my mind worked— be clever in undermining the system. In school I ended up not only disliking and distrusting authority, I distrusted women because they were the authority. I kept a series of underground notebooks where I illustrated the injustices my friends and I suffered at the hands of the nuns. These were pretty graphic drawings, nuns fornicating, that kind of thing. The notebooks were my revenge on the system. I passed them around to allies and sympathizers, which further enhanced my reputation as a rebel, which in turn became a foundation for my self-esteem, such as it was. You could say that my anger kept me on life support.

"To the school administration I was a serious hazard. I broke the all-time demerit record in my sophomore year.

At the end of my junior year I was asked by the head prefect not to come back. That's the moment I hit bottom. Mom and Dad made me realize that I had a choice: buck up and become responsible, or be labeled a screw-off, disappoint myself and my family, and give up on my future. They never said exactly, 'You're a failure, Barry,' but the message was clear. I gave the issue lots of thought over the summer. Thanks to lobbying from my parents, I got reinstated, but not before I had to sign a special contract with the school with a 'zero tolerance' clause. One mistake and I was out for good.

"I have a serious side to me that wants to do the right thing, to be successful and respected (my parents' values, for sure), and maybe that seriousness started to kick in during my senior year. I started to enjoy learning, and I also excelled in music and choir. I even got the lead in the school play. I filled out to six-foot three and 200 pounds, and became a decent hockey forward. As I went from C student to honor roll, people who had once called me a loser now rallied to my side. I would wake in the middle of the night, thinking, hey, is this for real? For the first time in my life I had real self-respect. At graduation I was even singled out for an achievement or two. That validation meant a lot to me.

"I got acceptance letters from several very decent, high-pressure colleges, but because my confidence wasn't that deep, I settled for a state school. In college my behavior regressed slightly—no drugs but lots of partying (*Animal House* remains one of my favorite movies). I started out being attracted to almost any girl who gave me a lot of attention, so long as she met my minimum standards for attractiveness. Call it the quest for validation from someone who still feared he was a geek inside. Even if my looks had now blossomed and I was no longer awkward and lumbering, I was still insecure. I could be charming one moment, but with my temper I could blow up at someone at anytime. Because of that immaturity I wasn't capable of committing to any one woman. I ended up cheating on several girlfriends, even though I knew it was wrong and I felt guilty. I got one girl pregnant and we had to arrange for an abortion, which did nothing to soothe my Catholic conscience. Overriding the moral aspect of my behavior, however, was the emotional logic that the more women I had relationships with, the more I was loved and validated, the more popular and desirable I would be, and the higher I could set the perfection bar for women I dated in the future. What amazed me was that most women couldn't see through me. As transparent, even desperate, as I thought I was, the women I dated got caught up in the externals. I was funny. I could dance. I was charming. I was a gentleman. What else is there in life when you're twenty years old and in the incubator called college?

"At the end of my freshman year I fell in love for the first time. Zoey was my age, and—incredibly—she met all my criteria for the perfect woman. Not only was she a gorgeous, athletic blonde, she was empathetic, kind, caring, and totally accepting of me, rough edges and all. She had not a bone of distrust in her. Zoey was an angel. I was too young to understand how lucky I was, too much on the prowl to settle down and make a commitment. I didn't even know enough to be sad about my loss when we broke up because I thought there'd be a million more Zoey's on the horizon, just waiting for me. I was so wrong. I don't know how many women I dated before I graduated, but none came close to Zoey. She definitely spoiled me. I was suddenly attracted only to tall, athletic, smart blondes who also had to be empathetic and kind. And of course they had to love me to death.

"I want to stress the absolute importance of a woman's

acceptance of me. At that time in my life I invested all my emotions in women. There was no other yardstick for success or self-esteem other than who I slept with, ate with, went to the movies with, and to whom I revealed my deepest thoughts and feelings. One of the ironies was that I wasn't overly revealing to any woman because I had that old trust issue dating back to the nuns and their authority. I was very cautious about what I exposed of myself—never my fears, God forbid—yet women found it quite easy to talk to me and trust me. I thought that was the perfect template for a relationship—women opening up to me while I coyly hid my insecurities.

"Although I didn't recognize it at the time, I had become in some ways quite controlling. I certainly fit the profile. If you've had a rough childhood, you know your pain spots and work hard to avoid them, consciously or unconsciously. If I had women trusting and confiding in me without me reciprocating—isn't that the ultimate control? Yet one of my contradictions, particularly after Zoey, was that I tended to fall for controlling women. I misinterpreted their control of me for a kind of maternal care, warmth and indulgence. While I was distrusting at my core, on the surface I was too trusting.

"That was my frame of mind when I met Georgia in my junior year. She was stunning, even more lovely than Zoey, and I was pulled into the gravitational field that I would call her 'feminine mystique.' Georgia had one powerful aura. I fell in love with her right away. I would come to realize she was nothing like Zoey—Georgia was selfish and manipulative—but sex with her was beyond description. By that I mean its emotional connotations far surpassed any physical pleasure, and that opened the floodgates for my total devotion to her. I kept thinking that I didn't deserve this woman, and even when her darker side became evident—she was, for example, always driving a wedge between me and my friends—I couldn't say no to her when she wanted something. In retrospect, a classic case of fatal attraction. The more elusive or unavailable she was—deliberately so, I came to realize, as she broke dates or failed to keep her word—the more I chased her. That was her power, or the power I gave her. She ended up cheating on me, more than once I'm sure, but I didn't want to believe it. Georgia was even more insecure than I was, and playing the same validation game with the same tools. She had the charm, the good looks, the intuitive/empathetic insights that you offer your partner when the lights are out, but Georgia used them even more seductively than I did.

"I don't think Georgia was even close to being in love with me, no matter what she said to the contrary. When I began accusing her of insincerity and deceit, she always had an excuse. More arguments ensued. I never did get her to admit that she was a phony, and I'm not sure she was convinced that she was. She probably still gets away with her same behavior. I finally broke up with her, but I still felt like a fool for being used. No doubt this was my karmic payback for all the women I had cheated on. I was chastened. I told myself I had learned three huge lessons. One, don't abuse or lie to people, especially someone you're intimate with, and think you can get away with it. Two, don't be too dependent on women; don't let them be your tape measure for success or validation. And three, using a combination of their sexuality and emotional reasoning, women have an incredible aura, a power than few men possess. Men are great bullshit artists but that 'talent' doesn't compare to a woman's bag of tools. She just has more junk in her trunk. She can manipulate and persuade you without your even knowing what she's doing. Sometimes she doesn't know either. Men may be deliberate liars but they usually know what they're doing. Women exaggerate (it's rarely called lying), often subconsciously.

170

"After my Georgia experience, I began to date with a lot more caution. I no longer looked for an outrageous beauty with all the cards. I looked for a woman who wouldn't threaten me. Often I found myself attracted to wounded souls. These were women who had had a bad childhood or, like me, had been scarred in a relationship. I would help them solve their problems, at least give advice, and be around when they needed someone for comfort. If you're with someone who's hurting, it's easy to play lifeguard, the wise father, the fixer...whatever is necessary. This made me feel great because I like to be counted on and looked up to. I think my hero complex goes back to my underground school journals—the rebel as hero—because it's me slaying all those authoritarian nuns and righting the world's wrongs. So here I was, adored and validated once again. It was a safe strategy for me, like going to state college instead of trying an Ivy. None of these women could reach my emotions because most were too vulnerable or needy to make that effort. Once again I was resorting to one-way relationships. I had plenty of fun and companionship with these women, but I didn't fall in love or even care to with any of them. Falling in love might take away my power.

"Rather that dating a lot, I put my energy into my fledgling career as a bank loan officer. This meant fifty- and sixty-hour work weeks, but the results showed with superior performance and accolades from my boss. I was feeling much better about my life. I had transferred my validation needs from women to work. The bank was a place to feel safe, and as competitive as it could be, the reward for honest, efficient labor was straightforward. I think, in general, men are much happier, and more productive, in a masculine work environment, as banks usually are. When a woman is the boss, or most of your co-workers are female, communication in general is a lot more emotional and circuitous. You need a higher level of intuition to do well in that environment.

"I met my future wife, Danielle, when I was 27 and had just switched careers from banker to executive head hunter. Within a year I became as adept in my new field as I had been in my old, but now I was making close to a six-figure income. If work is your validation, money can be your super-validation. Like Zoey and Georgia, Danielle was a blonde but hardly a '10' and not especially athletic or even a great dresser. What she offered was a winning personality, sincerity, friendship, kindness, self-confidence and humor. She didn't exhibit very many weaknesses. This was a turn-on for me, and another one of my internal contradictions. While I am attracted to women who need me and look up to me as a hero, as well as to women who control me, sometimes I'm simply drawn to strong, confident, independent women who treat me as an equal. The equality ideal brings out self-respect as well as respect for one another. It feels healthy. It *is* healthy.

"As silly as it may sound, Danielle became my own private vision of the Virgin Mary. As we got to know each other, her beauty radiated from within and I fell in love with her, not with head-over-heels adrenaline as I had with Zoey or Georgia, but slowly, as I came to feel secure around her. Trust was now a very big part of my search criteria. It was what ultimately made me decide on marriage. During our courtship there wasn't one incident of deceit, or even a case of Danielle letting me down. She was in love with me, she said, and she would always be there for me. Unlike Georgia, Danielle showed she meant it time and time again. I realized how lucky I was. Maybe this is a Catholic response, but I thought I was getting more than I deserved.

"When I got to know Danielle's family, I knew right

away that 'fitting in' was not going to be easy. These were brilliant but strange people. Her dad, an engineer, was a cold, unfriendly hermit who had the first nickel he ever earned but was too tight to put air conditioning in their home. I had the impression that in his eyes I wasn't good enough for Danielle, but at the same time he treated her with such indifference that I knew I would be a lot better for his daughter than he was. Danielle's older sister came across as friendly, but there was something 'off' about her; eventually she'd be diagnosed with a mental disorder. Danielle had two brothers. The older one was a Ph.D. and a ringer for the old man in his coldness and hoarding. The younger was socially immature. I learned that their mother had died when Danielle was only twelve.

"Danielle had no trouble blending into my family. My folks and brother and sister adored her. We didn't talk much about her family—it wasn't a subject she was comfortable with—though in the back of my mind I wondered how she had survived her teenage years in that crowd. Danielle was so responsible and self-confident I assumed she had somehow taken over the role of mother for her younger siblings, and being responsible had kept her sane and out of trouble.

"After we were married Danielle and I went about our lives with great focus and happiness. We had different sets of friends but everyone mingled comfortably. I don't think we had a serious argument in those first eight years. Danielle worked as a financial consultant and I did increasingly well as an executive recruiter. Money was never an issue for us. We got along on every level, including agreeing on things like who put out the trash (me), who balanced the checkbook and paid the taxes (Danielle), who went grocery shopping, washed the cars, and made house repairs (me), and who cleaned house (Danielle). While we talked of having kids, we were in no hurry. We traveled, lived well, had passionate sex, and thought the world was made of roses and daffodils.

"If there was a dominant person in the relationship it was probably me. I think it wasn't intentional, it just sort of happened that way because Danielle looked to me whenever a real problem or crisis came along. And being a man, I thought that was my role. She would never really thank me for coming to the rescue, and that bothered me at times, but I didn't dwell on it. I just assumed that this was what a man did—take charge, solve problems, show some leadership, even if I didn't always know what I was doing!

"Let us fast forward. After eight years of a contentment that I thought would last forever, something happened. The first sign of trouble was hardly noticeable. Danielle began to get up in the middle of the night to make sure the doors of our house were locked. Or she checked the kitchen to make certain the oven was off, the lights were out, and the car had been put in the garage. At first I attributed her behavior to fatigue and her admirable habit of responsibility. When she began to check the door or oven two or three times in one night, however, I began to wonder. At restaurants we would pay the bill and leave, then Danielle would rush back inside because she was sure she had left her purse behind (it was in the car.) On several occasions she was sure she had lost her keys, earrings, or driver's license, and became very nervous until they were found. She began looking into my wallet every morning to see how much money I had. When I inevitably came home with less, she demanded to know how I had spent it. Old friends, she complained, were standing her up for lunch dates. I didn't know what to think of this bizarre turn in her behavior. For a while I thought she was just frustrated with her job, or wanted a change in her life, like starting a family. Whenever I asked what the problem was, she said, cheerfully, 'what problem?'

"One night, however, Danielle tearfully confessed that she knew something was wrong with her. She said she wanted to get help. I was relieved. A therapist diagnosed her as suffering from 'OCD'—obsessive/compulsive disorder—and put her on some serious medication. O/C behavior, as I would learn, is all about control, and usually springs from deep-seated fears that you are not in charge of your life, or some pain or unhappiness that lurks below the surface. O/C is often seen in people who strive for perfection, and at times I wondered if I wasn't O/C as well. What was hard for me to understand was where her paralyzing disorder had come from, and why did it spring up after eight happy years of marriage? I knew her family was bizarre, but I had always believed Danielle had escaped that connection. I looked critically at my own behavior. Over the eight years I had definitely become the dominant personality in our relationship. Was I suffocating her with my big personality? Did she think I was too controlling? Danielle never really said anything. In the meantime her meds made her moody and depressed. Worse, she became convinced that by taking drugs her O/C disorder was now 'fixed' and her life would return to normal.

"Our lives did not go back to normal. Danielle's behavior grew worse. If I tried to help her clean the house, for example, she grew upset because this had always been her role. But cleaning now took on a new meaning. Every piece of furniture and knick-knack had to be in one place and one place only, and she alone had to make the choices. If she didn't like what she'd done, an hour later she would rearrange the furniture, then feel anxious and paralyzed about having made the wrong choices. After I put out the trash, Danielle would get up in the middle of the night and bring it back in the house, sorting through it to see if I'd thrown out something that I shouldn't have. Her medication also caused her to gain weight. Soon she didn't want to leave the house. She didn't look or feel good, she said, or she needed more time to get organized. When she did go out, I would catch her bringing home strange and useless objects—pieces of string, rubber bands, stacks of newspaper—that she'd hide in drawers and closets. She would never say a word, as if none of this was happening, or maybe somehow I wouldn't notice. For my part, I just rationalized that things would somehow get better.

"But Danielle's behavior became a nightmare. Had the bizarre behavior that ran in her family, particularly the hoarding, distrusting behavior of her father, or her sister's mental illness, had some impact on her life? The therapist couldn't give me a clear answer. There seemed to be many reasons for her fears, he said, implying that the process of ferreting them out could take years. I didn't have years. Danielle said she couldn't stop her behavior and begged me for help. And I wanted to help. The old role of playing hero to wounded women was familiar, yet so different this time. This time I didn't have any solutions. Comforting Danielle only went so far. So did imposing my will. Danielle grew suspicious, if not hostile, when I stopped her from bringing trash into our house. She also grew increasingly antisocial. One evening I invited over our closest friends, hoping that would improve Danielle's mood. She sat passively in a corner, barely talking. By now our house was a rat's nest of odds and ends. Our friends kept looking around the house, then to Danielle, then me. I could see the dismay in their eyes, like, 'what the hell is going on here?' As they said good night, they pulled me aside and asked what was wrong. I fumbled for words, claiming that Danielle simply wasn't feeling well. They urged me to get her some serious help.

"I was determined to hang in with Danielle because I loved her and took my marriage vows seriously. I also wanted to prove to myself that I wasn't the immature kid I'd been in college who fled at the first sign of trouble. I know a lot of men who run away emotionally when there's a serious problem, but I was determined to be different. We tried a new therapist, and Danielle began to speak in darker tones about her family, yet still told me nothing specific. When I pushed for more information, she pushed back. A wall went up around her. I grew increasingly frustrated, but never more so than when she tried to claim again, with her new doctor and new meds, that everything was back to normal. Her wishful thinking, her denial, seemed like the easiest place for her to go. I remember one evening asking her if she'd gone that day to her doctor, or paid our bills, or run specific errands—all promises she'd made that morning. She said of course, asking why I would ever doubt her. When I checked the next day, I found that nothing had been done. (I later learned, during our divorce, that she hadn't filed several years of tax returns.) She'd grown into a compulsive liar because that was part of her disorder, I learned. But lying and deceit were the very triggers that brought out the most angry, intolerant and controlling part of me. I sat with Danielle many evenings, trying to reason with her, but by now any rational communication was almost non-existent. If I couldn't control this situation, if I couldn't be of help, then what was the point of my sticking around? That's how I began to think. Despite my vow not to do a disappearing act, I was about to that very thing. If the roles had been reversed, I wondered, would Danielle have stuck with me—or would she have bailed? Those are the issues I still wrestle with today.

"I honestly believe I could have stayed with Danielle if her lying hadn't become epidemic. Where once I had trusted her implicitly, I was now in a state of suspicion about almost everything she said and did. My anger and frustration only fomented the same emotions in her. We virtually stopped talking to one another. In bed we slept back to back and never touched. I'm sure she thought I was the coldest asshole since her father. Each day the arguments and accusations grew in intensity, along with Danielle's hoarding and paranoia. Finally, I told her I couldn't live like this anymore. I knew she couldn't live with herself either, and that filled me with guilt. I still wanted to be the hero and save her. There was just no solution that I could think of. We tried a couple of separations, but each time we got back together, our old patterns resurfaced.

"By now I was frustrated, angry, and tired of being blamed. Why couldn't she blame her problems on her illness? Instead, she told our friends that I was cold, insensitive and uncaring. As she made herself into the victim, I lost respect for her. I felt sorry for her, but I didn't feel love anymore. When we agreed on a divorce, I thought most of my stress would be behind me. Then I found out Danielle hadn't filed our tax returns for the last three years. She told her divorce attorney that her lapses were due to my bullying her. I was stunned as she complained to our friends that she'd never been happy in our marriage. Did she really believe what she was saying, and if so, was that part of her illness?

"Since our divorce, Danielle has been in and out of a couple of romantic relationships, and is seeing yet another therapist. She admits to being unhappy, but still sees me as the villain. She badmouths me to everybody. But what hurts the most is the way she judges me. In Danielle's eyes I suddenly had been a bastard from the day we first got married. All my actions and motives were now described as controlling, selfish and cruel. She suddenly couldn't find a speck of good in me. This raises an interesting question. Do women approach judgment differently than men do? For my male friends and me, if we have a golfing buddy who is also an alcoholic and has missed some child support payments, we'll still play golf with him. Our disapproval of his irresponsibility to his children or his abuse of alcohol doesn't get in the way of a useful and fun relationship on the golf course. But in my experience—and Danielle is just one example—when a woman finds just one thing really creepy or objectionable about someone—man or woman—she goes overboard in her judgment. She tends to condemn that person lock, stock and barrel, and wants nothing to do with him or her. For women it's often black or white. Aren't men more likely to see shades of gray?

"As I've begun dating again, I've had a half-dozen fairly serious relationships. In my city the singles scene is pretty wild, but I imagine it's the same in most big cities. At any given time there are five or six 'hot' clubs where everyone hangs out. You see the same faces over and over. The ritual gets pretty familiar too. Your first date is almost always 'the interview.' You feel under the microscope from the first hello, and most times you only get one chance to get it right. I always overdo the intro—making a big splash to win the woman's attention before I really know what or how I feel about her. I want to be accepted, of course, but I also want to know that she likes me before I venture out on a limb and make the effort to get to know her. I also want to pass her test because rejection is so painful to me.

"After my divorce, I got myself in shape physically, bought new clothes, and tried to look as youthful as possible. We all have mental check-lists when we go out, but I think for most women their list is longer and more rigorous than a guy's. It's certainly a different list. For example, while looks are important to women, I think it's just one item on the list, while for most guys it's at the top. Women have a longer list, and it's got nothing to do with emotions, not in the beginning. Instead, a lot of women take one look at you and a half-dozen questions pop into their heads. Does he have a secure job? Is he generous or cheap? Does he open the door for me? Does he make me laugh? Does he have a lot of confidence? Did he win the NCAA tennis singles championship? As difficult and demanding as I can be, most women I have dated were even more discriminating and judgmental.

"Sex is definitely part of that test. Maybe not on the first date, but if you get a second or third, and the woman is trusting of you, you're on stage. I was shocked at how many women wanted to go to bed before they decided whether they wanted to develop a relationship with me. Were they thinking that if I wasn't good sexually, I wasn't worth a relationship? For a guy, jumping into the sack sounds like heaven but it's not. I did it because I was afraid of disappointing the woman and getting kicked out of her life, failing another test without even taking it. The whole experience is awkward and self-conscious. I felt one woman was evaluating me as she would a glass of wine: first there's the smell, then the initial taste on the tongue, then the body of the wine as it swirls in her mouth, and finally the aftertaste. You know the Wine Spectator? It's almost as if a guy gets rated in the same way. There's so much anxiety. After your 'performance' you want to scream out, 'How did I do? How did I do?' I was judging her performance too, but it took a back seat to wondering how *I* did.

"Drugs, particularly ecstasy and pot, are prevalent on the singles' scene, and so is Viagra. Women carry Viagra or Cialis in their handbags just in case you forgot yours. For many women, the idea is to get smashed in a romantic restaurant, make the guy pop a sex pill, then go somewhere to screw your brains out. Most women over thirty know how important and strategic sex is. Sex is their resource of choice for winning over a man. I think they often bring you into their life sexually for control. That's certainly what Georgia did. Few men I know can resist. It's not just the testosterone thing. You feel this incredible acceptance—dear God, she's letting me into the most intimate part of her body!—and like the Sirens singing from the dangerous shoals, you literally do have to tie yourself to the mast of the ship not to be pulled in. But who does that??!!

"Still, I'm leery of entering into a sexual relationship prematurely. Once you have sex with a woman, the fundamentals change. Communication between you moves from a plane of logic to one of emotion. I can't explain this alchemy. Maybe the woman is thinking, hey, I've shared the most intimate part of me, and I want the same intimacy back from him. But she doesn't mean just sex. The intimacy she wants is a lot deeper. After having sex, her expectations and needs change, and the man is held to a higher level of accountability. You often feel 'owned' by a woman. Then there's the unwritten 'exclusivity contract' that women demand after three or four dates and going to bed with you. They want you to date only them. Maybe this is a dark definition of intimacy because part of me likes this possessive quality in a woman; to me it means that I'm special, accepted, and she's taking care of me. Yet another part of me is wary and distrustful. I want to be possessed but I don't want to be owned. I know my current girlfriend defines our relationship as much by the future as she does the present. I look at it more as a day-by-day phenomenon. She is a wonderful person, and I'm beginning to fall in love with her (she says she is already in love with me) but I don't want to rush into a commitment. When I explain what happened in my marriage to Danielle, that I need time to heal, she acts sympathetic, but in the next breath she lets me know she won't wait forever. Does a man ever get out of this squeeze play?

"In terms of commitment, there is a strategic difference between men and women. I know Freud is famous for asking 'what does a woman want?' As brilliant a psychoanalyst as Freud was, he said the answer escaped him. If he were alive today, he might be asking 'what does a man want?' Because for women today it's pretty clear. Not all, but most women want long-term relationships. That, and having or raising children, are their primary definitions of happiness. They want commitment and emotional fulfillment. Some women want it all—if you believe romance columnists, they want to be adored, possessed and protected—so no wonder they get so frustrated. No man is going to give them all that.

"But that doesn't stop a lot of women for asking for the moon. On the other hand, men don't define what they want. They just don't know, or they're all over the map. Among other things (like a lifetime pass to Yankees' games), I believe they'd like multiple relationships. If they have a really, really good marriage, they will restrict their extra-marital activities to fantasies. But the truth is men aren't wired for monogamy. Maybe the younger generation of women aren't either. Whatever women want, they are a lot clearer and more insistent about getting it. Men simply go along because they're not as focused, or they're too afraid to stand up for themselves."

Summary and Interpretation

- Barry's depiction of the nightmare of being single and trying to find a new relationship is the same for women and
men. Perhaps, as Barry says, women are more focused
on what they want, but both genders have a deep fear of
judgment, especially in bed. Barry, like many men who
are driven to succeed, may be his own worst enemy. If
he wasn't such a perfectionist, he wouldn't put so much

pressure on himself. It's almost as if he's setting himself up for the very thing he dreads the most: failure. In his marriage, the pressure he put on Danielle to "get better" probably helped doom their relationship. While Barry says he wanted to be understanding and patient with his wife, perhaps his perfectionism led to an attitude of intolerance. Could he have fought harder to get Danielle more help? Maybe that's where some of his guilt comes from.

- The problem for most perfectionists like Barry is not just that they are driven by the need to live up to someone's expectations, but by a fear of failure. Men can be so consumed with their images and reputations that they are slow to trust their own instincts, or listen to any internal voice that complains of unhappiness and unresolved conflicts. In Barry's case, that would be his anger and distrust of authority. Barry has been hurt enough times in his relationships that his distrust extends to women. It's too bad his need for perfection and control becomes a diversion from his unresolved conflicts, a safety net to keep him from rigorous self-examination.

- Another tyranny of perfectionism is self-delusion. Men and women create in their imaginations, or from their own needs, an idealized version of the opposite sex. The Prince Charming myth gives a little girl a sense of destiny—and the notion that the perfect man is out there, waiting just for her—along with a sense of entitlement. At some level the myth stays in her consciousness until she dies. But that fantasy is no different than someone like Barry or his friends creating their list of attributes of the perfect woman. Men too have a hard time relinquishing their fantasies. Perhaps cultural values, especially celebrity worship, enforce the idea that one can never be beautiful, rich, smart, or happy enough. As many psychologists have pointed out, we push each other to impossible extremes to fulfill impossible roles, then tell ourselves that something is wrong with us or our partners if we don't reach those goals.

- Perfectionism, then, is a relationship buster not only because it leads to the need for control, but because it creates the tension in a relationship that one can never be perfect enough. Many men beat themselves up, and sometimes blame their partners in the process, if things don't go exactly their way. In Barry's case, growing up Catholic and believing in the ideal of the Virgin Mary, coupled with his perfectionist parents and the desire to overcome his "loser childhood," make him inflexible in his pursuit of success. He's still not totally convinced that the search for the ideal woman is an illusion, despite his admitted fear of judgment and the horrors of the singles' scene.

- When mental or physical illness occurs in a relationship, the wild emotional swings in the healthy partner may bring more instability to the relationship than the illness itself. Barry runs the gamut from sympathy to disbelief to guilt to despair to deep frustration. He never quite knows how to treat or think of Danielle—is the person he relates to in the past, or the present?—and no doubt his vacillation makes Danielle feel more insecure. When Barry finally gives up on the relationship, one reason may be that he loses respect for someone who is weak, or that he sees Danielle as an obligation. Does he actually fall out of love, or just decide to leave out of frustration? Barry isn't sure. The under-40 generation tends to believe that a relationship should not be based on duty, but on attraction, pleasure and emotional fulfillment. If something doesn't work out with one partner, you're entitled to seek fulfillment with someone else.

- Besides his quandary about how to perceive Danielle, Barry also may be confused about how he sees himself. He wants to have a positive self-perception—someone who's jumped from immature loser to respected businessman. Yet he sets himself up for disappointment—and being perceived as too demanding—by putting himself on a pedestal. Because he has to be perfect, everybody around him feels the pressure to measure up too. Single now, he would like to get some nurturing from women, but his negative experiences have led him to believe he can't count on the opposite sex because women have their own agenda. Ironically, by putting himself in the perfection box, by being afraid of risk, his chances of falling in love are greatly diminished. Until more men accept that pain and failure are not necessarily bad, there's little chance for growth and lasting change.

• Of the generation of working women in their thirties and forties, some have borrowed a page from the male play-book that equates perfection and control with happiness. By ascending to positions of authority or achieving high levels of success, many believe that men will migrate to them—and some do, just as women are attracted to men with power—but most men I spoke with said they wouldn't trade places with any of those women. Indeed, they thought everyone would have to learn the lesson that men have already learned about the demon of perfection-ism: it leads to exhaustion, frustration and an abiding sense of never being perfect enough. Although there is a difference between achieving and overachieving, between a quest for excellence and one for perfection, the line is so thin that many never realize when they cross it.

• Men value goals, independence, and being a go-getter as their definition of what one should do in order to achieve happiness. Women's values—presumably Danielle's—have more to do with support, closeness and connection. These are what make women happy. Unfortunately, most men tend to regard women's values as inferior to their own. Men have little chance of genuinely connecting to women until they accept that both value systems are valid. Women need to make the same acknowledgement. Creating a bridge between the two worlds takes effort and consciousness. While men tend to give up more quickly in this endeavor—and become unhappy in their relationships—women need to stop blaming men if they haven't first tried to teach them some relating skills.

Chapter Ten

Benjamin's Story

The first problem for all of us, men and women,
is not to learn, but to unlearn.

—*Gloria Steinem*

Benjamin is a 48-year-old artist, recently divorced, and shares custody of their teenager daughter with his ex-wife, Andi. There is a gentleness in his face and demeanor, but that is belied by an animated speaking style when he feels passionate about something. An intellectual, Benjamin can talk on almost any subject. He likes to dress casually, wears glasses, and while he carries some extra weight around his middle, he never worries about his image. With his "straight-arrow" values—reflecting his Midwestern upbringing—the lessons of his immigrant parents and a strong intelligence, he's always believed in brain power over emotions to guide him through life. Yet he acted on emotion when he became infatuated with Andi, a beautiful woman who was totally his opposite in almost every way. They were married for almost two decades. Believing in the infallibility of his values and a man's ability to be a master problem solver, it took Benjamin eighteen years to accept that his wife didn't love him and that this was something he could not fix. Even as the relationship deteriorated and he felt increasingly abused, his sense of denial was strong. It was Andi who finally asked for the divorce. What sustained Benjamin after the divorce were male friendships and a lot of self-exploration. His emotions turned out to be more layered and complex than he knew. He had mistaken infatuation for love, a mistake he believes that many men make because they don't know what they want from a relationship. How can they, he wonders, if they don't first know who they are and what they want from themselves?

* * * * *

"From my experience, women like to think of themselves as the more special of the two genders. They see themselves as exotic, mysterious, inscrutable, sensitive, intuitive—even sublime. When you read *The Da Vinci Code*, you learn about the 'sacred feminine.' I'm told that women readers devoured that book. They loved the concept that Mary Magdalene was not only the wife of Jesus, according to the novel, but that she's the Holy Grail. Maybe that's why the goddess label flatters them. Maybe that's why they love designer fashion labels: you're the best so treat yourself to the best. I think of the L'Oreal ad—'Because I'm worth it'—and how that must resonate with most women. High self-worth is great, but can any woman explain how she gets that label? Does she just give it to herself? Is this an assumption that just runs with the gender? If a man were to proclaim that he were a god or somehow ineffable, I think he'd be laughed at.

"It's not a stretch to argue that in the last few decades our society has become increasingly matriarchal. There's little doubt that, in some industries, in terms of salaries and authority, men are still the dominant gender—but who shapes the mores and social values of our culture? I think women have that power partly because they market themselves better than men. Eavesdrop on conversations at Starbucks, at the workplace, in the movie theater lobby. Women see themselves as smart, caring, open, fair and, when they make a mistake, misunderstood.

Men are perceived as needlessly jealous, possessive, distrustful, hyper-competitive, and often deliberately hurtful. Somehow, women have labeled themselves with the 'good' emotions and men often get stuck with the 'negative.' And when men get those labels, they often don't know what to do about it, so the labels stick.

"I don't know many women who like it when men analyze them. They like to believe that men can't truly understand their complex and subtle natures. Their exotic essence is one of their 'secrets.' (The name 'Victoria's Secret' is not without subliminal meaning.) Only women can understand women. On the other hand, continuing with this myth, men are easily understood by women because they are not nearly as complex or mysterious. Men are just men. Their emotions are not as evolved as women's. They are transparent. Yet, while women may claim to understand both themselves and men, I have had psychologists tell me that men don't understand men. As supposedly linear and transparent as we are, we are often still clueless about what drives us in life. And because men are so lacking in self-awareness, they need women to help them through life.

"A lot of women believe that myth and, unfortunately, men do too. I certainly did for a long time. It's only in the last two years, since my divorce, that I've realized that for men to have power—which means understanding and dealing with their own complexity—they need their own separate world. I mean not just some male hobby but a psychological world where happiness is a perception that I control. If I perceive that happiness means getting along with other people, then I have to get along with other people. If I perceive that my happiness has nothing to do with other people—if it means just getting up in the morning and working on a canvas or getting the oil changed or going to the library—then that's all I have to do. There's no duty or obligation involved. In the real world, of course, there're lots of duties and obligations, but if your primary perception of happiness is centered on yourself, that's where your power lies.

"From my own relationships, and from the men I know, we're drawn, at least initially, to a woman's physical attributes. Men stare at women as they walk down the street, in the supermarket, or waiting at a traffic light. They all have their favorite part of a woman's anatomy. As if there's a little bit of Keats in all men, the overall obsession with beauty is powerful. Why else are we seduced by the sleek, feminine lines of a car, a boat, a plane, a computer, or piece of furniture? Women know how important looks are. Most will do anything, and spend lots of money, to make themselves look as attractive as possible. They don't just do it for men. They do it for themselves, often in competition with other women. Whether the issue is self-esteem, cultural pressure, or the desire to 'pull in' a man—clothes, cosmetics, shoes, perfume and plastic surgery are as crucial to a woman's existence as food and water.

"I'm from the classic school of Midwest conservatism. Growing up in the Fifties, I was a scruffy, outdoorsy kid who could have posed for a Norman Rockwell painting. I was a 'boy's boy' who had lots of practical and mechanical skills. I was taught to be patient and thorough with every assignment or job I tackled, to do it right, and see it through to its end. I'm also an optimist in the sense that I believe almost every problem has a solution, if you just think hard enough about it. I also developed a sense of individuality as I grew up. I have rarely cared about social conventions, judgment, or gossip. I remember going to grade school wearing a coat and tie and toting a small briefcase because I wanted to look like my father. Kids made fun of me, but I just blocked out the noise and kept my eye on the prize:

good grades and learning as much as I could.

"I went to Catholic schools and toed the line in every respect. In second or third grade the nuns showed our class a picture of a man standing on the edge of a cliff. He was in a business suit with a briefcase and a hat (that could be me one day, I thought), and his family was clustered behind him. An angel was pointing down toward a flaming abyss; one poor guy, briefcase and all, had already teetered off the edge and was diving into the flames of Hell with this horrified look. I've never been able to forget that picture.

"My dad was from a poor German family, and around 1935 emigrated with my mother to the United States. Like a lot of immigrants he associated the American Dream with a ceaseless work ethic and material success. He put himself through med school, became a practicing doctor, and later acquired an engineering degree as well. He worked fourteen-hour days, six or even seven days a week, and had little to do with raising me and my three sisters. I was the second child but the only boy so maybe it was natural that my dad was my role model. Excellence through diligent, hard work. That became my marker for masculinity.

"While I had great respect for Dad, he was an emotionless, authoritarian man whose focus was on winning respect, wealth and social status. I felt I was often an underperformer in his eyes. But I just wasn't driven like he was. I do pursue excellence by giving my best effort, but I'm far from a perfectionist. A perfectionist is someone who gets down on himself (or someone else) whenever there's failure or disappointment. I don't mind my failures so long as I've tried. Failure is a great teacher.

"My parents recently celebrated their sixty-sixth wedding

anniversary. They have not changed one iota in their attitudes and behavior in those six-and-one-half decades. Even today I'm not sure how their relationship 'works' or what emotions mean to them. If you came of age in the Depression, I think marriage was seen as one of life's duties, like a medieval vow.

"Growing up in our very regimented house was easy in the sense that my sisters and I knew the rules and that there were no exceptions to those rules. Everyone had a role. Father was the breadwinner, children did their chores and homework, and Mom wrote the book on housekeeping. A typical immigrant's wife, the house was her kingdom and she was determined to administer it at the same level of excellence that my dad applied to his medical practice. But how many times can you scrub a bathtub? My older sister remembers Mom bleaching the hell out of everything she got her hands on.

"My mom was a problem solver, a 'fixer' more than a nurturer. I wouldn't ever call her warm and fuzzy. Looking back, I realize that my father never gave my mother much latitude for personal growth, and perhaps her anger at her repressed life showed both in her obsessive housework and in her strict discipline in raising us kids. I think a lot of boys bear the brunt of mothers who are really angry at their husbands but take it out on their sons. There was almost zero physical affection in our house, and a fair number of slaps across the face for breaking rules or acts of disobedience.

"Down deep, I was afraid of my mother. I loved her but I can't discount the fear factor. A lot of men, if they feel safe enough, will tell you they have mixed feelings toward their mothers. My wife had lots of childhood issues and anger toward both her parents. I think that's why she picked on me often and without provocation, just striking back. I

192

wish I had challenged her about who she was really mad at, but my own anger was so repressed that, rather than speak up, I just buried my resentments.

"When you're a child you're aware of none of this, of course, including the seeds of discontent and rebellion that are planted in you. If you're lucky, as I was, you escape for a time into play and fantasy. Because my folks lived in a rural area, I had hundreds of acres of meadows, forests and streams as my backyard. My friends were all boys and we did the Daniel Boone thing. At age twelve I built my own mini-bike out of scrap parts. I gravitated easily to Cub Scouts, then Boy Scouts, and as an Eagle Scout I was honored at one of the national jamborees for my achievements. Life wasn't all seriousness. My friends and I loved playing practical jokes—but deep down there had to be purpose to most things I did. Equally important, I was never boastful about my accomplishments. In keeping with my Catholic, Boy Scout, immigrant upbringing, eventually I became valedictorian of my high school class, scored 1590 out of 1600 on my SATs, and was admitted to more than one Ivy League college. Yet I never talked about any of it, believing that modesty was a virtue.

"But modesty can be code for lack of self-knowledge and courage. Not speaking up for yourself, I believe, begins with not defining or exploring yourself internally. If you don't feel safe speaking up as a child—if your parents fail to give you that special space—you won't develop a voice for your emotions. It doesn't matter how intelligent you are if you don't understand your emotions. You're going to be ambushed. Maybe I just followed my parents' lead of quiet stoicism, but for most of my adult life I've had difficulty getting things off my chest. That weakness played a key role in undermining my relationships with women, especially with my wife, Andi.

"In high school I had only one girlfriend and we went steady for three years. When I first laid eyes on Marjorie I knew I wanted to be with her and only her. I've had this pattern with women all my life: while I'm very selective, once I'm attracted to someone I go all out—flowers, lunches, love letters, poetry. My second pattern is, once we're in a relationship, I stick with a woman through thick and thin. I am impervious to temptation. Is it my fear of violating the Seventh Commandment or just my habit of being single-minded? Then there's the family history. Not only have my parents never been divorced or separated, but my grandparents on both sides exhibited the same fidelity. Monogamy is only one of several 'ideals' that I have been drawn to throughout my life.

"While we were not quite twins, Marjorie, my high school flame, was very similar to me. She was brainy, a cheerleader, a student body officer—in brief, overachiever *extraordinaire*. She was also drop-dead gorgeous, and more than any of her other characteristics, it was her beauty that I focused on. I didn't lose my virginity until we'd been dating for two years. This was before the sexual revolution, so we moved from first base to second to third at a snail's pace. My friends and I believed you didn't sleep with a woman unless you intended to marry her.

"I thought Marjorie and I made the ideal couple. I assumed that because we were so compatible and because I was in love with her that we were going to get married. It never occurred to me that eighteen years old was too young, because I basically envisioned life as a series of duties. Once you found the right woman, you married her and moved on to your next duty—college, career, whatever. In our senior year, while I was wondering where and when we would tie the knot, Marjorie fell in love with the star basketball player. I was dumbfounded. I could barely breathe. Cool as ice, Marjorie told me, "he's just better

194

than you, Benjamin." Today Marjorie has both law and medical degrees, and has been married and divorced three times. I think no achievement is ever enough for her.

"Losing Marjorie was my first experience with deep emotional pain. Her unexpected rejection was like a right hook from Muhammad Ali. I didn't share my grief with anyone, nor did I try to understand it. I just let it grow inside me like a tumor. I was so devastated that I didn't date again for two years. By then I was a sophomore in college. I joined an eating club, which at our school was the equivalent of a fraternity. Women were not permitted to join most eating clubs at that time. This allowed for sharing thoughts and feelings with just men, creating our own male universe without worrying about what to say or think in front of women. Men act differently when women are around: they're less forthright, more artificial, more cunning, more prone to jealousy-inspired competition. I developed terrific male friendships during this period, many of which have lasted throughout my life.

"College was a great four years for me. My friends and I devoured the seminal novels of the Fifties and Sixties— Kerouac's *On The Road* was my Bible—and we all dreamed of being free to challenge bourgeois conventions. My summers involved tough manual labor, including work on oil fields and in coal mines. I loved it. The money was good and I made friends with roustabouts, cowboys, hobos—tough, independent men, uneducated but very smart in their own way. I'm an unabashed romantic when it comes to the outdoors, traveling around, living the rugged life, using my ingenuity, being independent—that's a big part of my definition of manhood.

"Later, when I studied different cultures and their initiation rituals, particularly those of the American Indian, I was drawn to the fact that there were specific tests for bravery, honor and survival. You passed the tests and you never worried about your self-esteem again. You had made it! You were a man! One reason I loved the Boy Scouts was that there was a relatively clear path to maturity. There were skills you acquired and that were validated with each merit badge. Skills defined manhood. Where else in American culture do you find this clarity?

"In my junior year at college I met a co-ed named Isabel and zeroed in on her. Isabel's looks were even more stunning than Marjorie's, she had an incredible work ethic, and what started out with innocent intellectual discussions ended with my falling in love with her. We had a three-year relationship and this time I did talk about marriage. I told Isabel I wanted to spend my whole life with her, and the next one too. Isabel said she liked that I wore my heart on my sleeve. She also liked my sense of humor, my art, and my imagination. She said she wanted to get married too. I realize now we should have talked a lot more. I trusted Isabel at her word, instead of picking up on little warning signs that flashed in the last year of our relationship: missed dates, broken promises, moody behavior. Was I just horribly naïve? One night I went to her dorm to surprise her with flowers and found her in bed with another guy. Another right hook from Ali!

"Days later Isabel showered me with clichés—she was too young to marry, needed to grow and find herself, sorry she hadn't had time to tell me, she wanted us to be friends, blah, blah. I don't think she had any idea of the pain she caused me, and somehow I couldn't tell her because I just buried it inside me along with all the other pain in my life. Dumping me meant little more to Isabel than a change of mind, a practice every woman in my life has handled with great facility. I know men can change their minds too and cause plenty of pain (and are quickly branded 'heedless cads'), but when women do the breaking up they seem to forgive themselves more quickly and are largely spared social judgment.

"After graduation I took a high school teaching job in a small California town. Removed from the Ivy League pressure cooker, I happily occupied my free time by hiking, camping, working on my motorcycle, and successfully building a plane with a friend. This was a very defined, self-explanatory world where I felt safe and validated. During these years I was into music, writing, and my art. I also read voraciously about the Chumash Indians, who at one time represented a thriving culture in California. By now I had abandoned Catholicism, but I still considered myself a very spiritual person. The Chumash believed in sweat lodges, the importance of visions, and they had a concept of the earth as mother goddess, not unlike other ancient cultures. I began to think of women in this positive role, not just as goddesses but as protectors, guardians, these special beings of sentience and warmth. I even said a prayer that I could meet a woman that had those characteristics.

"The next day, right after my prayer, I met my future wife. In every serious relationship I've been in the woman has to be physically attractive. She certainly has to be more attractive than I am. I was so blinded by Andi's beauty and femininity that I barely considered her character, background, or mood swings. I trusted that my strong attraction to her femininity would be enough to keep us together. Trust has been my downfall with women. Once I fall in love, I trust a woman implicitly. I'm like a puppy in her lap.

"Except for being stunningly beautiful, Andi was very different from Marjorie and Isabel. There was nothing hard-working, self-effacing or overachieving about her. She was a college dropout who could barely balance her checkbook. Andi had little ambition. She was the quintessential California babe with her vintage sports car, a deep tan, and a sparkling personality. She lived moment to moment, day to day. That's not to say she was dumb: she was as clever and intuitive as anyone I've met. After we were married, when we began to argue, her debating skills ran circles around mine.

"I didn't know what she saw in me, and I didn't particularly want to ask. I just wanted Andi. Her sexy smile, the way she dressed, her perfume—it was all part of an irresistible package. While I was normally a careful, patient and organized man, Andi was spontaneous, free-wheeling, outrageous and unpredictable. We were living proof that opposites attract. It was her wildness that I found so liberating, the perfect escape from my straight-laced past and the pain caused by over-ambitious, perfectionist women.

"As our courtship progressed, Andi took me to parties, bars, all-night clubs, homes of her crazy friends and, ultimately, to meet her family. Unlike mine, Andi's family had a history of multiple divorces and remarriages. She was from a wealthy and (as I would eventually learn) highly dysfunctional family, but for the first year of our relationship I was blinded by my infatuation. Was I finally breaking out of my old, repressed self? I was spellbound by her family's wealth. Everyone dressed well. They were incredible athletes. They even had their own plane. It was hard to keep track of all the step-brothers and step-sisters, uncle and aunts, with everyone coming and going. There was so much unsettling change and chaos around Andi. It didn't seem to bother her like it eventually upset me. Even with my infatuation, I wondered in the middle of more than one night if I wasn't in way over my head with Andi.

"After dating for a year, Andi showed up at my studio one

afternoon and announced she was moving in. Just like that. This was the same studio where my friend and I had built parts of our plane—our sacred male space, if you will—and the moment Andi entered it with her suitcases, declaring her intentions, everything felt different. I was upset by her arrogance, yet I was too hooked on Andi ever to turn her away. She said she found my digs "different and exotic." I knew they were really quite plain.

"By now it was clear what Andi saw in me. I was her port in the storm, the only stable thing in her kaleidoscopic, chaotic life. Trust was very important to her, she confided, almost tearfully. I would always be there for her, wouldn't I? Yes, I promised, I would. When she told me stories of past boyfriends chasing her for sex or money, or how involved she'd been with drugs, I understood that I was supposed to save her from all this. And being the quintessential Boy Scout, not to mention the lapsed Catholic who was nevertheless still informed of the dangers of hellfire, I was prepared to do exactly that. Was there a merit badge for this? Yes, I would save Andi from herself.

"Our first year of marriage was special. A year of great sex, fun, racing around in her sports car—Andi saving me from geekdom, I suppose, and me saving her from her aimless, destructive ways. (Sex later would be anything but great. It was either non-existent or it felt forced and mechanical.) I got to know her family better and Andi opened up to me about growing up with unloving parents, health issues, sibling rivalries, bitter divorces, betrayals, and damaging gossip. I tried to shield her from that past. Determined to have our own life, we bought a small house together. Andi took some courses and qualified for a job with a state social agency, counseling people in abusive relationships (something she already knew well). We talked about having kids. We were happy. Maybe, I thought seriously, my prayer of finding the perfect woman had been answered. I could never live without her, I thought.

"I could, however, easily live without her complex and agitated family, though this proved impossible. Andi's many relatives were forever visiting us, often unannounced. Even though she didn't get along with many of them, she would never ask anyone to leave. Despite all our intentions, Andi and I had little privacy. As it turned out, the more chaotic things were, the better Andi liked it. Without my consent, she invited her father, recently divorced, to live with us. From Andi's perspective, the more people in our small house, the better.

"After our honeymoon year, I think, something in Andi changed. Maybe she thought I wasn't quite the Rock of Gibraltar she had first envisioned. Or maybe she didn't covet or need that stability as much as she thought. Or perhaps she just surrendered to her wild side and didn't want me to cramp her lifestyle. But all of a sudden I felt she didn't love me. Somehow I was still useful to her—companionship, advice and the ever capable handyman—yet there were so many times I felt I was on the outside of our relationship looking in. With her verbal skills and sparkling personality, Andi was deft at convincing me of her needs while also convincing me that my own needs weren't as important. And Andi had lots of needs—for attention, flattery, friends, or just activities. She made a big point of saying she valued her independence, but if I ever brought up the same issue for me, wanting to spend time with my friends, she was annoyed.

"As things cooled between us, Andi began to drift back to an old boyfriend. First it was just lunches and dinners, then she'd be gone overnight. Rather than risk a confrontation, I just let the matter go. When she was home at night she drank wine, stayed on the phone, or isolated herself in a room. She began to complain that I was a really dull guy who never took her to exciting places. Yet when I tried to spend time with her or be intimate, Andi would push me away. I didn't probe further. I wasn't good at dealing with hidden emotions. And frankly, I didn't want to believe our problems were insurmountable. I was brought up to believe that every problem could be fixed. That's what a man does: if something is broken, you find a way to make it work again.

"Andi loved to provoke arguments, and not just with me. While fighting wore me out, it energized Andi. Arguing was the outlet for her anxiety, which seemed to come out of nowhere. I had now learned that this was her family's way as well. There was lots of yelling and screaming, threats, and tantrums. When I came home from work there was an inevitable knot in my stomach because I could never anticipate Andi's mood. She could find fault about anything—the way I was dressed, how her family treated her, why we didn't have flowers in the house, or the wine I'd brought home was the wrong kind. If I argued back and raised my voice, even one decibel, she would snap back, 'why are you yelling at me?' She could go from aggressor to victim and back to aggressor with lightning speed. While I stumbled from one defensive position to another, Andi had her end game in mind from her first word. She always knew what she wanted out of our arguments, usually some concession from me, even if it was just to agree with her point of view. Why couldn't she just come out and say in a normal voice what was on her mind? Everything had to be complicated and charged with drama.

"Her linguistic skills were formidable, as had been Marjorie's and Isabel's. Language is an art form, and I believe women have a genetic head start in that department. I've read that when girls are born, they are more open than boys to receiving information and emotions, and I would guess that somehow the two—information and emotions—get intertwined neurologically. I've also read that mothers with newborn daughters make more eye contact and talk more to them than they do with boys. If you combine a woman's body language with her voice inflections, and the nuances and subtexts of her messages, isn't a man at a communications disadvantage?

"I think Andi's temper and penchant for arguing ultimately became a form of abuse. The more inept or passive I was in arguing back—sometimes I was just too exhausted to fight with her—the more confident and bolder she grew. One time she was so angry that she didn't use words—did she think I was no longer listening? (probably true)—but threatened me with a beer bottle. Another time she took a swing with her fist and broke my glasses. Once, out of spite, she vanished for a whole month from the house and never called me. If I were smarter, if I hadn't been in such denial, I would either have walked out and called a divorce attorney, or at least figured out that somewhere in her past Andi had suffered from some kind of terrible problem and needed help. Her low self-esteem was camouflaged by her femininity and big personality, big enough to fool me and many other men in her life and to help her get away with some outrageous and aggressive behavior.

"Andi also had what I call the goddess complex. Perhaps like a lot of women, especially women with big careers, incredible beauty, or great talent, she really thought that men should worship her just because she was this special, inscrutable, mysterious being. A friend told me he was watching a television show called *The Big Idea* and listening to a high-powered women executive elaborate her views on men. She said, without a sliver of irony, 'Every man lives to make a woman happy. Every man loves to serve us, you know.' That was how Andi felt. It's hard to imagine a man saying those exact words today, about women being born to serve men.

"The long and short of it was that I treated Andi like the goddess she thought she was. I gave her total empowerment. No matter how abusive she was, how many times she stormed out of the house, I always forgave her. If she disappeared from my life and wandered back a month later, I took her in without hesitation. I was happy to have her back. Was it because I was so in love with her beauty and femininity? Was my loyalty a kind of self-abuse? Or was I just in denial, certain that I could make things better somehow? Relationships are complex, organic entities, and for all the arguments and misunderstandings, sometimes there are periods of real love and contentment. During one peaceful interlude in our marriage, Andi and I conceived a child, a girl who is 13 today and a source of joy to both of us. But after our daughter was born, Andi's behavior grew even more erratic. She could be warm and nurturing one moment, then narcissistic and aloof. More than once she went into her disappearing mode, sometimes for weeks at a time, leaving me with most of the child-rearing duties. While it was lots of responsibility and a juggling act with my career as an artist, any time alone with my young daughter turned out to be a blessing. If I had a choice between going to work every day or staying home and being Mr. Mom, I'd chose the latter.

"No matter how much comfort and joy my daughter brought me, however, I couldn't ignore the problems in my marriage. After one of her petulant explosions, I told Andi she had to get professional help because she was damaging her relationship with our daughter. To my surprise, Andi listened to my plea. For a while I felt some hope as she began seeing a therapist. The problem was, she never told me what happened in her sessions. She insisted they were private and confidential. When I tried to insert myself into the equation, thinking that I could help her solve any problems, she would sometimes grow furious. 'How could you possibly understand me?' she demanded. 'How could any man understand a woman?' She ultimately quit one therapist and tried another. I was sympathetic and understanding but that wasn't enough to help Andi. It was as if too much damage had been done in her past for anyone, including me, to unwind. I had clearly disappointed her because I hadn't saved her, despite my 'mission,' and no therapist ultimatley could help her either.

"Andi had several reactions whenever she became overwhelmed with stress or anxiety. One was to explode with unfocused rage, often at me. I was to blame when things went wrong or she careened from one crisis to another. Another was to keep herself in motion, running to or from something, or working long hours at her job. The third was to go out and buy a *haute couture* wardrobe at Saks, take her friends to expensive restaurants, or splurge on new furniture. But she wasn't the only one with multiple personalities. I kept flipping back and forth as well. One side of me was the romantic, emotional guy who was still hooked on Andi's feminine mystique; the other side felt rejected, abused, and helpless. Andi was drawn to chaos like the proverbial moth to a flame. I eventually understood that there always had to be a crisis in her life because she'd grown up with nothing but crises. I was from a steady, quiet, church-going family who rarely said a cross word to one another. Where we buried our feelings, Andi disgorged hers at every opportunity.

"I was aware of problems, and that my emotional needs were not being met, but I didn't know how express that to anyone. I had no outlets. I never cheated on Andi or even thought of it. I was just as steady and dependable, and silent, as a plow horse. Even when I eventually attended some of the therapy sessions with Andi, I never got many insights into my own behavior and feelings because Andi was always making the therapist focus on her. Yet—another irony—she hid the truth from the therapist as adroitly as she had from me. She could giggle one moment and cry the next—how did you ever penetrate that kind of behavior? Either you embraced it or it repelled you. For twenty years I embraced it.

"Today I sometimes feel ashamed of my long history of passive behavior. One or two good years out of twenty? How can I explain that to anyone, including myself? Was I just dependent on Andi, just like abused women are dependent on abusive men? She made me so happy in the beginning that I thought that even when things got bad we could find that happiness again. I don't know if Andi was ever really in love with me or just needed me, and ultimately she was the one who walked out the door because she had met someone else.

"If Andi hadn't insisted on a divorce, maybe I'd still be married to her. I'd like to think not, but the truth is I let her get away with a lot of unacceptable behavior because, like my mother, she was the authority figure in my life. That was the pattern established in my childhood. I looked up to my mother with a certain amount of fear and blind obedience, and I did the same with Andi.

"With my divorce two years ago, and lots of time for contemplation, I no longer blame Andi for the two decades of mostly misery. I let her do it to me, so I accept responsibility for that. I accept responsibility for my life. That way I become more cognizant of what I need from myself in the future (and from a woman): self-acceptance, space, respect, tolerance, and speaking up when I need to. I know that would make a very dull reality TV show, but TV is part of the problem. It distorts with adrenaline and instant gratification. What is truly real is more subtle, more powerful, and under the surface."

Summary and Interpretation

- Andi hides behind the goddess label, claiming full privileges to act as she pleases with exemption from blame. She's the aggressor when she needs to be, the victim on other occasions. Unlike a lot of women, Andi *likes* being on the pedestal. For many men this would be a huge turn-off because they fear they'll get blamed whenever their partner falls, just as Andi blames Benjamin for her various crises. That Benjamin waited twenty years to be free—and only because Andi forced the issue—may seem inexplicable, even to him, until he looks at his childhood and a lack of nurturing parents. Lack of nurturing leads to an adult male who doesn't know or trust his emotions, and often lacks self-confidence. Perhaps that's why men like Benjamin give authority and control to their partners. For Benjamin, ceding control to someone who is out of control seems illogical, but there was an emotional dynamic that kept him and Andi together in a dark way. Benjamin simply assumed that when things went wrong it was somehow his fault, or at least his duty to make them right. He describes himself as "a fixer." No matter how abusive Andi's behavior became, Benjamin wanted to tough it out. While he was more than entitled to leave the relationship on many occasions, *his* controlling nature was to fight that impulse and to pretend that everything would be fine.

- Like other men in this book, Benjamin confuses a magical moment—the fact that he prayed to meet a spiritual, earth-goddess of woman and, the next day, he ran into Andi—with a sense that this is destiny and that falling deeply in love is inevitable. This infatuation was so strong that even when his relationship began to disintegrate, he clung to the hope that the magic would resurface and rescue him.

- Benjamin is one of those rare men, refreshingly, who does not fear or secretly worry about failure. However, perhaps he took that attitude to an extreme with Andi by not acknowledging his painful reality. If he'd admitted early on that his relationship was breaking down—and why—he might have set the boundaries for Andi that she badly wanted from him. Her attraction to Benjamin was the idea that he was someone who would save her from herself. As he gradually grew frustrated by that role along with her erratic behavior, Andi became vindictive because she thought Benjamin had betrayed her. What initially attracted them to each other—her femininity and his seeming stability—was really never enough to sustain a marriage.

- Benjamin is astute in his overall observations about gender behaviors and the psychology of women—almost in exact disproportion to his awareness of his own situation with Andi. He said he was lured into his relationship by the powerful mystique of Andi, but he didn't recognize that the beginning of most relationships is the accommodation phase, where a woman pleases a man to gain a foothold or even control. He also didn't pick up on Andi's methods of communicating until it was too late. Creating crises, or being physically intimidating, or storming out of the house after a fight, is a manifestation of her anger over not being able to control Benjamin, or make him respond to her need for boundaries. Instead of admitting her vulnerabilities, she just walked out on him on numerous occasions. This "cut and run" is more typical of male behavior. Probably in her teenage years, Andi learned she couldn't show her vulnerability or pain, and resorted to her attention-getting behaviors, possibly imitating her father.

- Like a lot of men, Benjamin throughout his relationship had an intellectual awareness of sick or unhealed aspects of his masculine conditioning, but he couldn't seem to integrate that awareness on an emotional plane. There was no off/on switch he could find when it was time to find the appropriate *emotion* to convey what he was *thinking*. Again, many men simply don't know how to maintain themselves in a relationship—except to repeat the patterns of their caregivers.

- Benjamin is more of an optimist and an idealist than a perfectionist. Besides the no-win control dance with Andi, he fits into this chapter because he's an example of the anti-perfectionist and the consequences of living with a good deal of emotional chaos. He doesn't seem to mind when the system is breaking down because this gives him something to fix. Instead of investing his time and talents in preventing the breakdown, Benjamin becomes micro-focused on the perceived remedy. It's hard to have a successful relationship and stay in love if most of your emotional energy is invested in waiting for something to go wrong, and then reacting when it does go wrong. You begin living more in the past—thinking of things you should have done or said. Since his divorce, Benjamin is in a new, positive relationship, and reports that he is now learning about give and take, and not getting stuck in residual anger and dredged up emotions.

- The way Benjamin was raised by his Depression-era parents, he thought it was irresponsible to give up on any task. In analyzing his relationship with Andi, Benjamin feels she took advantage of this trait. If he saw himself as the problem solver, and the quintessential stoical male who never complained, this gave Andi license to abuse him not just because she knew he wouldn't fight back, but because he would ultimately blame himself. Many women criticize men for being too withdrawn and not

intimate enough, only to end up exploiting those qualities, as Andi does with Benjamin. Do women really want
their partners to change, or does male passivity offer them
the chance for control? Many men I talked with believe
that for a woman, the issue of "controlling her man" is
paramount in a relationship, even more important to her
than feelings of love. The same men also pointed out the
fine line between being "taken care of and nurtured" and
"controlled" by a woman. Once the line was crossed, they
said, the impulse in their partners was to take control of
almost everything. This may be no different than a man
assuming "ownership" of a relationship through male
methods of control, such as intimidation and bullying,
but in either case it's an invitation to fall out of love.

- When Andi formally ends their relationship, Benjamin
  finally comes to the realization that happiness for him lies
  in being *less* controlling and *more* assertive. Assertiveness
  reflects confidence and self-awareness, and represents
  true power. For many men, to release control is probably
  the smartest thing they could do for themselves and their
  relationships. It means abandoning a role they think they
  are supposed to play but generally distrust. Too often
  men confuse control with power, when in fact the two are
  opposites. Having power means not needing to control
  anyone.

- Unlike a lot of men, Benjamin is not hung up on success
  any more than he is bothered by failure. His definition
  of masculinity is determined by his role models—men
  who live in the outdoors and make their living with their
  hands, who prize their intellect and the world of ideas, who
  choose spiritual solutions when rationality doesn't work.
  He takes a middle road in a culture that is bookended by
  polar opposites. While men are portrayed in sitcoms and
  commercials as bumbling, clueless and self-centered,
  in more serious depictions they are seen as brainiacs,

209

philanthropists, or fearless leaders who strive to both improve themselves and beat the competition. Particularly in business and athletics, men are encouraged to be masters of the universe. The image of Lance Armstrong crossing yet another finish line with his arms raised in the air is Hollywood-perfect. Then we turn on the television to *Married With Children* and see Al Bundy struggle to get to dressed in the morning. This contradictory image of men confuses both genders largely because men are so silent about defining themselves. Who are they, and who do they want to be? In the ocean of conflicting expectations and images, the short-term remedy for many men is simply not to answer those questions. They choose instead to seek validation—from whatever source they can find—that they are one kind of success or another. Even Al Bundy, despite his self-deprecation, sees himself as a loving and devoted father. Not every man may be a master of the universe but at least he is recognized for *something*. If a man doesn't get acknowledgement from his peers, his boss, his partner or his children, he has a new problem to deal with. Either he has to work still harder to find approval, or write himself off as a failure. Or, like Benjamin, find his own path, which is one of the best definitions of success.

- Benjamin eventually learns that in relying on people like Andi to make him happy means allowing the same people to make him miserable. His thoughts on having a separate universe—a world that is not too full of duty and obligation, or dependent on others' approval—is a world where he feels powerful and in control. He may be right that happiness is about perception, but how does one wean oneself from being totally dependent on others for happiness to becoming the center of one's own universe? As children we're totally dependent on our caregivers, and our emotions are shaped by that dependency. Perhaps the key to some separation as an adult is, as Benjamin learns, to accept responsibility when things go wrong, and to stop blaming others.

Chapter Eleven

Hugh's Story

"How am I going to keep myself away from me?"

—*Counting Crows.* Perfect Blue Buildings.

In his mid-forties, Hugh is over six feet tall with thinning hair and an intelligent face that always appears alert and eager. A stylish dresser, he keeps his car immaculate, his house clean, and the papers on his desk in perfect array. He is unfailingly polite, thoughtful and articulate. He describes himself as competitive, and gives the impression of thinking several steps ahead of everyone else. A sales executive who lists his goals as money, success and security, Hugh was married for almost twelve years before he and his wife Deborah divorced. Deborah, short and trim, is more than attractive with strawberry-blonde hair, a quick smile, and emerald eyes flecked with gray. But there is also a hint of pain in those eyes, and in the way her mouth sags when she's under stress. Today, Hugh and Deborah share custody of their only child, Cindy, a precocious 11 year old. Hugh attributes his emphasis on money and security to being an only child and having parents whose frugality denied him the opportunities enjoyed by other kids in his neighborhood. Deborah, whose parents also struggled financially, shared Hugh's goals. Besides being in love, one reason they married was they thought they were so much alike.

* * * * *

"Without always realizing it, I think a lot of women want very much to be in control—control of themselves, their romantic partners, their children, their overall environment. That was true for my wife, Deborah, and quite a few women I've known over the years. The more specific things they fear, the more control they want to exercise in all areas of their lives. Some women have a pretty long list: fear of fixing a flat tire, fear of violence, fear of any darkness in their past, fear of strangers, fear of not looking attractive enough, fear of being hit on, fear of not being popular, fear of not being good enough to make the cut. The list goes on, but just maybe their insecurities boil down to a fear of any task that a woman doesn't have the confidence or experience to tackle, or a fear of anything not directly in her control. For better or worse, our culture allows women to have their fears. That's why a lot of women make themselves into victims. Men, on the other hand, are expected by society *not* to be afraid. They're quickly labeled cowards or sissies if they don't step up to the plate. A woman can jump on a chair if a mouse scurries across the room and be lampooned but she won't be judged. A man jumping on a chair when the mouse runs by will be judged a pathetic wimp.

"I think women channel their fears in various ways: by denying them, getting angry, or blaming someone else. Anything but facing their fears head-on and saying, 'hey, I'm scared.' It's so much easier for some women to go into that control mode, or pass the particular task on to a man, like fixing a flat tire, or figuring out how her Blackberry works, or dealing with the spiders in the garage. Men of course have their share of fears—they especially fear emotional pain, and many, like me, fear conflict—but in the end, if they're honest, they admit their fears. A lot of women don't like to admit anything. They just won't. In my opinion, so many women, like my ex-wife, are escape artists.

"I didn't settle down and get married until I was thirty-three. Not because I didn't meet some terrific women along the way, or because I was into the stereotypical male sexual conquest mode. I just wasn't ready emotionally, nor did I particularly want to give up the single life I enjoyed after college. That life could best be described as a sharply honed work ethic with very fixed goals of success. I didn't want to marry until I felt secure in my career and I also wanted to be with someone who was equally secure, equally motivated and focused, and with whom I was in love. I was in no hurry. I wanted things to be right, to fall into place, and to be as perfect as possible.

"I grew up in the suburbs of a large Indiana city, the only child of hard-working parents—my dad was a high school guidance counselor and my mother was a housewife—in a predominantly white middle-class neighborhood. My life was pretty conventional. My parents were loving but strict. I was pretty much a model child, as straight-laced as a choir boy. I knew I wasn't supposed to argue or talk back so I didn't. Why break rules unless you really have to? It's always easier just to get along. I had good friends, was popular with girls, and was a strong athlete, so I enjoyed peer respect. For most of my life I considered myself well adjusted, without any deep resentments or special self-esteem needs, but in the last few years, especially after the last year of my marriage with Deborah, I've done some reassessing.

"While I loved my parents and respected their values, something gnawed at me as I grew up. My parents didn't have the means to send me away to camp for summer, much less on trips to Europe, so I knew I was missing something that some of my friends were enjoying. There were also other things, like my parents' frugality, that made me think I wanted more from life than they'd achieved. That's where my ambition came from. No doubt being an only child also shaped my values. I wanted to belong, to be accepted, yet I also wanted to stand out and be noticed. Sometime in high school or certainly in college I became a very motivated student, and I put pressure on myself to excel and be the best I could at whatever I tried.

"College was a terrific experience. I loved academics, especially literature and history, learning about worlds to which I'd never been exposed. I had different jobs during the summers, and lots of entrepreneurial ideas even if I didn't act on them all. In addition to learning, my goal was to save as much money as possible during those years. Money eventually became one of my benchmarks for success and self-respect, as well as a criterion for respecting others. I realize now that on many occasions I was too tight with my friends, but I thought I had a good reason. I was on my own in the world—that's what being an only child growing up in a frugal household teaches you. How many times did I hear 'money doesn't grow on trees, Hugh.' So I coveted it. Money was what made me feel secure. I think many women feel the same way. Money is something you can trust. Deborah and I shared that view.

"Sometime during college I became pretty judgmental and critical of just about everything—politics, ideas, value structures, behaviors. It was my cynical phase. Maybe not all idealists are perfectionists, but I managed, at least for this time in my life, to fit into both camps. I was hardest on myself, but also on the women I dated. Not in any mean or overt way, but it was too easy for me to find their flaws, give up on them without getting to know them, and move on to someone else. I didn't want to compromise. I wanted to have the 'right' car and eventually buy the 'right' house and always wear the 'right' clothes and eat at the 'right' restaurants and listen to cool music and do other cool things. And of course I wanted the 'right' woman. And to have an idealized lifestyle you needed money, which only reinforced the idea that money was the appropriate benchmark for success and self-respect.

"Like anyone who prizes discipline and moves toward his goals, I also had some control needs. To me it was all logical. The more you can control your life, the more focus you have, and the easier it is to meet your objectives. I definitely wasn't into controlling others. Even if I was critical of the women I dated, I didn't try to shape them into what I wanted them to be. I just said goodbye, walked away, and kept looking. I didn't want the chore of being responsible for someone else's life. I wanted to find someone just as self-assured and independent as I was.

"Once out of college, after a few hits and misses, I found a niche in sales at a large company. I enjoyed not just the people I worked with but the act of making a deal. The feeling of closure, of accomplishment, was terrific, as was earning a commission. By my late twenties, I was making good money and buying some of the material things I'd always wanted, essentially living the life my frugal parents didn't, but one that I thought they'd be proud of. Being a success in your parents' eyes is what drives most men and women, isn't it? I didn't see how you could separate my need for money from my need for approval, security and control. At that time it all blended together. Besides gaining my parents' respect, it was important to me that I was liked by my peers and customers. I had decent looks and a pleasing personality, but that led to some problems.

"The first was that I had a hard time with confrontation. In fact, confronting anyone and risking their anger, or any emotional turbulence, was a turn-off for me. It rattled me. You could say it was the epitome of loss of control, or a blemish on my idealized, perfect world, or maybe that's just how I was raised. So usually I would worm my way out of any conflict.

"My second problem was that when I made a mistake or error in judgment, I got down on myself. A screw-up meant I wasn't trying hard enough. Besides, I always found it easier to blame myself than to pick a fight with somebody, even if they were at least partly responsible for the error. That only led to conflict, which inevitably got in the way of meeting my goals. The less resistance, the better.

"I met my future wife, Deborah, at a party in 1990 and we hit it off right away. In addition to the indisputable physical chemistry between us, Deborah met all my criteria for the ideal woman: she had been a Fulbright scholar, was on the marketing team of a prestigious car manufacturer, and currently worked in sales in commercial real estate. She was a winner. The second oldest of six children, her family were third-generation farmers, hard-working, down-to-earth, and while financially they tended to struggle, they were the types to look you squarely in the eye and tell you the truth. Deborah had a kind of dazzling confidence and independence to which I was intrinsically drawn. She was a great dresser, she had a sense of humor, and she also shared my dream of upward mobility and material success. I suppose I saw my twin in Deborah, a safe emotional harbor for an only child who wanted validation for his idealized world. We got married 15 months later. I was in love, I had risen even higher in my company, and I was in total control of my life. So I thought.

"After we were married, Deborah's first piece of bad luck was to lose her job with her real estate company. I was sympathetic but had no doubt she'd bounce back.

217

Instead, she struggled for months to find new work. Nothing seemed to gel. For Deborah there was always someone or something to blame. The economy was still recovering...her interviewer didn't really listen to her...the job requirements didn't quite fit her talents. It took me time to understand that while outwardly Deborah was blaming others for her string of disappointments, she was really blaming herself. She didn't have confidence that she could land a meaningful job. She didn't think she was good enough. As the months went by, she'd let slip little comments that indicated she thought her life was rife with failures—setbacks in high school and college, in her family relationships, with friends, at her previous jobs—things she'd never told me before we were married and that utterly belied the aura of outward confidence to which I had been attracted. As these stray admissions grew in frequency, they affected her overall attitude and personality. Basically, she stopped believing in herself and her gifts. Deborah also became increasingly dependent on me—both emotionally and financially—and took solace in material comforts.

"I didn't say much during this difficult period except to give Deborah continual encouragement. But as she wore her mantle of defeat more openly, and her dependency on me grew, I became anxious. Our immediate problem was that we were about to buy a house and really needed two incomes. Deborah, finally giving up on the job market, told me she wanted to stay home and be a housewife. I explained that we couldn't keep up our lifestyle without both of us working. She essentially avoided the question about her confidence, and our crisis of overspending, and accused me of being too dramatic. Somehow she thought everything would turn out just fine. But I didn't have that confidence, and I couldn't hide my anxiety.

"Whenever I pushed the issue, Deborah said I was trying to

control her. That just made me more uptight. I resented the financial pressure that fell on me, and I also had difficulty with the idea that Deborah never dealt with her own issues. What suddenly made her so lazy, so indifferent? Where was all the confidence I'd seen when we first met? Was she afraid of failure? As I got to know her parents and siblings, I could see that emotions were never part of any family discussion. They were nice, straightforward people, but their underlying stoicism made me think that perhaps Deborah had never been given the opportunity to express herself. When I brought up that possibility to Deborah, she denied she had anything but strong feelings of love for her family.

"To afford our new house and meet our financial obligations, we finally agreed it would make sense for Deborah to work for my company, where I held a management position and could easily get her a sales job. For a while her spirits picked up and she made decent money. But her appetite for an even more lavish lifestyle grew, and despite our additional income, a monstrous renovation on our new house virtually depleted our savings. To make even more money, I left management and joined Deborah in sales. While we did bolster our joint income, the pressure of working together put further strain on our relationship. Deborah felt we were in some kind of competition. She was unhappy whenever my commission checks were larger than hers. 'But all the money goes to a common goal,' I told her. I was getting frustrated because I could never seem to please her. I was also worried not just about her overspending but mine as well. That seemed to be another area of competition between us—who had the best taste and who would spend the most money to prove it. From big things to little, we were like two junkies egging each other on. Who would find the most expensive china, the best lawn mower, the top-of-the-line lighting fixtures. My own discipline began to erode, eclipsed by this insane desire to be the perfect couple living the perfect lifestyle and hiding the truth from the world.

"I can't say it was one single factor that loosened the first thread of the tapestry I had woven for my future. And it certainly didn't happen overnight. But in essence, the Deborah I courted and fell in love with, the Deborah I thought I knew so well, turned out in many ways to be a front for a very different person. It was as if I'd fallen in love with a mirage. For a long time I never knew where reality was with Deborah, what was important to her, when she was posturing and when she was being sincere. Were my early perceptions of her simply incorrect—had I been blinded by love—or did Deborah change? If the latter, did she know that she was changing, or was it something out of her control? Was I helping her or was I making things worse?

"One thing was for sure: our internal relationship was being replaced by an external one. One of my weaknesses was that by ducking confrontations I also ducked discussing the touchy subject of our dissipating intimacy. I was lousy at communicating. That may be the price you pay when you're fixated on achieving a goal and you don't want anything to get in the way. Like truth. But knowing we were in trouble, I diplomatically suggested that something felt wrong between us and that we should consider counseling. Deborah didn't really respond. She lived in this increasingly private world to which I felt I was denied access. Her periods of moodiness grew more frequent. I ignored them, hoping that the problem, our problem, whatever it was, would simply go away. Our tacit solution was to become more wrapped up in our external world of parties and spending. But in truth, we were both miserable. Even when Deborah became pregnant, what should have been one of the happiest moments of my life was tempered by my fading attraction to my wife. I was starting to fake all my emotions for her.

"When our daughter Cindy was born, I hoped things would stabilize and return Deborah and me to some level of happiness. Cindy was colicky and never slept more than a few hours at a time. I wanted to do my share with the baby, but Deborah was insistent that since she was the mother, Cindy was her responsibility. Deborah was up at all hours, and with sleep deprivation her moodiness deepened. When I suggested she needed a prescription for a sleep aid, she coolly denied there was even a problem. Except for discussions about the health of the baby, our communication was dwindling down toward subjects no more consequential than the weather. The subject of our still wobbly finances was never brought up. When we got into bed at night, we didn't touch each other. Denial was the order of the day.

"Cindy seemed to take up all of Deborah's time. When I came home at night there was often no dinner because there was some issue with the baby. Deborah was too busy even to ask how my day was. I felt like a third wheel. When I grew more insistent that we seek counseling, Deborah became upset, even furious. Unlike me, my wife had no trouble with confrontation. Her behavior was cyclical—periods of pouting and moody silences alternating with out-of-control anger. Though I'd seen previous glimpses of her temper, now it came as a tidal wave of fury. What nerve had I touched? Was this just a case of sleep deprivation or had Cindy's arrival touched on some deeper issues? When I arrived home at night, if the slightest thing had gone wrong at home, Deborah would be screaming. Sometimes her voice grew so hoarse that she couldn't talk the next morning.

"I often blamed myself during this period—even if I couldn't identify what I'd done wrong—because I thought that would pacify Deborah. Also it was my old habit to avoid fighting. But nothing appeased Deborah: not my apologies, not my offers to help her with Cindy. Deborah was so fixated on the baby's well-being that she developed frequent migraines and finally an ulcer. Still, it was hard to broach the subject of getting her help. She was playing the role of martyr all the way. Just as she denied that she was sleep deprived, she denied that her physical ailments were anything to worry about. Maybe she thought she could hide them from me, from everyone, just like she hid from her fears. I would come to believe that my wife's fears, whatever they were, had such deep roots, and that her strategies for denial and masquerade were so ingrained, that she had little chance of ever seeing herself realistically or getting healed.

"As much as I loved our little girl, I soon found myself competing with Deborah for who gave Cindy the most affection, who could be the most perfect parent. Deborah and I had competed before in the workplace, and now it was happening at home. Since I worked all day, no doubt Deborah's bond with Cindy was stronger. What was also clear was that Deborah and I had virtually nothing in common anymore except for our love for Cindy, and the same hollow, expensive lifestyle that both of us clung to like a life raft, as if to compensate for our lack of intimacy. Once more I asked Deborah to see a therapist with me. By suggesting counseling, she said, I was implying that something was wrong with her. I was invading her privacy. I didn't love her enough. I was, in short, making needless trouble instead of enjoying our new baby daughter and being thankful for all that we had. I think she was mouthing what her stoical parents had told her. Always be thankful, don't complain, don't make waves. Anyway, she had a dozen reasons why our lack of intimacy was either unimportant or was my fault.

"In the meantime, she became the perfect mother. I say that with both admiration and jealousy. Deborah doted on Cindy with such affection and joy that our daughter flourished because of it. I was happy for Cindy, but to say that I felt excluded from Deborah's universe was an understatement. For sure, there were fun times when we both took Cindy on strolls and trips, and Deborah, when she felt secure, could be as caring as she was in the early days of our marriage. But she could turn off those loving emotions in a wink, and I felt stranded again. I resented always being at the mercy of her moods. At times I got really angry about it. I wanted Deborah to recognize that I had emotional needs too, that I wasn't the just Great Hunter-Gatherer who stoically, perhaps like her father, provided the means to meet our material needs and that was all I was needed for. I wanted something more. I wanted attention and affection.

"Whenever I spoke up for myself, Deborah's eyes usually glazed over. It was as if Deborah felt she had to make a choice between paying attention to Cindy or to me—as if she didn't have enough love or energy for both of us—and she chose our daughter. It was a good example of Deborah seeking control over a very limited world that was safe and secure and where no one could threaten her. But if she'd paid more attention to me, if she'd been honest about our lack of communication, trust and intimacy—if I'd been honest too—maybe the marriage could have been saved.

"For the next eight years, almost all our free time was so child-centric that Deborah and I rarely saw friends, went out to dinner or a movie together, or considered a lost weekend. Everything revolved around Cindy. There were so many toys and play structures inside the house and on the lawn that we looked like a nursery school. Deborah and I virtually gave up on sex. That should have been a clear warning sign that we needed to separate, but Deborah and I both ignored it. Cindy was the bond that would keep us together, she said once, and I wanted to believe that too. But in effect our beautiful little daughter was depleting the last dregs of energy and passion from our marriage.

"As Cindy grew older, my perception of what was right for her changed. I suggested to Deborah that we were beginning to spoil her. Deborah grew defensive and put up another wall between us. Tired of futile conversations, I retreated into silence. That just emboldened Deborah to lash out at me and others when her mood darkened. You hear a lot of talk about unresolved anger in men, but women can be that way too. What was becoming apparent to me was Deborah's negative perspective on life. She would repeat what her father had told her and her five siblings: 'the little guy always gets screwed.' I think that's how Deborah felt. She was the 'little guy,' the one the world tended to overlook or trample on. Her bravado, her seemingly indefatigable confidence, the one I had been so attracted to when we first dated, was turning out to be just a smokescreen. Whether conscious or not, it was a clever way to fool the world and me, and maybe herself as well. Underneath all that bravado was low self-esteem and the feeling she was never going to succeed at anything except being a mommy. Cindy was perhaps the only thing that kept her going.

"Even if Deborah wouldn't join me, I knew I needed counseling. Why was I living with a woman who made me miserable? In therapy I learned a lot about myself relatively quickly, about my own need for perfection and achievement and being validated by money. And that to admit that my marriage was a failure would be a breach of my perfect world. Also, maybe I wasn't the easiest person for Deborah to live with because I was not making her feel good about herself. She was comparing herself to me and thinking that she came up short. I didn't do enough to support her and maybe that reflected my overly sharp focus on my own needs. I acknowledged to myself all my weaknesses and insecurities, and set out to work on them. If I could change, I thought, our marriage could also change for the better. But whenever I went home and confided to Deborah what I had learned about myself, how liberating it felt, I was greeted again by that faraway gaze. Either she thought I was suggesting she needed therapy too, or my self-revelations triggered unhappy memories of her own childhood.

"When I told my therapist about Deborah's background, more pieces of the puzzle fell into place. Because my wife was from a large farming family that struggled, she was imbued with a dawn-to-dusk work ethic where everyone pitched in. That lifestyle also was characterized by an unflinching stoicism where one never complained, never whined, never asked for or received special attention. Along with not having a voice among six children, the work ethic on a farm makes you an adult before you're ten or eleven. I think Deborah felt she never had much of a childhood, even less of adolescence. She had lived most of her life in a state of material and emotional deprivation. Her desire for an affluent lifestyle was more than understandable, along with a lack of self-confidence because she never had the opportunity to blossom on her own. It was easier for me now to understand Deborah's motives in raising Cindy with such affection and devotion. Besides wanting to be indisputably good at something—motherhood—Deborah also needed to lavish on our daughter all the love she thought she had never received. I think she also believed that if she wasn't overprotective of Cindy, something bad was going to happen to her. Maybe that fear came directly from Deborah's father's negative philosophy about the 'little guy.'

"As long as she had our daughter as her escape hatch, Deborah wasn't going to enter into a world of painful self-examination. So ultimately, nothing really changed between us. To me it was incredible that Deborah could turn from the most gentle and constructive play hour with Cindy, then close our daughter's door and, in the privacy of our bedroom, lash into me for one infraction or another. During one screaming tirade, she put her hands around my neck and pushed me into the wall. Incidentally, we never fought in front of our daughter. We gave Cindy the impression that everything was fine between us, that her world was as safe and secure and perfect as we all wanted it to be. We basically raised her with a terrible lie.

"I'm not trying to assess blame in this story. If anything, I put blame on myself for not speaking up, and for perpetuating the lie of our perfect universe. I think men in general internalize blame and criticism more readily than women, and that this is a conditioned response from childhood. A boy is more likely than his sisters to feel a parent's pressure to be mature, responsible and successful, and is held (and holds himself) to a higher standard of accountability. It's the 'you're the man of the house' syndrome. Out of fear of criticism, or trying to project an image of superman, a man tends to hide his mistakes. He will even lie to hide them.

"Long before Deborah and I were actually divorced, I knew that our relationship had nowhere to go. I just couldn't make myself tell Deborah. A divorce would mean the end of my Ozzie-and-Harriet universe. And I think Deborah stuck with the marriage for a similar reason. She had been raised with the notion that you just don't quit or give up on anything. It was the farmer's way: no matter what the adversity—your crops could turn to dust and the bank could foreclose on your house—you just hung in there with a poker face. In my opinion Deborah never understood what real happiness meant, unless it was defined as the opposite of a negative—in her case material deprivation. Women are supposed to be the ones who really understand their emotions, but that wasn't the case with Deborah. If they were under the surface, she didn't want to go near them.

"One day we both had just had it. Deborah asked for the divorce first, but I was finally in the mental state to want it as well. Many of our friends were shocked. Despite our internal upheavals, and Deborah's retreat from the world, we had maintained the façade of the perfect couple. The divorce was relatively quick but emotionally tough on both of us. In my opinion, Deborah continues to be devoted to Cindy to the point of denying recovery for herself.

"I don't know whether Deborah and I will ever be friends. I'm open to the possibility, but she has to want it too, and right now I believe there's too much anger and lack of self-understanding on her part. As for Cindy, I worry about her as well. She is eleven now, very mature, smart, but driven and perfection-oriented. I spend as much time with her as I can. I worry about whether she can weather the trauma of her perfect world being cracked open like an egg. We had inadvertently taught her that perfection was not only the ideal to strive for, it was the norm. I hope as she gets older she can understand some of the issues and lessons that it took me until mid-adulthood to learn."

Summary and Interpretation

- According to Hugh, Deborah hid from her darkest emotions and kept Hugh away from them too. She claimed a shield of complexity that she said Hugh couldn't possibly penetrate—as the wisdom goes, only women can understand women—and therefore he couldn't help her. She didn't let her family or her women friends close either, and did everything possible to keep her pain private. Hugh didn't pick up on the fact that it's just as difficult for men to access and deal with their fears, and not just the fear of emotional pain or confrontation. While Hugh did sincerely try to help Deborah, he was often an inadequate communicator, and his emotions were so guarded that I wondered what he might be hiding. Like other men in this book, he didn't seem to know how to relate to his partner when she began to change. Worse, Hugh's own prejudice—and Deborah's—that their lives had to be perfect ultimately made everything worse. In being intolerant of mistakes, they reinforced each other's sense of denial. Eventually, they got so caught up in their artificial, make-believe world that they became strangers to one another.

• Many women are leery of "angry" men without understanding where and how that anger originates. Hugh is so guarded that, like many men, he doesn't let anyone know what's really bothering him. Perhaps, like Deborah, he didn't develop his own voice in his strict, by-the-book middle-class home. His dislike of confrontation may really be a fear of being exposed or shamed, or a fear that his anger will come out and overwhelm him. Looking at Deborah's life, her template for anger is the same as for a lot of men: a childhood where she never spoke up or got the attention she needed; an adolescence lost to the common family goal of labor and survival; the overriding message that you can never work hard enough or be virtuous enough; the defeatist attitude that the little man always gets trampled; and the rationalization that it's okay to be an impostor—pretending to be confident and happy, if not perfect—to impress your partner. Women are no different than men when it comes to putting up a smoke screen of confidence to gain a foothold in a relationship. However, while a lot of men will explode from their anger, or run away, according to most psychologists, the majority of women will process their anger differently. It is often turned inward and manifests itself, for example, in eating disorders, obsessive-compulsive behavior, physical ailments (like Deborah's ulcer and migraines), self-mutilation, alcoholism or anxiety disorders.

- Deborah's anger was directed both inward and outward. Her often explosive rages at Hugh were probably meant in part for her strict and inflexible parents. Hugh doesn't say, but perhaps in Deborah's mind his passive, judgmental nature reminded her of her father. Deborah put added pressure on herself by trying to be the perfect mother when it was clear that she and Hugh were losing the crown for the perfect couple. The future raises some interesting questions. Desperate for validation and investing everything in her daughter, what happens when Cindy grows up and interprets her mother's smothering love and perfectionism as control? Just as Deborah felt controlled by her family, will she pass that anger onto Cindy when she enters into her adult relationships? If Deborah does let go of her daughter, what emotional resources does she have to fall back on?

- For Hugh, having a controlling, judgmental nature may have created in Deborah, at least in the early stages of their relationship, a corresponding submissiveness and desire to acquiesce. This may have started when Deborah asked Hugh to be a leader and make important decisions for them when she lost her job and things got tough for her. Most men want to meet women's expectations and will assume that role if asked. When Deborah came to interpret Hugh's leadership as domination, however, her own need for control became obvious. She had to do something to keep from feeling suffocated. How could two people who failed to communicate their strong needs and deep secrets possibly keep a relationship together?

229

- For Deborah and Hugh—and so many others in this book—hiding in the silence and pain of their pasts does them and their relationships irreparable harm. Why didn't the men—if they did perceive themselves as leaders in their relationships—choose to speak up? That Hugh didn't confront Deborah more openly reflects the behavior of men who dislike a controlling partner but dislike confrontation even more. In the end, control in one or both partners becomes a means of not having to deal with conflict, which ultimately leads to even greater conflict, unhappiness, and the likelihood of falling out of love.

- "Constructive conflict" is usually healthy in a relationship. When one partner expresses what he or she really wants, in a safe environment, it eliminates a lot of irrational anger, fear, and passive-aggressive behaviors on the part of both partners. Hugh wonders at one point what keeps the spark in a relationship. There are many things, but one is certainly the security and freedom to express all your emotions. It's a primary definition of intimacy. The caveat is not to be threatening but to let your partner know that you trust him or her and that you're asking for help. Tolerance and forgiveness are also part of the equation. Both of those were missing in Hugh's and Deborah's relationship.

- Instead of experiencing true intimacy, many men—bored or frustrated in their relationships—fantasize while making love about previous lovers or a colleague at work or even a stranger. When a man grows too dependent on those fantasies, intimacy with his partner is in serious jeopardy. Sensing his emotional distance, his partner may become increasingly unhappy, angry, moody or depressed in the relationship—or one day she just leaves. This disengagement process may have happened between Deborah and Hugh. For a lot of women, were it not for their economic insecurities or other dependencies, it's doubtful they

230

would remain in their relationships where they perceive their partners as emotionally absent. A man might argue back, as Hugh would, that he wouldn't be so emotionally distant if his partner wasn't so controlling.

- Hugh points out that women can be very selective when and with whom they share their emotions. He believes this is one of their primary tools of control over men, along with sex. Sex has always been a woman's basic trading card. Most women surrender sexually only when the card they get in return has real value, such as a relationship commitment, emotional support, or some material advantage. Bundling sex and emotion together—and the ability to withhold them at will—gives women an incredible leverage that men do not have. When men are "shut off" from what they crave and need, women may not be aware of the anger and resentment this creates. If the pattern of deprivation becomes willful and consistent, men will fall out of love.

- After all the negotiating that turns a relationship into a partnership, if one side ultimately feels he or she has been treated unfairly, the partnership won't endure in a healthy way. The back-and-forth use of control and leverage is the underlying foundation of any working relationship, yet love, which presumably initiated everything, needs to be there too. Love means acknowledging the need to be flexible and a willingness to renegotiate. Yet, some men have a hard time with this process, not because they lack negotiating skills but because they don't know how to relate to their partners in any way except in the masculine, linear, non-emotional fashion. Women, with their gift for "emotional reasoning," may be much better at getting, keeping or changing what they want. Men like Hugh need to adapt if they want to find more leverage in their relationships.

PART FIVE

LOSS OF ATTRACTION

Chapter Twelve

Andrew's Story

We teach people how to treat us.

—Dr. Phil McGraw

Like Steven, Bill and Barry who, in various parts of the country, fritter away their Saturday nights in solitude, worrying about their relationships and what makes them happy, in Seattle we find Andrew dwelling on similar thoughts. It's the wee hours of the morning now and the 59-year-old psychologist can't fall asleep. Andrew is fair skinned with fine, unkempt hair and soft brown eyes. Of average height, he is for the moment on the thin side—on a careful diet after surviving a health crisis—and his expression is more somber than usual. Andrew describes himself as extremely analytical, someone who's always peeling away another layer of the onion and not quite satisfied with what he finds inside. But there is also a softer, romantic side to Andrew, one that is on a quest for love and harmony with another soul.

As he lies in bed absently watching television, his thoughts drift to his sixtieth birthday coming up in less than a week. Turning 50 was bad enough, he remembers, and now ten years have passed in what feels like days. What's life all about? he wonders. Separated from his wife, frustrated with his career, it's hard not to feel a certain loneliness. Despite earnest attempts with on-

line dating services and networking with friends, he's not found anyone that he clicks with. Twice married, the doting father of two daughters and a son, Andrew still doesn't fully understand why his two serious relationships fell apart. Both Marie and Lucy were great women. They accepted and loved him. Why couldn't he love Marie and Lucy back? The simple answer is he just lost interest in them. They stopped being the fascinating or nurturing or funny women that he first knew. In addition, they began to do things that annoyed him. But more than anything specific, there was a general, pervasive tedium in the relationships that, honestly, made him want to scream. Eventually, bored and restless—and perhaps responding to some internal compass—he moved on. All his life, he thinks, he's been searching for a deeper happiness that no woman has provided him.

Perhaps his unhappiness started with his parents' divorce, when he was about fifteen. It came as a shock to him and his brother and sister. Until then, Andrew thought they'd had a very together family, and he certainly was a model teenager: selfless, hard working, well behaved. He'd done nothing to break up the family. After the divorce, he became more guarded and circumspect, and particularly shy around women. He also became very tough on himself, quick to accept blame when things went wrong, and prided himself on helping others and making them happy. Usually Andrew is drawn to a woman because she's grounded and stable, like his mother. But after a while, the very things that attract him to someone seem to work against the relationship. That's what happened with Lucy and Marie. Sometimes he wonders if he's just acting out from his parents' divorce. Once free, however, he feels lonely, and not a little guilty for breaking up his family. Andrew wonders if he's hopelessly tormented, or if he should keep trying, keep dreaming, looking for that deeper happiness that was taken from him by his parent's divorce.

* * * * *

Andrew is divorced from his first wife, Lucy, a pleasant, down-to-earth brunette with pretty skin and a pleasing smile, and separated from his second wife, Marie. With high cheek bones, sweptback hair, and deep-set brooding eyes, Marie's warm and forgiving nature has been tested by Andrew on more than one occasion. Each of Andrew's marriages lasted over fifteen years, and between them he is proud to have successfully raised two daughters and a son. While athletic as well as brainy, Andrew has never been caught up in competition, and he shies away from any aggressive behavior. Quiet and introspective, he considers himself an existential romantic; at different points in his life, in his search for happiness he has taken up painting, gone into therapy, and binged on literature on religion, philosophy and spiritualism. He adores women and often looks to his relationships for the happiness he craves, but much of the time there's disappointment. The older he gets, the more thwarted he feels by a lack of solid answers. He wonders if he is just too critical and judgmental, too much of a narcissist, or is he on the search for some truth that is too complex and elusive ever to grasp.

When he was around two, Andrew moved with his mother, at the time a housewife, and his father, an academic and economist, to Washington, D.C. His brother was born a year later, and a sister two-and-a-half years after that. Andrew's earliest memory is of sitting with his grandfather on the edge of a bathtub in his new home, hacking away with whooping cough and having a terrible time getting his breath. "My grandfather couldn't help me," he recalls, "but I felt caring and compassion from him, and his presence comforted me."

* * * * *

"I have many pleasant memories of Washington, D.C. We lived in a housing development on the edge of a large wood. I remember hikes in what to me was a slightly scary but fascinating forest. We caught snakes and turtles and there were always new areas to explore. My father loved the outdoors and knew all about animals, birds, trees and plants. He was always teaching me about the things we encountered. I remember one Christmas going out in the early evening to find and cut down a tree for the house. The ground was covered with snow. It was dark but a full moon was out and there was plenty of light to travel by. I was worried because I didn't know where we were going, but I had confidence in my father that he knew the way. We cut the tree and brought it home by sled. It was truly a magical night. In those early days, my father made my life exciting and I felt he cared for me deeply.

"My memories of my mother in this period are less clear. I had the sense of her caring and doing a lot for me, but it did not seem as exciting as what I did with my dad. While my mother loved me a great deal, I think she also wanted me to be well behaved and to reflect well on her. She told me that she was sometimes embarrassed when I was quicker and more capable than some of my playmates, so she put an emphasis on me learning to share with others. I think I took these lessons to heart and worked at being well behaved. This kind of obedience came relatively easily to me—I've never been a rebel—so from a young age I developed a concern for pleasing others and not showing them up. This pattern of wanting to please has run throughout my life.

"As I grew up my male role models were hard-working, considerate of others, intellectual and responsible. My father and both my grandfathers were this way. My own work ethic and pride in my professional accomplishments were seeded in my teenage years. I did not have any aggressive or strongly sexual role models that I can remember. In addition to my father, grandfathers and some male teachers, probably my most influential models were heroes in books I read. In my early teens I was particularly drawn to Western novels and felt an affinity for the prototypical frontier hero: a tall, lean, strong and quiet man, often a loner, who believed in righteousness and who suffered endless trials and pain before vanquishing the evil foes arrayed against him. In most novels there was also a beautiful woman to fight for, yet she was typically in the background and often something like a goddess to be worshipped from a distance. These men rarely voiced their feelings of love and attraction to these women and acted almost as if that was not appropriate or manly. These novels seemed to be saying that when a man loves and cares for a woman he should make a commitment to take care of her forever. Anything sexual came after that commitment, and usually after marriage. Sex without honorable intentions was inappropriate. This was my early concept of how a man was supposed to behave and to some extent it is still with me.

"As an older teenager, I liked Ayn Rand's *The Fountainhead* and *Atlas Shrugged*. Both novels were thinly veiled stories to promote her philosophy of personal independence and responsibility and striving for perfection. In Rand's universe, less competent or irresponsible persons were considered unworthy of compassion and undeserving of support. Love was highly prized, but even in a relationship it was crucial to maintain one's individuality and separateness. I believed strongly in this philosophy in my late teens, but by college it put me in conflict with some new friendships I had developed. I decided Rand's standards were too idealistic and I became more accepting of the give and take that is necessary for any friendship to grow. However, I continued to believe in striving for high standards and always doing my best.

"To backtrack for a moment, when I was around seven our family moved to Europe because my dad got a job with a United Nations agency in France. This was a bit of a shock for me, as I had to make all new friends, and my teachers spoke only limited English. However, I learned French quickly and in school I was an adequate student. I was somewhat shy, and though I made some friends, I tended not to be very assertive in socializing with others. Sometimes I felt on the periphery, but I just took this for granted and accepted it as how things were. I did notice that a few of my male friends were more sociable and seemed to have a talent for talking to girls and making them laugh. I was impressed but didn't think it was something that was learnable. In my preteen years I got into thinking of girls as persons to avoid or not play with. That was the attitude most of my male friends were taking, and it seemed a natural thing to do at that time.

"As I was growing up, my parents were consistently positive, and devoted a lot of time to me and my brother and sister. They rarely got angry and gave us the message that anger was considered an inappropriate and socially unacceptable emotion. My younger brother was the only one in the family who became angry or provoked me or my mother. As we got older, he began competing with me more and more. This was a losing cause because, being three years older, I could easily defeat him in just about any contest, including physical fights. This did not deter him, however. He was jealous of me and wanted to beat me in games or contests and would get visibly annoyed when I beat him. In the end my parents insisted we stop fighting and learn to get along. So I got a lot of messages that fighting and being angry were wrong. I think I gradually developed the belief that I shouldn't compete with persons who were less capable than I was. My strategy with my brother was that as long as he didn't attack me physically I would not attack him. He then became adept at verbal insults and insinuations, pushing my tolerance to the limit. But I became good at restraining my impulses to attack back. While this solved my immediate problem with my brother, it again strengthened my tendency to control my anger and think of others before myself.

"At lunch one Sunday, when I was fifteen, my parents

calmly announced to my brother, my sister and me that they were getting a divorce. This came pretty much out of the blue. While I had recently noticed that my parents weren't getting along that well, they never argued or fought in front of us. I was frightened and overwhelmed by the news. I knew this meant my parents had significant problems with each other but I didn't know to what extent and I felt afraid to find out. My parents also seemed to want to present the divorce as no big deal, as if it wouldn't make much of a difference in our lives. They asked us if we had any questions. I didn't have the courage to say anything, but my brother did ask what would happen to the three of us. As if reading from a script, my parents calmly explained how my dad would be moving out but he would continue to see all of us. Trusting my parents' judgment, I was happy enough to buy into the notion that this wasn't such a big deal, but psychologically I began to withdraw further into myself, to keep my feelings private, and to believe that ultimately I had to take care of myself. No doubt it was at this point in my life that trust became an important issue to me. My parents did indeed conduct themselves responsibly in keeping their promises to us, but I did not feel comfortable opening up to either of them ever again.

"About a week after the divorce announcement, I experienced for the first time a migraine headache. It included numbness in half my body and blurring of my vision. The doctor didn't know what I had and to rule out cranial problems I underwent a variety of brain X-rays and neurological tests. He prescribed bed rest for me for that summer, which was quite weird because, except for the headaches, I felt fine. For a number of years I continued to have periodic migraines, which I learned to endure in solitude.

"A year and a half later, my dad married my physics

teacher, which was another shock and put my family situation squarely in front of my classmates. In those days divorce was rare, and I felt somewhat stigmatized by it, though at another level I was able to maintain the belief that it didn't really change who I was. Here again I just hid my feelings and felt I had to endure these events with a stiff upper lip.

"In high school I felt very confused about how to express my feelings of attraction to girls. As I mentioned earlier, in grade school, along with the other boys, I looked down on girls and sometimes made fun of them. Then I skipped sixth grade and by eighth grade, when most of my classmates were going into adolescence and starting to relate to each other, I was behind the curve. All through high school I was a year younger than everyone else in my class, and had trouble catching up socially. I think my parents' divorce and Dad's remarriage had the indirect effect of making me even more shy and unsure around girls.

"I did fall in love with one girl and later still another. I thought about these girls all the time, but I never really ventured to talk with them. I suppose it was a relationship I carried on mostly in my head. In the few instances when I attempted to communicate, I bungled it badly and only made myself look foolish. In my junior year, a new girl joined our class, and briefly showed a lot of interest in me. But I felt paralyzed and frozen with her, even though I liked her a lot, and she soon moved on to another boy who was willing to show more interest in her. I diverted myself with academics, developing a great interest in math and science, and took pride in my accomplishments. When I took my SATs, I did extremely well in math and science, and that boosted my self-confidence. But it didn't really help me with girls.

"Those last few years in France, before I left for college in the United States, my mother became a stronger influence in my life, and my dad, now in his new relationship, less so. While I liked my stepmother, she was often quite emotional and it took some adjusting to get used to her. My dad wanted to keep her happy and didn't assert himself a lot with her. By this time, my mother had for several years been taking classes to become a psychoanalyst, and began seeing her first patients. Unlike when I was growing up, she was suddenly very interested in talking to me about feelings and why people behaved the way they did. This caught my interest on some level, yet it scared me too. On a number of occasions my mom asked me about my own emotions—for example, did I feel a lot of jealousy toward my brother (I did not), and why did I think I was so shy around girls? I didn't open up much—that was my pattern after the divorce, and the answer to her second question—but I appreciated her efforts. They helped me start paying more attention to my feelings and how feelings dictated so many of our decisions and actions. These are pretty obvious observations today, but forty years ago this was novel stuff.

"As much as I enjoyed Europe, I definitely wanted to get back to the United States. In going to college I felt I was getting away from the embarrassment of my parents' divorce and could make a fresh start in my life. College really did give me a new beginning. I attended a prestigious all-male science college where I had the good luck to get in with a great group of friends who eventually became the leaders in our dormitory. This was a considerable improvement over high school, where I was not really part of the status crowd. In college I often ended up in some leadership position that I hadn't particularly sought, but I enjoyed the respect that it conferred on me. Along with being in my new group of friends, the leadership role helped my self-esteem considerably. I also discovered at this college (not known for its athletic prowess) that I was one of the better athletes and got involved in a lot of intramural team sports. More accolades came my way.

"The downside of a male college is that it's hardly the ideal environment for meeting women. My interaction with the opposite sex consisted of blind dates or mixers at other colleges. I had several girlfriends but no relationships that really took off. With these girlfriends I tended to be tongue-tied and shy, and a number of them got tired of my timidity and moved on. While I had strong feelings for some of these women, I felt a great anxiety over expressing those feelings. I continued to feel that I had to be respectful of them (which translated in my mind into not making physical and sexual advances). Looking back, I was probably protecting myself from sexual relationships, which were both attractive and scary to me. I typically tried hard to be a 'nice guy' because I thought that was what was needed to attract a woman and to sustain a relationship. I had little idea about how relationships worked, though I thought I did at the time.

"During a sociology internship program the summer after graduation, I met a woman I liked very much, but she was dating someone else. Had I been more forward, I think she would have left him for me, but I ended up leaving for graduate school. My career interests had shifted in the last two years from the physical sciences to clinical psychology. I'm not sure of my motives for this change of heart. Perhaps my mother was a force, as well as my own need to better understand myself. I also found people's behavior interesting in general.

"Graduate school was co-ed, but our immediate class was small and didn't have any women that I was strongly attracted to. There were lots of other women around campus, of course, but there was no easy avenue for

243

meeting them. The summer after my second year of graduate school, however, while I was working as an aide in a psychiatric ward, I met Lucy. I liked her from the start. She had a warm, communicative side that I lacked—bringing me out of my shell—and as things progressed between us I developed my first real, deep, long-term relationship. Lucy and I went together for two years while I completed my Ph.D. and arranged for a post-doctoral internship on the other side of the country.

"This impending move made it necessary for me to make a decision about Lucy and our relationship. In those days it wasn't common for a man and woman to live together without marrying. I thought I either had to marry Lucy or break up with her. I was pretty sure I was in love and felt very comfortable with Lucy. I also felt that Lucy was strongly attracted to me and that it would be very painful to both of us if I chose to break up. This thought—and the anxiety of moving across country alone to a new place—ultimately led to my asking her to marry me. I can explain my actions by simply saying it was a combination of doing the honorable thing, getting married at the right time (for both of us), and my expressing genuine feelings for Lucy.

"After we were married and I completed my internship, we returned to our original city. Our relationship was going well, and two years later we had our first child, Ann. Becoming a father turned out to be a wonderful experience. I really didn't know what it would be like, but I found myself tremendously bonded with my first daughter and delighted to spend endless hours with her. A great deal of my time and energy went into activities with Ann, as they did with our second daughter Sue, who was born three years later. My relationship with Lucy remained good, but because so much of our time was centered on our daughters we had less time for each other. Over the years, our relationship lost some of its excitement and emotion. I would say that Lucy became less appealing to me, but we did not have any major conflicts.

"Around the time Sue was born, I met a woman named Marie. We both worked at a large residential psych facility, and our paths crossed periodically. I gradually became more and more attracted to her and arranged my schedule to see her as often as possible. Initially I had no thoughts of leaving Lucy, but as I became aware that I was thinking about Marie day and night, I confided in Lucy about my feelings for Marie. She was very upset, but later was willing to discuss the subject with me. For a while I had the notion that I might be able to continue my marriage with Lucy yet have a second relationship with Marie. This was the 'open marriage' concept that had become popular in the mid-Seventies. However, it soon became apparent to me that I was not emotionally able to carry on a relationship with two women simultaneously.

"I really didn't know what to do, and for a while I let things slide, continuing to see Marie at work but not doing much else. Then I experienced an episode involving an irregular heart beat, which, like my migraines, no doubt was another manifestation of stress. I was hospitalized for three days, and took medication to get my heart stabilized. I did tell my cardiologist what was going on and he strongly advised me to make up my mind between Lucy and Marie, and then stick with that decision. I agreed with him and entered a period of trying to sort out my feelings, which lasted another year.

"Lucy had done nothing particularly to upset me. I was reasonably content in my marriage, but it had become mundane and routine. Marie was very beautiful, lively, intelligent and friendly. She also did an excellent job at work and I greatly respected that. She seemed much more

245

exciting to me than Lucy, although comparing the two was unfair, considering the very different roles they had in my life. I went to a couple of counselors in that two-year period, including a nine-month stint with a Gestalt group. Twice I moved out of the house and twice I returned to be with Lucy. Each time I moved in one direction I started to feel overwhelmed and changed my mind. Eventually I felt that I had damaged my relationship with Lucy to the point that it was not salvageable, and that there was no choice but to get a divorce.

"I felt very guilty about the breakup of my marriage, in particular for the hardship and turmoil it created for my daughters. I worked hard to maintain my involvement with them. They visited Marie and me regularly and I also volunteered weekly at their school. This led to some stress with Marie that, naïvely, I had not anticipated. I took a very strong role in setting the standards for how we treated my daughters, and didn't really discuss it much with Marie. In recent conversations she has told me she felt left out and sometimes criticized by me in dealing with Ann and Sue. Also, when they did visit us, she said, I tended to focus nearly all my time on them and neglected Marie.

"Nonetheless, I was very happy to be with Marie and had expectations of a deep and fulfilling relationship. We got along well, but from the beginning there were some issues that we weren't able to talk about. These included money and spending patterns, what love meant to each of us, and sharing our deepest feelings, as well as how to relate to Ann and Sue. We dealt with these topics mostly by avoiding them and by attempting to "read" the other and then do what we thought the other wanted. Looking back on it now, I don't think we always read each other very well.

"After living together for a year or so, we decided to have

a child. When Marie became pregnant, it seemed the appropriate time to get married. We were really happy. After a difficult pregnancy, Marie delivered a baby boy, John, and his birth brought us even closer together. While John's presence in the family mostly changed things for the positive, there were stress points too. The same pattern I'd experienced with Lucy happened with Marie. Taking care of the baby left less personal time for Marie and me. When Ann and Sue visited us, how to spend time with them and John together became complicated. Often it ended up with me doing something with the girls and Marie staying home to look after John. This wasn't very satisfactory to Marie but it just became another issue we didn't discuss. When John was about twelve months old, I had a discussion with Marie about some plans and her response gave me the sudden realization that she would be using John as an ally in some power struggle against me and Ann and Sue. I felt very helpless and didn't know how to react. True to my pattern of denial, I didn't say anything to Marie. I did not want to pit John's needs against the needs of Ann and Sue because I loved all three. But I also did not want to get into a constant tug of war with Marie.

"Looking back, this began a long pattern of what I would call background tension and conflict. On the surface we continued to get along well, but there was still, for me, an absence of full trust between us. Marie has recently told me that she too felt a distance and lack of trust between us. Yet neither of us talked about it in any depth. At one point, while John was still very young, I did tell Marie that one of my main hopes for our relationship was that we share all our emotions, even if they weren't always positive, and that we accept each other for who we were, faults and all. Marie's response was that she didn't feel a need to do this. I was surprised. I was trying to be open while Marie was choosing to go in the other direction.

Was I just too much of a romantic—maybe a demanding one—or was she reacting to being hurt and excluded in the way I dealt with my daughters?

"I felt rejected, and basically retreated into myself. I gave up further attempts to reveal my deeper feelings, or to expect Marie to be open. In so doing, no doubt Marie felt rejected by me. I very much wanted to make this marriage work and not subject John to a family breakup as I had done with Ann and Sue. I resolved to keep moving on and accept a relationship that was suddenly less than I wanted, and no doubt less than Marie wanted. We were two people who both tended to hide rather than face the unpleasantness of confrontation. Communication was not our strong suit.

"I remained married to Marie and we raised our son successfully despite many bumps in the road. Our relationship seemed to go through cycles of better and worse. After awhile I became aware that whatever state we were in, it would eventually change—that is, if it were bad for awhile it would eventually get better, and if it was good at some point, it would surely get worse. I took a certain comfort in the predictability of all this, that at least there was some stability to this pattern in that it never got too far out of control. It also gave me a reason to ignore some of Marie's complaints, believing that they would blow over in a few days. I realize that over the years I developed more and more the pattern of trying to anticipate Marie's reactions to what I did or said, and spent more and more effort trying to avoid antagonizing her. With the lessons learned from my childhood, I also believed that anger was unproductive, and I worked repeatedly and successfully to control mine. I had also made significant progress in learning not to blame others for things that might upset me. Overall, however, by repressing these different feelings, I had diminished my other emotions and energy for life.

"Another area of conflict between Marie and me was money management. I came from a frugal family and valued saving money and looking for good bargains. Marie thought of expensive possessions as a way to judge one's confidence and station in life. She also believed that how much someone spent on you was a gauge of how much he loved you. On the other hand, I believed that earning and saving money was a way to express love in a relationship. So we had a lot of divergent and entrenched feelings around money matters. It didn't help that in the early years of our relationship we didn't have a lot of money. After staying home with John for three years, Marie went back to work and eventually was earning a good salary. However, we kept separate bank accounts and we never really worked out a good spending plan. I felt that Marie spent a lot of her money on herself and her interests and only contributed a limited amount to joint expenses. But any attempt on my part to discuss money or ask for an accounting of her spending resulted in Marie getting angry. This became another issue I learned to live with.

"About fifteen years into our marriage, I resumed an old interest, oil painting. I had painted some in high school and college but was never very good and finally gave up because I couldn't really paint what I wanted. Marie gave me a book on drawing one Christmas and I went through all the exercises in the book. To my amazement, this gave me the ability to draw accurately in a way that I had never been able to do, and inspired me to take art classes. I found painting very soothing and comforting, not to mention a kind of therapy, and it became somewhat of a refuge for me.

"Five and a half years ago I learned I had prostate cancer. I was shocked because I had always been very healthy and thought I would be immune to cancer. I was frightened, but rapidly got into researching my disease and its various forms of treatment. I consulted a number of doctors. Marie was extremely supportive and accompanied me to these consultations. I eventually selected a choice of treatment and, while successful, the whole process was wearying, physically and emotionally. Facing the possibility of death was a mind opener. On the one hand, I could tell myself that I had already experienced a full and rewarding life, and could die without complaints. On the other, I felt a deep fear of dying and a strong desire to keep living. It probably took three years from the time I was diagnosed before I began having a fair degree of confidence that my cancer was gone and that I would live. In this process I lost the feeling of invulnerability that I previously had, and I realized that there were things I would like to experience before I died. This led to me questioning how much I wanted to remain in my relationship with Marie. Should I leave her and explore the possibility of trying other relationships? Still, the thought of leaving Marie made me feel very anxious and guilty. We got along well on many levels—and she had been very supportive during my illness—but ultimately I was after some kind of happiness with a woman I had yet to experience.

"I didn't take any immediate action. Marie and I continued to co-exist in separate orbits. One thing I did do was to spend more time on my art. I had gone to a half-time work schedule after I was diagnosed with cancer, and began working on a series of paintings which had to do with men and women. Most were about a man, a woman and a convertible car (mostly 1950's cars) and expressed the attractions, longings and fears that go with relationships. This was a significant outlet for my feelings of uncertainty about Marie and thoughts of possible relationships with other women.

"Then, about three years ago, I began feeling quite attracted to a younger woman in my office. I had known

Rita casually for several years, and we had gradually become friends. She was very lively, sociable and had a sense of humor that I loved. She seemed to like me and welcomed our conversations. I began thinking about her a lot and looking for excuses just to drop by and talk with her. I reached the point where I began to think of approaching her for more contact outside work, to explore the possibility of a relationship between us. This thought frightened me because I felt I couldn't try to see Rita behind Marie's back. Just as I had done with Lucy when I first became interested in Marie, I decided to discuss my feelings about Rita with Marie.

"Equally predictably, Marie was surprised and upset when I told her about Rita. But she really pulled herself together and made it clear that she wanted to work to resolve the issues between us. She didn't voice a lot of anger at me and really put some effort into being caring and understanding. We went to a marriage counselor for about seven months. In the beginning I was not optimistic, but over time Marie and I made solid progress, and I found myself losing interest in Rita. We stopped seeing our counselor and life seemed to be going well. Then about eight months later I began feeling an interest in Rita again. The intimacy that I had rediscovered with Marie seemed to be wearing off, replaced by my old doubts.

"At work I felt Rita was showing an increased interest in me. She had been living with her boyfriend for two years and I had assumed that this, along with the difference in our ages (over twenty years), precluded any serious relationship between us. But when she showed a higher level of interest, it made me wonder if something might be possible between us. Through several coincidences at work, we found ourselves going out to lunch often. She confided that she was planning to get married to her boyfriend, yet simultaneously she conveyed how much I meant to her. There was also a lot of touching and hugs from her. What message was she trying to convey?

"I chose the typical vain male interpretation: Rita somehow felt she had to marry her boyfriend but he was lacking in the emotions and sympathies that only I could offer her. I soon entered into a state of delirious euphoria in which I was constantly thinking about Rita. Maybe all I had was a crush on her. I didn't actually know her well and, rationally, the odds against a successful relationship were high. But at the same time I felt that this might be my one chance in a lifetime for a great romance and I didn't want to lose it. By now my new emotions had taken control. I tried to suppress them but found that almost unbearably painful. I came to believe that my subconscious mind was giving me a powerful message that I needed to do something new and different, that I had been trying to please Marie and others for too long and it was time to do something for myself, even if it was crazy. I felt alive and energized in a way that had only happened perhaps two other times in my life (both because of women, one of whom was Marie). Finally, I told Marie what I was feeling and that I wanted a chance to get to know Rita. She was again caught by surprise, but she didn't fight me much. Maybe she too was acknowledging that down deep our relationship wasn't working. But I think both of us had a fear of letting go.

"A few days later I found an apartment and moved out. When I next had lunch with Rita and told her what I'd done, as well as about my feelings for her, she expressed shock and dismay and reminded me she was planning to get married. She said she hoped that my move to my own apartment was inspired more by my problems with Marie than by my interest in her. I felt a little stupid. Was all this a fantasy in my head? Or had Rita been coming on to me, only suddenly to get cold feet? Composing myself, I tried to explain that I wanted what was best for Rita, and that I wasn't asking her to give up her plans to get married. I was hoping, however, that if she got to know me better, Rita might change her mind.

"Shortly thereafter, I went on a pre-planned ten-day vacation. While I was away, one of Marie's co-workers— who had heard Marie talking about my leaving her and my interest in a younger woman—called a supervisor in my office. Marie's friend wanted information about the woman in whom I was interested. As it happened, the supervisor was a close friend of Rita's, and told Rita about the inquiry. Rita felt this was an attempt by Marie to orchestrate a smear campaign against her. Very agitated, Rita decided to protect herself by going to another supervisor and filing a claim of sexual harassment against me. I spoke with Rita by phone the day before I returned from vacation, and she told me what she had done. She said she didn't really feel I had harassed her, but that was the only way she could think of to stop what she felt were attempts to hurt her reputation.

"I was caught off guard, to say the least. I listened to Rita and tried to be sympathetic. I assured her that none of these machinations by Marie's friend had anything to do with me, and probably not with Marie either. I then tried to prepare myself to accept whatever came out of this situation. But never in my wildest imagination had I conceived of a scenario involving being accused of sexual harassment. Rita warned me that my supervisor would want to see me the next morning. She expressed regret again for all this chaos, but said she was also under orders not to have any contact with me. I said I understood. I said goodbye on the phone and felt that things were over between us.

"The next day my supervisor did call me into her office

and informed me of the allegation that Rita had made. She told me I was to have no contact with Rita either at work or outside of work. She also expressed some sympathy for me, conveying that she doubted I had really harassed Rita, but that this was a serious charge and any further allegations would lead to an investigation and potentially serious consequences. She also indirectly alluded to the fact that Rita had had similar situations in the past with other men, and that I should be very careful in dealing with her.

"I carefully avoided Rita for the next four weeks. Then I answered a phone page one day and it was Rita on her cell phone. She again apologized for the harassment charges, said she missed talking with me, and asked if I would be willing to meet her outside of work. Clearly, she was manipulating me, and I knew it, but I had this deep desire to see her again. I really felt powerless to stop myself. I agreed to meet her. Over the next five months, this led to a number of phone conversations and to seeing each other at lunch once a month. Rita was always warm and cordial at these meetings, hugged me, and expressed an interest in continuing to see me. She got married as planned, but even after that she still called me and wanted to get together. On several occasions she talked about how her harassment charges against me were wrong and that she planned to withdraw them. But she never did. Each time I saw Rita I felt a strong attraction, and actually a great deal of openness with her. I continued to be pretty direct about what I was feeling and doing. I guess I was so needy that I felt I could trust her and be open with her. That my behavior was that of a lovesick adolescent didn't escape me, but we don't always understand how powerful the process of attraction can be.

"About two months after Rita got married, I began seeing a counselor on my own for Eye Movement Desensitization

Restructuring (EMDR), a therapy involving bilateral stimulation of the brain. The theory is, roughly, that our early, strongly emotional experiences are stored in the middle or lower parts of the brain, which are not very accessible to the more mature reasoning parts of our brain at the cortex. EMDR somehow connects these different parts of the brain and enables them to work together to resolve early childhood patterns and conflicts. In my case, I had some really strong and emotional experiences with EMDR, and felt that I did gain access to a lot of feelings and painful past experiences. These sessions seemed to help me express my feelings more fully and also to be more comfortable in expressing them. A number of my family members have told me that I am now more relaxed, spontaneous and emotionally accessible.

"After my second EMDR session, I felt a clear change in my feelings for Rita (though my feelings for her were not involved in that session). I felt like I had outgrown these feelings and that they were immature and were no longer very important to me. In some ways I was upset to have lost the intensity of my feelings for Rita. They had energized my life, even though what had happened reputation-wise was fairly disastrous for me.

"Marie and I have now been separated for a year. In the beginning I did not have much contact with her, but after I started some counseling and doing EMDR, I began recovering some interest in her. More recently we have been seeing a different counselor together, and she has had us communicate directly about conflicts and feelings that we've hidden. I think we have both changed a good deal and are finally able to voice our differences without getting into a hostile or hurtful interchange.

"During the time I've been separated from Marie, I have made many attempts to meet other women. But I realized after a time that I kept finding reasons not to get involved. Why I'm holding myself back, I'm not sure, but I suspect that I've come to the point in my life where I need more self-discovery. It may sound absurd at my age, but I really don't fully know who I am or what I want. In addition, I still feel some connection and responsibility to Marie. I am not able to free myself from feelings of guilt about having a relationship with another woman. I am also worried about getting into a relationship and finding out I don't care for her, and then having the unpleasant job of breaking up. I still am fearful of conflict. I have felt very frustrated with myself for being unable to move clearly in any direction.

"I also realize that I have to find a better way to balance my own needs as well as those of others with whom I get involved. I think for a long time I have downplayed my own needs to please others, especially Marie. The effect of this has been to take energy out of me and my relationships. I am clear that I want to express my feelings more fully and directly, and need a relationship with a woman who wants that as well. The dilemma I face is whether to return to Marie or maintain my separation. This brings me back to trying to figure out how I want to spend the remaining years of my life. I've been stuck in the middle of this conflict for some time, and don't see a clear solution emerging.

"I do not believe in life after death so I want to use what time I have left well. Part of me wants to explore unpredictable and exciting new realms of life (though I am not sure exactly what those are). Sometimes I believe I have to conquer some inner demons—and then I can break through to wonderful joys on the other side.

"Through all of this turmoil I have gained a greater appreciation of the deep—and in many ways crazy and unfathomable—attraction that men have to women. Certain women bring out in me great feelings of energy and trust, seemingly beyond all reason and good sense. In some ways I yearn for a hypnotic engagement and merging of the flesh and senses that would take my breath away and give me an ultimate experience of existence, of being alive. Am I chasing a fantasy? Perhaps, but I don't want to give up seeking it."

Summary and Interpretation

- Andrew lives in a state of low-grade anxiety because he can't quite forgive himself when things go wrong. Any setback or rejection is taken personally. Terrence Real, author of *I Don't Want to Talk About It*, might describe Andrew as suffering from covert depression, someone who knows something is wrong but can't quite put his finger on what or why. Andrew might be the first to agree that there is a great disconnection between who we know we are and what we project to the world. To be assertive means narrowing that disconnection—being honest, proud of oneself, and not afraid to make or admit mistakes. Andrew has made efforts to be assertive —from going to therapy to reading voraciously to expressing himself in his art—but still remains deeply frustrated. One problem is that he is an inconsistent communicator. On the one hand, he had the courage to tell Lucy and Marie of his interest in other women, but on the other he was largely silent about the anger and loneliness he felt from his childhood and adolescence. Like a lot of men who prefer self-isolation to relating to their partners, he lives a very protected, almost self-censored life. Andrew is an example of someone who never learned relating skills as a child or adolescent, and he's forever playing catch up. For most of his life he's seen himself as a fortress, believing that the enemy is on the outside trying to get in. But the enemy is already within. In Andrew's case, it's the pain of his parents' divorce and overall feelings of abandonment and rejection.

- Andrew is strong intellectually—a strength that perhaps is in inverse proportion to his emotional resources—so it's natural for him to rely upon reason when he confronts problems. In his relationships he thinks, "Look, I'm doing my best, and things aren't working, so what am I supposed to do? Whatever I do isn't good enough, according to my partners—so why should I stick around?" The defensive attitude reflects in part the tendency of many men to feel isolated in our culture, that when things get tough in a competitive, judgmental world, they're on their own. Support from other men is often fickle because, underneath any surface sympathy, men judge their successes by the failures of other men. As simplistic as it sounds, the limits of reason in solving emotional issues is never clearer than when men give up because they can't "think" of anything else to do. It's not that men aren't emotional; it's that too many don't know how to access those emotions or are comfortable trusting them. The sad irony is that men trust reason and rationality even when reason and rationality let them down. As someone once said, the definition of insanity is taking a strategy that you know doesn't work and using it over and over.

- Andrew is highly critical of himself and feels guilty when his relationships collapse, especially when he does the collapsing. Whether he's in rebellion and acting out his anger from his parents' divorce, or he really is driven by a search for a deep and elusive happiness, in order to feel good about himself he benchmarks his life by other things: his professional accomplishments, being conscious of other people's feelings and always being polite and helpful, and being a good father to his three children. He's also desperately looking to be loved and validated. He's most confident and comfortable with himself when he has peer acceptance, as in college where he's a sports star, or when he's praised for exceptional work in his profession. He finds self-discovery and solace in his art. He is most stressed when, despite his best efforts, things go wrong, as with Rita and the sexual harassment charges. The fact that he wasn't more outraged by this betrayal indicates how deeply he has buried his feelings. Perhaps he's too narcissistic to let something like this affect him. Or perhaps, when he comes to grips with his anger and feelings of loss from his parents' divorce, he'll learn to speak up and assert himself—the way he never did as a teenager. That might be his best way to find happiness in a relationship.

- The cliché about men is that they are the aggressive gender, a pack of alpha dogs who have a limited range of emotions that centers on power and self-preservation. But the vast majority of men are not power-hungry; they are more like Andrew, driven by an internal and cultural mandate to survive and succeed, meet female and family expectations, and find some kind of nurturing—be it sports or fantasies or from their partners and peers. There will always be some behaviors dictated by testosterone, but most men crave love and intimacy every bit as much as women do. Their key failure in not getting what they want is not being assertive enough, and not knowing how to relate. Why don't men like Andrew speak up? Is it a fear of losing control? Do they want to deny they have vulnerability and dependency needs? Do they simply not know what they want? Sometimes it's all three. Sometimes, intimidated by a woman's complex mode of communicating, men become "pleasers" and "enablers" because it's the safest and easiest way to get love and attention. Men also turn to music, books, television, movies, pornography and their own fantasies for their emotional "fix." But rarely are these strategies deeply satisfying. They don't achieve the level of intimacy that men really want. Men need to come out from hiding and stop living double lives.

- Part of Andrew's frustration in his search for a fullfilling relationship is due to his lack of real closeness to friends, family members and peers. He mentions nothing of his brother and sister or even his parents once he is married, nor any get-togethers with male friends. Most of his free-time activities, like reading and painting, are solitary. By living such a guarded, self-protected life, Andrew not only shuts himself off from emotional nurturing (except, presumably, from his children), but his fantasies of finding the right woman become too intense and narcissistic to be realistically satisfied.

- The art house movie *What the Bleep Do We Know?* is a fascinating look at the origin of emotions, relying on quantum physics to explain human behavior. A film that presents many complex ideas, including the possibility of simultaneous universes, also asks the equally baffling but more practical question: why do we do the same inexplicable things over and over, such as choosing the wrong partners, making the wrong career decisions, eating the wrong foods, or abusing ourselves in countless other ways? Looking to science, the talking heads in the film suggest our brains are a complex web of neuron receptors, which translate our external experiences into chemical reactions that produce emotions. Attraction, abandonment, anxiety, envy, fear—all have their origins when we're very young, in a precognitive state that is made up, essentially, of neurons. That is, we feel before we learn to think. Those emotions, negative and positive, only get reinforced, over and over, by our life experiences. Getting fired from your job, rejected by someone you adore, failing to meet your teacher's expectations—these may be different experiences but they stimulate the same neuro-receptors and produce the same emotions. Hostages to chemical reactions, we are in a state of addiction, whether we know it or not, and the only way out is a strong will, consciousness of the process, and a belief in the power of the mind to override our chemical receptors. While achieving this level of consciousness requires a significant amount of discipline, it can be a healthy way to overcome anger, fear and self-loathing, and can lead to stronger relationships. This path is not dissimilar to the Buddhist quest, where control of one's emotions is one of the first steps toward enlightenment.

Chapter Thirteen

Eddie's Story

*All happy families resemble one another, but each unhappy family is
unhappy in its own way.*

—Leo Tolstoy

Eddie is in his late fifties and retired from several business
careers. His build is stocky, his hair thinning, and his pallor on
the gray side. Like Jim Carrey, he can make his face into a comic
mask, which is appropriate for his sophisticated wit and sometimes
caustic humor. He has been married and divorced twice and has
no children. By his own admission, no relationship—and he's had
many—seems to last more than four years. Either it implodes or,
feeling hurt and abandoned, Eddie moves on. Besides being drawn
to ideas and politics, he describes himself as charming, extroverted
and sensitive, but also cynical and distrusting. High strung, he
admits to being his own worst enemy at times, and looks at his
childhood and adolescence to understand why. Unfortunately,
he says, explanations don't equal solutions. Falling in love with
women becomes more complex and difficult as he gets older, and
he believes it's the same for women. He wonders if this is just the
natural byproduct of accumulating too much pain, or does our
culture raise our expectations to such a high level that everyone
ends up disappointed with everyone else.

Eddie grew up in the late Forties in an old, crumbling New England mill town. His family was Jewish in what was mostly a Catholic, blue-collar suburb of Boston. Eddie and his older brother Arthur were offered a blend of public schools, values that aspired to be middle-class, and conservative politics. American flags and bumper sticks urging prayer in the classroom were rampant, "just as they are today," he says. Eddie was raised mostly in the presence of women: mother, aunts and grandmothers. "During the Jewish holiday 'bake-fests,' the house would fill with relatives both known and unknown, great aromas, and all of the bakers' chattering," he says with a smile. "Those are some of my fondest memories."

* * * * *

"Before she married my dad, my mom was a runway model at Filene's (then a fashionable Boston department store) and old photos of Dad and her from the Fifties show her to be quite a dish. She was curvy and had legs that most women would die for. The day after she married Dad, she quit her job and never worked again professionally. When I was about three years old she had some sort of emotional breakdown. It was all a big mystery what the problem was; even to this day I don't understand it. In general our family had one of those quiet, secretive lifestyles. This was a period in history before some shrink came up with the term 'communication.' My grandmother (on my mom's side) more or less did the parenting until my mother had convalesced to the point of resuming her duties as mother-in-charge. I think she mostly recovered but never quite had her wheels under her again. I can't remember much from that period. I do recall the smell of my grandmother's perfume, White Shoulders. To this day it reminds me of old women. That, and her breath. She died in 1959 of a painful, wasting cancer that made a grotesquerie of her once gentle, 'grandmotherly' face. It's her breath that I'll always remember.

"Despite my mother's emotional frailness, our home seemed to run okay. But it was not a very cheerful place. It took me years to realize that television life as depicted by Ozzie and Harriet was fantasy. My older brother had already figured this out but he didn't clue me in. No hum in our household, no radio, no pitter-patter of little feet. Shades down, a calm, cool, flat-line atmosphere. There were degrees of quiet, some decidedly cooler than others, but I can't recall an argument between my folks that ever spilled into my earshot. I couldn't figure out my folks' emotional connection, and as of today, I don't think I'll try. They were fairly social, and had occasional dinner parties with a large group of friends. They dressed well, and the women all looked like Donna Reed. I was always made to come down to the living room and say goodnight to the guests. The mixed aroma of cigarettes, Chanel No. 5, and aged scotch still triggers a few primal responses in me.

"My dad was a handsome guy, and financially successful, but neither he nor my mother ever really went in for displays of public affection. I like to hold hands, and can think of few things more re-affirming than your girl giving you a squeeze or a 'claiming hug' in public. Our whole family was on the undemonstrative side when it came to emotions. Even though as a grownup I tried to hang with Arthur from time to time, our seven-year age difference and our family's temperamental reticence probably doomed us. We were never close after we grew up. In family terms, being born so 'late,' I believe that I was the gift that couldn't be returned. Jewish families don't really plan to have children seven years apart. Arthur's childhood antics were probably what spawned *Dennis the Menace*. He just took my folks screaming to the edge of the precipice once too often for them to be interested in revisiting the terror that childrearing could be. Maybe I wasn't planned at all. But once I arrived, I think, thanks to Art, I was destined for benign neglect.

"Mom and Dad seemed never to have a grip on what kids needed. Somewhere along the way they decided the less parental involvement, the better for everyone. Or maybe they lost the parenting handle when mom had her breakdown. Maybe my brother and I caused her breakdown! In any case, my arrival was just the marriage damper that couples dread. They acted like I'd learn whatever I needed by the time I got to wherever I was going in life. 'Eddie, what would you like to be when you grow up?' 'A fireman,' I would answer. 'Are you kidding? A fireman? You think you can just *be* a fireman? You have to do a lot of work for that job. You can't be lazy!' At six years of age all I wanted were hugs and kisses. Instead I got a lecture on professionalism.

"To my folks, who'd endured the Great Depression and God knows what else, everything, down to the smallest and most simple task in life, was like walking through a minefield. Maybe it's a Jewish thing, but even a successful bowel movement seemed out of my ken. The negative reinforcement ploy as a child-rearing aid will never get a ringing endorsement from me. It's been that way with my mother (I think it's how she was raised) for most of my life. I also believe that aspect of my upbringing, that kind of negativity and doubt, helped dampened my self-confidence to such a degree that it never completely recovered. Someone said, 'Happiness comes in moments, and then it's gone until the next time. Sadness, on the other hand, settles in.' That's my mother, all over.

"Dad, on the other hand, was smart, athletic, and a much more positive person than Mom. A local man in his town saw him play baseball and helped get him a full scholarship to a good New England prep school. His brains and his baseball skills got him into Brown, Georgetown Law, and Boston College Law. He even received two "letters of intent" from baseball scouts from the Boston Braves and the Brooklyn Dodgers. Just the things a kid would want to hold onto, wouldn't you think? My mother tossed the letters in a near-fatal housecleaning attack, just after my dad died. My memories of Dad are scant but generally warm. Amazingly, he never spent a moment teaching me to throw or hit a baseball. Never a 'let's sit down and read this book together,' or 'let's go to watch airplanes land at Logan.' Not purposely neglectful, not mean, just kind of emotionally absent. A terrible loss I see now, a terrible waste to a kid who needed some attention. Dad was there occasionally, to be sure. 'Make the honor roll, Eddie, and I'll get you a motor to work on in the basement.'

"I can say that I always liked girls. Even in grade school they were a magnet. I liked their silliness, their spontaneous smiles, the way they whispered to one another, especially in the presence of boys, and just the way they walked down the hall alone or together. Throughout late junior high and high school I was a serial dater. I managed to stay with one girl or another for a few months at a time, and then move on. At that age, the combination of raging hormones and tender egos make relationships just one big treacherous lake covered with thin ice. I was always trying to be cool, but it was a learn-as-you-go environment.

"I lost my virginity at fifteen in the back seat of my dad's '65 Bonneville. Paula was sixteen and a half but looked and acted like she was already in college. We had been dating for about a month or two when my parents went out of town one weekend. Dad left the Bonneville keys on the entry table. I didn't even have my driver's license, but given the opportunity before me, was I going to sit home and watch TV? Paula was a somewhat experienced sixteen-year-old. I knew she'd had intercourse with several guys, and I had a sense that if I just hung in there, with a little luck I was going to join that elite group. It was raining and cold outside that night. We parked on a dark side street in a quiet, residential neighborhood. Clothes started to be peeled off, and the groping got to a heated level when out of nowhere Paula said, 'Stop!' I froze on the spot. It was as if a giant hand had entered the car from outer space and grabbed me by the collar. I stepped out of the car to take a few breaths, assuming that when I returned Paula would be all put back together, and things would be over for the night. I opened the door and to my delight Paula was naked from the waist down, sort of sprawled on the seat. Just when you think that God doesn't answer prayers... I even remember the song that was playing on the radio: *All Day and All of the Night* by the Kinks. The song can't be more than two minutes and 24 seconds long. It gives you a fairly accurate idea of the duration of our sexual encounter that night. But it felt like an hour, thank you. Wherever you are today, Paula, thanks!

"Two years later I had my first real, fall-in-love, go-mental, high-school attachment. I was a senior. Sandy, a junior, was five-foot five, and had a tight little body, dark green eyes, long auburn hair and a few strategically placed freckles. I thought that she was one of the best kept secrets in the entire school. Another outsider like me, bright and really pretty. I can't remember our first few dates, but after a while, we just clicked and quickly became inseparable. It's amazing how, when you're young and not hung up on judgment, how well things can go. Art, who was 25 by then, had an apartment that he let us use, and Sandy and I were like two minks. Her parents liked me too, and her mom took Sandy to a doctor for birth control pills. That kind of trust just never happened in my house. My mother was in my life so little at this point that I really was living at Sandy's house most of the time. My mom barely asked where I was. I left her a phone number, and she seemed just to be happy that I wasn't breaking into any Seven-Elevens.

"With Sandy in my life, my attitude, grades and friendships improved dramatically—thus the influence of a woman on a man's self-esteem—but when I finally left that autumn for college, the relationship fizzled out. Not my choice exactly. Sandy said she was sure I would immerse myself in my new environment, making new friends, meeting new women, and anyway she wanted time to think things out for herself. I was stunned, not to mention naïve. I had thought after a few months with Sandy that our relationship would last forever. I didn't want to break up. I didn't even want to meet new women. Sandy made me happy and secure. What's the lesson I eventually learned? That women can be so incredibly tidy about their emotions and self-assured about their decisions. The stereotype is that women are the emotional gender, but most of the ones in my life have been incredibly rational and direct when they want something. It's guys who are emotionally a mess. Even though I was only 18 and the whole world was before me, I took Sandy's decision hard. I was left with the pain of loss that one can only experience the first time you lose someone you're in love with.

"I think I've always been a little naïve about, and oblivious to, the idea of planning for the future. Maybe it's my existential leanings. Live for the moment and don't worry about tomorrow because it might not even be there. My brother believed that and passed down his personal wisdom along with all his existential books to me. But they didn't help me at this moment with Sandy. I was devastated by her decision, and the emotional loss I felt was only compounded by another life-changing event that happened around the same time.

"My dad suffered a heart attack in his early fifties and spent time in the hospital. My mom wouldn't allow my brother or me to see him. Even when he came home from the hospital and our dining room was converted into a first-floor bedroom, Art and I were told to keep away so as not to disturb Dad's recovery. Instead, I'd get pronouncements like: 'Your father says to do your homework.' Or, 'Eddie, make sure that the walk and driveway are shoveled for guests.' They got an audience and a clean front walk; I got second-hand messages from Dad that I wasn't that important to him.

"A year later, things must have been going well because my folks decided to go to Europe. At the time we had a comfortable home, a house on Lake Winnipesauke, a beautiful Victorian home in Maine, and a new house under construction. Then Dad went to the doctor for a pre-trip checkup and was told he had to have surgery to repair an aneurysm on his aorta. It wasn't the routine procedure that it is now. Two days later, he was dead. I still have the condolence letter from the surgeon and the hospital.

"Between my dad's passing and breaking up with Sandy, I was thrown for a double loop. To this day, every time I break up with a woman the loss is never a simple matter. It's always associated with other losses. Maybe that's true for everyone; their losses are entwined and hooked together like a string of paperclips, and with each new one the pain burns a little deeper.

"I didn't have the guidance or personal motivation, or the balls, to seek help. I thought I'd appear weak if I told my mother that 'I think I need to see a shrink.' She needed one far worse than I did, and if I spoke up, I thought it would just add to her stress and throw us all into a deeper tailspin.

"Instead of therapy, I chose a man's path for dealing with emotional pain. I ignored it. I lost myself in the physical world. I'd saved money for two years to go motorcycling through Europe, do the Hemmingway thing in Spain,

269

and try the beaches of Ibiza. It was great fun, though there were not a few moments when I was flooded with thoughts about Sandy and my father. When I returned to Boston a year later and got to our house, I didn't have a key so I rang the doorbell. An unfamiliar woman came to the door. 'Where's Mom?' I asked, startled. The woman explained that she and her husband had purchased the home several months earlier. She didn't know where my mother lived now. I was finally able to reach my brother. Art apologized—he'd forgotten to tell me about the move too! Mom later explained that she hadn't expected me home so early, and her new apartment had a den with a sleeper sofa. She said it was mine anytime I came home from school. Somehow that didn't ease my sense of loss, or make me feel less discounted. When moving, Mom had also thrown out virtually all of my and Art's belongings without wondering what we might want to keep. That woman could really clean when she put her mind to it. Ever since, I've had trouble unpacking anywhere I've lived. I have nightmares about waking up in a room that is absolutely bare.

"I kept in touch with Sandy after I started college. No other guy was in her life for a few years after we broke up, but that didn't make me feel better, not enough to raise my morale. Sandy was simply determined to meet her educational and career goals. I wasn't in the same camp. If I could only pass this exam, or pay that bill, or climb that next hill—God, I'd made it! I was content to just get by. I think most men, certainly at this age, just aren't as focused as women.

"I had many relationships throughout my college years, but few went deeper than the physical. I was always looking at the next girl, and down deep I told myself that I didn't trust any woman to really care about me. In the back of my mind I kept thinking I wasn't worthy. No doubt some of that distrust came from my mom's attitude and behavior, but what I'd gone through with Sandy didn't help matters. The truth was, I lacked confidence in myself, and if I didn't believe in myself, I really couldn't see anyone else volunteering for the job. A very insecure man, I regretfully admit. I didn't feel like I had anything behind me to prop up my confidence or my emotions. No role models, no mentor, no one to speak with along the way.

"After college, I lived in Boston with a woman named Lorna for four years. She was a buyer for a big department store, and came home every day with a purchase from that store. She'd watched her mother wilt under the domineering behavior of her dad, so the moment she left home and moved in with me she set out on a personal quest for freedom by exercising her purchasing power every chance she got. I worked hard to try to make her happy with what I considered to be very civil, loving, cooperative behavior, but there was no way that I could— unless possibly I bought her the entire department store. At the time, I couldn't quite see the destructive, obsessive, narcissistic behavior in her, nor did I realize its impact on me. I think I chose my mother's worst traits in the woman I was living with. That's been a pattern with me. I seem to seek out the 'difficult' cases.

"Lorna became even more acquisitive in our last year together. Tensions grew between us, and she began an affair with her boss. I had strong feelings for Lorna, so her affair really hurt. It's not hard to fall out of love when you've been betrayed and are bitter. But I'm not sure which I was hurt by more: the realization of my failure to please Lorna, or the ego blow of another relationship failure. Lorna and I have kept in touch over the years. To this day, she still exhibits the same self-destructive traits, hasn't been in a solid relationship for twenty years, and still can't see that she's hurting herself more than proving anything to her (now dead) father, who was forever oblivious to his own behavior. It's not any less painful when it's obvious that the circumstances from which we come are strong indicators of which way we'll go in our adult lives.

"More relationships followed, more disappointments, but I was still young (in my mid-thirties) and I saw the future before me, even if I couldn't define it. I began seeing my first wife-to-be, Kay, after she called one afternoon looking for my old girlfriend, Lorna. I gave Kay a brief history of Lorna's and my breakup, earned a little sympathy, and the next thing we knew we were having regular lunches. Kay had just graduated from law school and was determined to make a life for herself in Colorado, where she had interned the previous summer.

"Kay and I spent the best part of a year getting to know one another. This one felt like the 'healthy relationship' that you read about in women's magazines. I knew I was Mr. Right for Kay. Our personalities and interests meshed, the sex was fantastic, and she endlessly attracted me in her slightly distant, self-interested and independent way. I felt like I was constantly chasing her, which was a turn-on for me. Besides making clear her strong feelings for me, and mine for her, she was forthright about leaving Massachusetts and setting up a life in the Rockies. I was torn between following her or staying behind, where I now had friends, a good job, and a comfortable way of life. Very reluctantly, I told Kay I wanted to stay put, at least for the moment. I don't know why I said this. Maybe I was testing her feelings for me. Maybe I wanted her to beg me to come with her. I wanted to be wanted. But she didn't really comment, except to affirm her plans to move. We didn't discuss the future of our relationship, as if somehow that would just take care of itself.

"One day we packed up Kay's things in a U-Haul and had a misty final dinner. Afterwards there were more choked goodbyes. As she was pulling her U-Haul out of the drive, Kay abruptly stopped and ran over to my car. She leaned into my window, pulled a ring off her finger, and asked me to marry her. I couldn't believe my ears. I was stunned. It was a genuine Hollywood moment. This was my fantasy come true. I was wanted! We talked like crazy for a few minutes, and planned to speak the first time she stopped on the road.

"Mysteriously, I didn't hear a word from Kay while she was en route. Neither did her family. This was the era before cell phones so I couldn't call her. I grew frantic after the four days it was supposed to take her to reach Colorado. This was the woman who said she wanted to marry me—why wasn't she calling? I imagined some terrible tragedy. Finally, ten days later, I heard from Kay. She explained that after she left Massachusetts she'd picked up a 'friend' to make the drive with her. She'd never mentioned him to me over the past year. During the trip she'd had a change of heart about us, she said, and 'needed time to think about our relationship.' Guys, when you hear that phrase, make like it's a fire drill—keep low to the floor and head for the nearest exit. Trouble is brewing. For those ten suspenseful days, despite my anxiety, I was living and dreaming of a future with the woman I loved. Suddenly, with one phone call, I'd been reduced to a state of anguished waiting.

"This was a kind of warning sign about Kay's personality, I think, and if love weren't blind (as it certainly was in this case) I might have seen my future more clearly. Kay was leaving behind a core group of people, including me, who loved her! Most of us might find that exceedingly hard, but not Kay. She could cut off the past and fearlessly jump into an unknown, insecure universe as easily falling off a log. She liked it!

"For the next year I traveled back and forth between Massachusetts and Kay's new digs in Colorado. Slowly, our relationship got back on track. Kay loved her new job and I also knew what she wanted from me—a commitment not just to love her but to move to Colorado. I didn't understanding the meaning of the word 'control' then. Maybe the better word was simply 'fickle.' I was so happy to be reunited with Kay that I just signed on the bottom line.

"We married a few months later, after I had completed my move to Colorado. I really did come to like the wilderness and mountains of the Rockies and the small-town ambiance. However, I was never as happy as Kay. I missed my old friends and hang-outs but tried to hide my feelings. Kay grew wary whenever I became too moody or quiet (though she could be quite the mood queen herself). I got a job in antiques restoration—something I'd done successfully back east—but the money wasn't great, certainly not what it was back home, and nothing close to what Kay was bringing in. It was also insufficient for the standard of living we desired. Frustrated, I suggested to Kay that I should go back east for a few months, where a friend had promised me a large commercial job, then return with a good sum of money to take the pressure off. Kay gave her reluctant blessing. That is, she said yes, but she really meant no. I'm not sure whether this was an abandonment issue for her, or loss of control, or if she genuinely loved and missed me. Maybe she wondered why I couldn't find a decent job in our new town, as though I wasn't trying hard enough or was taking the easy way out. The net result was that the phone calls between us grew briefer and cooler while I was away, and when I did return to Colorado with a healthy chunk of money, instead of being praised and congratulated, the temperature between us grew even cooler.

"I finally landed a decent job, but something inside Kay had shifted, an internal compass that now pointed in another direction. I didn't know where. She could shut down her emotions with the snap of her fingers. Kay would never win the Pulitzer for communication skills. More and more she would work late at the office. Staying away from our house one weekend, she came back on Monday to tell me there was someone new in her life and she wanted a divorce. We'd been married exactly four years. Before I could open my mouth (actually, my jaw was already on the floor) Kay said she didn't want to talk about it. She added that there was no way for me to change her mind. I wasn't allowed a single option but to accept her will. I couldn't remember feeling this level of hurt, abandonment and loneliness since my dad died and Sandy left me. After a few months I pulled myself together but felt diminished by the whole experience. When I called home and finally told my mom and brother what had happened, it didn't help my morale. No words of consolation or compassion from Mom—I might as well have been giving her the weather report—and my brother had just ended a six-year relationship, so he had little advice or solace to offer.

"Kay and I didn't speak for a while, but we gradually developed a post-divorce friendship. I like to stay connected to people, even after a relationship is over and even if I've been hurt. I don't know whether that qualifies me as a masochist, or someone, unlike Kay, who just has a hard time letting go. Maybe it's a fundamental loneliness. One day, years after our divorce on an otherwise pleasant spring drive, Kay said to me out of the blue, 'Have I ever apologized to you for ruining your life?' I bit my tongue. What I wanted to scream was, 'You broke my heart into a million pieces!' But what would be the good? I had begun to internalize a lot of the blame that had been tossed my way over the years. I had begun to think automatically that if something went wrong in a relationship, because I'd had so many disappointments in the past, it just had to be my fault. I couldn't separate personal feelings of inadequacy from actual culpability. Kay never really gave me objective reasons why she'd fallen out of love with me, or what I'd done wrong. I craved information as much as she craved her privacy. Major stalemate.

"I can spend an inordinate amount of time philosophizing about my life or life in general, about the choices that are presented to us and the ones we make. I take it very hard when I make the wrong choice. I hear about women who beat themselves up because they have negative self-images, but do they know there are an equal number of men who suffer from the same unrelenting self-scrutiny? No, I take that back. I think there are more men.

"This leads me to my second, and final (to date) marriage. Four years (my karmic time space) after the divorce from Kay, I was still in Colorado, finally adjusted to my new environment, when I met a woman thirteen years my junior. Cali had recently joined the sales company where I was now one of the top producers, and as a rookie she would come to me for advice about clients. She was previously married, and shared custody of her toddler-daughter with her ex-husband, a local contractor. After a year of office socializing, one afternoon she asked me to lunch. In one of those perfect settings—the cloudscape, the outdoor café, the food, the cabernet sauvignon!—she told me she had a crush on me, and asked how I felt about her. Imagine, you're looking at a woman thirteen years younger, her eyes as sparkling as the wine you're drinking, her smile as beatific as a Raphael painting, and she's wearing tight jeans that showed off a pair of hips any model would covet—how would you respond? Plus she was sweet, gentle and kind. She wasn't the uncommunicative, calculating, aloof, willful woman I usually gravitated to. Cali laid it right on the line, and her eyes backed it up—she had a crush on me! What's wrong with this picture? I'm a big, dumb male, lonely and hurt from the past, as easy a mark as they come. A little flattery at the right time from a very pretty woman and I'm on the floor, like a dog waiting for its belly to be scratched. Defenseless? You bet! That's the reason I'm here today in divorce court, Your Honor: I plead guilty to being flattered into willful submission. I was charmed. I was seduced. I don't think many men have looked at Cali and not thought about sex. My heart ached and in one magic moment she healed it. Talk about the emotional power of a woman.

"Cali and I lived together for two years before deciding to get married. Getting burned in past relationships will make anyone cautious. But we were in love and told each other that over and over. I was devoted only to her, I swore, and I meant it. The afternoon of our wedding, Cali suddenly got cold feet. I had to keep our guests waiting for half an hour until I talked her out of her anxiety and fears, which she couldn't articulate, no matter how sympathetic I was. This would prove to be a sign of a troubled past that Cali hadn't yet revealed to me. That would come later. The wedding ended up as a happy day, and we were now man and wife.

"I was never more determined to make a relationship work. Cali's daughter, Elizabeth, now five, was a charmer, and I had been bonding well with her. It's not to say Cali and I didn't feel some stress as we set up house and planned our lives. Money was one problem. The sales market was softening, and Cali, in order to be a full-time mom, no longer wanted to work. To economize, we moved into a small house on a very pretty lot—complete with trees and a year-round stream—that was owned by Cali's Aunt Gloria, who gave us what she called 'a favorable rent.'

A mistake, in retrospect. We would have been better off staying at Motel Six. Aunt Gloria just didn't like men, and she had no bones about telling me about it. Whether I wasn't considered 'good enough' or I was too old for her niece, Aunt Gloria was domineering, bigoted, racist and mean as a rattlesnake. When I asked Cali why she put up with this woman's tyranny, I began to learn about Cali's childhood, something she had concealed from me—and for good reason. I believe she thought it would repulse me. Her parents were manipulative, selfish and deceitful, in my opinion, and basically used Cali as bait in their divorce. At the tender age of 13, she had to choose which parent to live with—the abusive, alcoholic mother or the philandering, alcoholic father. In the end, she was whisked off to another town where she knew no one, and her bedroom was in a cramped basement with no windows, with no personal possessions, and no sense of belonging to anything. She was raised by an insensitive half-sister, a teen bride with children and issues of her own.

"Cali's upbringing was significant in how she viewed raising Elizabeth. To say that Cali was overprotective was more than an understatement. It was a living, breathing reality that in my opinion ultimately helped undermine our relationship. Cali constantly worried about Elizabeth's happiness and well being, and virtually sacrificed anything for her. In my opinion it was a classic case of a parent reinventing her childhood through her own kid. Initially, I thought one of my attractions to Cali was as the 'father figure,' the good father she never had, so I naturally assumed I was to have a role in helping raise her child. I wanted a family just as much as Cali did—maybe even more than she did, after my own dysfunctional upbringing. But anytime I made a suggestion about how she might discipline Elizabeth, Cali almost always vetoed it. She would bark, 'no one is going to tell me how to raise my child.'

"In retrospect, I can't blame her, based on her own pretty wretched childhood, but she had no idea how she was shutting me out of a process that was critical for my own happiness and our happiness as a couple. Combine that with our chronic money shortages and things began to fall apart. Aunt Gloria, despite all my efforts to bow and scrape, considered me barely worthy to take out the trash. How many times did I come home, tired and frazzled and in need of companionship, to 'our' house and find Aunt Gloria there on the couch, like she was the one paying the rent.

"After only eighteen months, despite trying to control our stress and reassure each other about the future, Cali and I ran out of energy. Maybe neither of us cared enough to keep the marriage going. Looking back, neither of us were able to deal with our own childhood issues and therefore had no way to deal with each other's. To this day, as with Kay, I am in touch with Cali. She has a long-term boyfriend but doesn't seem to be eager to try marriage again. Like me, if you're burned twice, the third time fills you with more dread than you want to admit.

"After the divorce I moved back east. These days I content myself with what I call 'the life of the mind.' It grows in importance as one gets older. I like what people throughout history have thought, what bold and inventive ideas they came up with. I like sharing that with a woman. I can say with some confidence that I'm wired pretty well in the intellect department. I 'get' some ponderous issues, and can converse with confidence on quite a few. I like the origin of the forces that power life, evolution, behavior, consciousness, and everything else from economics to governments. I'm interested in a universe of things and love the pursuit of knowledge. Here's a tidbit: geneticists have discovered that women are far and away the more important of the two sexes. Apparently, new analyses of the human genome have shown that women were only a few small bits of DNA away from not needing men at all in their reproductive cycle. I'm told that one tenth of one percent of all women are born with penises—no kidding! I think I know which way evolution is going. Kind of leaves us men with just the heavy lifting and trash duties, doesn't it? Maybe Aunt Gloria was right. Women are now goddesses, and children are the new gods. Stop looking for other deities. Just listen to the way people carry on about their kids today. They treat them like Baccarat crystal. I mean, talk about over-protection and creating a sense of entitlement.

"Some things I know for sure. Women want to be loved and appreciated, coddled, and perhaps most importantly, listened to and understood. Funny—just like men! But they're emotionally wired in a fashion so open and yet so complex that sooner or later many men can't deal with it. I'm emotional but, like most men, my emotions would likely burn through my guts and on towards China before I'd let them be a part of casual table talk. But we never catch on to that soon enough to avoid the damaging effects. Some days I understand women pretty well; other times I'm as clueless about their logic as I am to particle physics. To me, women are unfathomable creatures hidden in human skin. I love them. I like their smell, their feel, and the way they make me feel. I like the way they dress in autumn. Cashmere and perfume were invented for women, or for the men lucky enough to feel them in it. If you can get in synch with that, it's aces for you. The killer is, we all have personalities and as we age, a few personal peculiarities throw the romance off-track for just a fraction of a second. But that's enough for a total derailment. It confuses the objective, and pretty soon the cashmere starts smelling like a big wet dog and that whiff of love dies.

"Of course, I'm no walk in the park either. In the late Seventies I was dating a beautiful attorney. She later became a managing partner of a prestigious firm, married well, had a few troubled kids, and was big in the Republican Party. But I somehow managed to interest her for several months of blissful dating in an otherwise bleak New England winter. She was a high-maintenance princess, but the sex was great, and it was a no-stress situation. One cold Saturday morning after a rather satisfying and spirited roll, we were lying in bed just looking at one another. I knew something was boiling up in her, so I bit and asked the question. 'What are you thinking?' It's a question a man should never ask a woman unless he's truly desperate, and then you have to be prepared for something akin to nuclear annihilation. I'm hoping her answer is sex-related, of course, but honestly, in your dreams! After several attempts to cajole it out of her, she dropped the bomb: 'I was just thinking that if you had money, you'd be perfect!' I was stunned. Why the sudden meanness? What does money have to do with love and companionship and affection? If I'd said that line to her, I'd be digging shell fragments out of my skull for a year. I thought for a moment and replied vengefully: 'If I had money, I wouldn't be interested in anyone like you.' We started to drift apart in about 20 seconds. That is among the worst conversations I've ever had with a woman.

"But a lot of women do like money and hence wealthy men. Part of it is the age-old attraction to power. But chasing money is also an insurance policy if the love thing goes out the window. Just ask any divorce attorney. In retrospect, most if not all the women in my life (except for Cali), whether they liked money or not, were emotionally distant, intelligent, strong-willed, inflexible and demanding. None of them have been able to maintain long-term relationships and, my guess is, they don't have a very high opinion of men. But I found these women! I

281

found just the type of woman who is like Kryptonite to me! And as damaged as they may be, I've chosen several! What does that say about me? As much as I'd like not to believe it, maybe I've chosen my mother, over and over.

"Here's one you'll never find in a fortune cookie but should: 'Relationships are like damaged china. Sometimes even when you work your hardest to repair it, and you feel that it's as strong as it ever was, the crack is still there.' I tend to focus on the crack and question its fragility, rather than marvel at the piece's overall strength. Maybe that's how I give up on women."

Summary and Interpretation

- The "loss of attraction" argument may be the most common rationalization for men who want out of a relationship. It doesn't involve a great amount of introspection, nor does it summon much emotion, and perhaps only minimal pain. "I just lost interest in her" or "we weren't getting along anymore" or "she suddenly changed" is enough of a *reason* for many men to move on without feeling any guilt. When communication about emotions is difficult, men resort to clichés like "hey, it's nobody's fault, things just happen." In the case of Eddie, and a lot of men, no matter what *reason* they give, the *cause* of their breakups may be an unwillingness to deal with their own anger, feelings of distrust, a lack of childhood nurturing, and certainly a lack of self-love. Do some men, especially those with abandonment issues, set themselves up to fall out of love by setting impossible standards for their partners to live up to? Do they want their partners to fail and disappoint them so they can leave the relationship with a clear conscience? Some men will go to great lengths to win their freedom without feeling guilty. It's understandable that the fear of being put on a pedestal becomes, for many women, an act of self-preservation.

- Among the men I spoke with, many said they fall out of love when they feel their partners becomes too self-important, or take their men for granted. This was how Eddie felt much of the time. This often occurs when a partner appears no longer to be the same person you fell in love with. She stops giving you a kiss at breakfast, doesn't care how she dresses, forgets the errand she promised to run for you, or is late for the dinner you fixed and doesn't apologize. Perhaps this is partly the fault of men who pretend that there is no problem they can't solve, that nothing—no setback, no disappointment—fazes them. They act this way in part because they think this is what women expect. They try so hard to be capable, autonomous and self-sufficient that they give the impression they don't need special attention. But they need the recognition as badly as women do. When men tell their partners that they're no longer attracted to them, it is often code for "I'm not getting enough love."

- The feeling of being taken for granted may also be due to women, especially the younger generation of professionals, who place their careers ahead of their relationships. Eddie certainly feels this is what Kay did. Suddenly, the man feels like the "accessory" or "bauble" that Gloria Steinem once alluded to as the exclusive plight of women, and that shows like *Sex in the City* exploit for humor. Much has changed in forty years. A lot of men have co-opted what were once perceived as strictly feminine values— empathy, sensitivity and nurturing—while women have adopted the so-called male attributes of competitiveness, dominance and power. What is amazing to many men about this transition is that women wielding power elicit mostly praise from other women, while men in power are still regarded skeptically.

- Much has been written about a woman's "secret garden," a special and mysterious place, an oasis of self-intimacy that is healing and empowering. Whether its meaning is sexual, spiritual or a state of being, the "secret garden" hints at a core identity that has no equivalent in the lives of men. In the novel *The Da Vinci Code,* reference to "the sacred feminine" is made repeatedly and supported by an argument that invokes not just history but the order of the cosmos. If someone were to talk about "the sacred masculine" it's unlikely there would be many believers. Yet is there not, somewhere, a hallowed place for men to affirm their uniqueness and authenticity? Most men, consciously or unconsciously, seek out an emotional support system to help them through life. Religion, sports, male groups or clubs, or the love of their children, for example, are ideal systems because usually there's little chance of betrayal or rejection. Men need a place to feel safe. Unfortunately many never find it.

- Until a man finds that kind of sanctuary, or has a deep passion, a vision, or some kind of strong internal compass, his emotional resources are narrowly focused, and can be exhaustible and finite. That women have at their disposal a deeper level of self-intimacy, something to fall back on when a relationship crashes or tragedy enters their lives, is probably one reason their rates of suicide are significantly lower than men's. Statistically, according to Terrence Real in *I Don't Want to Talk About It,* a far higher number of women attempt suicide than do men, but their efforts are nowhere near as violent or as successful. This might mean that women know how to "send a message" while still surviving. Men, when things go drastically wrong, often lack the capacity for self-forgiveness as well as a support system to get help. Too many would rather literally kill themselves than be publicly disgraced or admit defeat. Or they are so filled with anger—with themselves or someone else—that their suicide is an act of revenge.

- Eddie makes reference to a scientific study asserting that in the spiral of evolution women were only a few bits of DNA away from reproductive self-sufficiency. Are women the superior gender? Because of their evolutionary role as givers of birth, their gift for nurturing, the necessity of knowing how to survive if her partner dies before her, the ability to bond and seek help from others, women seem better equipped than men to endure pain, to socialize, to love, and to simply exist. The physiology of the brain, and genetic and biological explanations of gender differences, are still far from clear, but it can be argued that the integrated emotional circuitry of women allows for greater flexibility and adaptability than men possess. The expression "women bend, men break" is just another metaphor for a man's reluctance to venture into areas where he's not comfortable, engage in battles where he fears he might not win, or to take on emotional pain for which he's not prepared. It's as if the rational part of his brain is not only overdeveloped but quite separate from his emotional lobe. The apparent gap between his ability to reason and his ability to feel sheds light on why it may be more common for men than women to struggle with love. Women can connect reason with emotion. They also seem to know, unlike men, that reason can't solve all emotional issues. Some emotional issues simply aren't fixable, and therefore women make other choices when there aren't solutions. Men are biased toward decisive solutions and not letting go. They are often leery of having to grapple with new choices and nuances for fear of having to master new facts and possibly making a mistake.

PART SIX

WHAT EVERY COUPLE SHOULD KNOW

Chapter Fourteen

Ten Warning Signs

Love does not consist in gazing at each other, but in looking together in the same direction.

—Antoine de Saint-Exupéry

We are at once a culture that talks too much and doesn't talk enough. What makes us happy or unhappy in our relationships is so crucial, yet most of us don't ask the question, at least with any urgency, until we're already unhappy. When a relationship becomes a "crash and burn" scenario, we suddenly question everything: Why does this hurt so much? Whom should I be mad at? Was it my fault? How do I make myself feel better? How do I make sure this won't happen again? Our self-esteem is often uprooted, and we search everywhere, sometimes frantically, to fix our "happiness problem."

Popular culture markets the idea that not only is happiness an entitlement, but something must be wrong with us if we don't achieve it. When your life changes dramatically, the first question a friend asks you is: "what are you doing now?" The second question is, inevitably: "are you happy?" We are a living, breathing happiness culture. Nothing means more, even if we don't always know what happiness means. It's no coincidence that the "smiley face" is still around after decades of parody. It's

288

now used, sincerely, as an e-mail icon (with multiple variations), as well as on T-shirts, bumper stickers, shopping bags and umbrellas, to indicate one's emotional state. Emotions are us, and there is no emotion worshipped more, or more sought after, than happiness.

The next grand equation that we are sold is that happiness equals love. Your soul mate is out there, and if you don't find him or her, well, you're not doing something right. Let Hollywood, the media and infomercials point the way: lose some weight, look younger, buy the right car, dress the right way, have the right friends, drink the right vodka and, of course, make lots of money... If you follow the formula, you'll be so inescapably attractive that you're almost guaranteed a lasting, gratifying relationship. Just in case it's not working, don't worry: lose a little more weight, make more money, keep on shopping... If that still doesn't work, there's always therapy, support groups, on-line dating services and dating brokers, church, sports, medications—something— anything—just keep searching. At the end of the rainbow is your soul mate.

If that doesn't happen—if we can't find our soul mate (let alone the rainbow)—we realize that perhaps our unhappiness cannot be fixed with externals. It lies within. How to get to that unhappiness, analyze it, and change it is perhaps the hardest thing any of us will ever do. When their relationships collapsed, the men in this book questioned their behavior and attitudes, endured a lot of pain, and most became stronger for their journeys. Changing ourselves doesn't necessarily mean keeping our relationships, or jumping out of them either. Anything can happen. What's crucial is that we don't necessarily need to lose weight, take a new job, or buy a sports car. We *do* have to be willing to question our behavior and the emotional choices we make. We have to go through a little pain. The men in this book notwithstanding, for most it's far easier to hide in the traditional masculine shelters of work, achievement and denial, even if few men are happy doing so, than take on the pain and the hard, sweaty work of self-exploration.

Traditional definitions of masculinity, we rationalize, were good enough for our fathers, uncles and brothers, why shouldn't they be good enough for us?

The answer is because the world has changed, women have changed, and men need to change too—if they want to escape their low-grade misery, to live longer and healthier lives, and to pass on to their children a more sensible and sustainable definition of masculinity. Just as in the Fifties, Sixties and Seventies there were too many unhappy women—women who didn't know they were unhappy until someone told them—today there are too many men who don't know they are unhappy. Through struggle, the ten men in this book began to understand some of the reasons behind their unhappiness, and tried to do something about it.

If we're vigilant, and believe our relationships are worth holding onto, here are *ten early warning signs* to watch out for. While these signals might pertain to either gender, they particularly apply to men and are written in that context. As a list they may seem obvious, but with the stress and responsibilities of daily life they can easily go unnoticed.

You need to pay attention if—

- He loses interest in you physically, no matter what his excuse.

- His general behavior begins to change, either slowly or abruptly, in small ways or large.

- He picks arguments, or finds fault with you, for no perceived reason.

- He communicates with you less and less on important issues, or refuses to discuss subjects that you think are important.

- He suddenly changes his schedule, comes home later and later from work, or chooses to spend his free time away from you.

- He defers more and more decisions to you, or insists on making all decisions himself.

- He shows a lack of confidence in himself, gets depressed, or grows angry without apparent provocation.

- He complains openly that no one respects or loves him, or he's being taken advantage of, or he's overworked, or not feeling well.

- He spends an unusual amount of time at work, or talks continually about the importance of his career, or has some other interest that takes the place of you or the children.

- He talks about his life before he met you, or an old girl-friend, or the times when "he was really happy."

Any of the behaviors cited above could mean, for example, that your partner has become infatuated with another woman or is vulnerable to doing so; angry with you or disappointed in your relationship; coming to grips with some personal trauma, past or present; feeling that his masculinity is threatened; or slipping into depression. If he becomes too talkative or too silent, drops old friends, has bouts of insomnia, gives in to anger over things that he once never even noticed, resists physical intimacy—he is disengaging from you for a specific reason. He may also be putting up walls because your behavior has changed. Maybe he's not getting the attention he is accustomed to because you're giving that to someone or something else, or you're suddenly assuming more power and control in your relationship. Don't confuse his silence for "everything is just fine."

Chapter Fifteen

Help for a Troubled Relationship

Our way is not soft grass, it's a mountain path with lots of rocks. But it goes upwards, forward, toward the sun.

—*Dr. Ruth Westheimer*

It is usually adversity that sets us on our inward journey. Without our relationship setbacks, perhaps we wouldn't arrive at the truths about happiness that are worth holding onto. The dilemma of a partner who senses something wrong in his or her relationship is whether to speak up, or to "wait it out" under the theory that all relationships have their ups and downs. Sometimes waiting *is* effective if the tension is tied to a temporary problem— an end-of-the-month money crunch, for example, or a disciplinary problem with a child. However, it's a very blurry line between giving a problem time to resolve itself and denial that something is serious enough to require special attention. Virtually everybody in this book was presented with this dilemma, and most fell into denial rather than confront their problems head on.

Of the relationships in this book that crashed, could any have been saved? I would suggest that if not all, then many might have, if the partners had been more aware of their issues and been better communicators. Almost everyone—man or woman—was too defensive, unsure about their needs or how to express them, and

292

unwilling to explore and learn. For anyone reading these stories and facing a similar crisis, what is critical is that at least one person be intuitive enough to recognize the storm clouds. The problem is compounded because some men may not understand the reasons behind their unhappiness and will never speak up. For other men (and women), the pain of dealing with an emotional trauma is simply too high a price for saving a relationship. It is sometimes less painful to let the relationship end. If we were all realists and not romantics, the vow "Till death do us part" would be replaced by "I'm in this relationship until one or both of us feels otherwise." As one of the men in this book mentions, our culture is permeated by the hope that if things don't work out with one person, take solace. It's not your fault, and around the corner is someone new, something better, to meet your needs. Is it really a hope, or an excuse to leave? Around the counter, first and foremost, is the same old you.

One of the keys to relationship rebuilding is the need for men not only to be conscious of the reasons for their unhappiness but to act on that consciousness. They need to challenge old stereotypes of masculinity that have for centuries put them on a wobbly pedestal, and to find a source of power that has little to do with control, aggression or linear problem solving. Most of all, they need to listen to their partners as much as they need to be listened to. Rehabilitation is about open-mindedness and compromise. In ancient cultures, many of the deities that were worshipped possessed a blend of male and female characteristics. In the new paradigm, the blending of traditional feminine values with masculine may be the mean tide line on which future generations meet and coexist.

The imperative for a woman who loves her partner is not to wait for the explosion of the volcano or to endure its endless smoldering. If you feel your relationship is in jeopardy, here are *ten suggestions* for putting it back on track.

- Even before you spot the warning signs listed in Chapter

293

Fourteen, from time to time conduct your own "relationship audit." What does your partner mean to you? What do you mean to your partner? How much has your relationship changed over the last year and are you closer now or further apart? Relationships are rarely static. If you're moving apart, try to determine what is driving the separation. For example, if you're taking a spiritual journey to "find yourself," or your career has become more demanding, or your partner has grown preoccupied or emotionally absent, explain to him what you think is going on. Keeping bad news to yourself is a huge energy drain and only inflicts more damage on the relationship. Also, hearing your partner's point of view is essential to your decision-making about whether to stay or go. While some discretion in what you reveal may be necessary, the general rule of thumb is to trust your partner by telling him what's really bothering you and expect the same honesty from him. Many in this book tried to do that. If you can't find that trust, this is probably not the right relationship for either of you.

- Be aware of how a man's emotions work and let him know that you care. Learn as much about him as you can, asking about his childhood, his parents, and especially his adolescence. Accept that his emotional wiring, while different from yours, is just as complex and equally crucial to his happiness. Recognize that the person you fell in love with may not be the same person you end up sharing your life with. His real self, slowly revealed, may be twenty- to one-hundred-and-eighty degrees different. That surprise can be a positive. Be flexible and open minded. The more open you are with him, taking the lead, the more open he will be with you.

- Be conscious of the impact on your partner of your own image, power and lifestyle. While they are not likely to admit it, most men feel at an inherent disadvantage in their

294

relationships simply because relationships are about emotions. The nest is perceived as a woman's territory. Until they learn to be more assertive with their emotions, men need opportunities to feel important on that turf and to get acknowledgement from their partners that their opinions and feelings count. Men need to feel secure. If you want intimacy and attention from your partner, be prepared to give it back to him in equal measure. In addition, while you might be madly in love with each other, for a man to commit long-term to a woman who has, for example, more friends than he does, is better educated, or is more successful professionally, he has to be very confident in his masculinity. Don't be reluctant to ask him for his definition of masculinity.

- In the firm I used to run, I was always struck by the difference between how male and female employees related problems to me. A man would come into my office and give the facts in a straight, direct manner, leaving nothing out but taking as little time as possible in his rendition—then ask for my opinion. A woman with the same problem would first ask how I was doing, how my family was, and if the company was prospering. Then she would explain the problem to me starting somewhere in the middle, jumping ahead to the end, and slide back to the beginning. She would repeat parts of her analysis, and offer a point of view of events other than her own, and go off on several more tangents that might seem to me irrelevant to the decision-making process. Altogether it takes her twice as long as the man to complete her story. It took me years to grasp that, in general, when women give information, it is a process that involves both emotion and reason, that it is circular and not linear, and that in repeating themselves it's not to make sure *I* understand their point as much as making sure *they* understand all the facts and angles. At the same time that they are giving information, women are processing and reprocess-

ing—problem solving as they speak—coming up with
their own solutions. My opinion almost doesn't matter.
It is the same for relationships: while women can multi-
task as they give information, men usually cannot. They
need to give and receive information in a linear fashion.
Emotional reasoning from a woman sends mixed signals.
Subtlety is sometimes misunderstood or just ignored by
men. Be very explicit in making your point, specifically
about emotions, your needs, and the direction you think
your relationship is heading.

- While it may run against your instincts, support your partner when he seems to be drifting away from you. When
you tap into your courage, the emotional satisfaction you
feel is more powerful than the fear that comes from not
dealing with the problem. Show that you're worried about
him, not just about yourself. If you become defensive and
accusatory, the breach between you will probably only
widen.

- If your partner is in crisis, or just turning away from you
emotionally, prod him gently but persistently to let you
in on the problem. While there is no stigma in asking for
professional help, many men will deny there *is* a problem,
at least one that they can't solve themselves. Sometimes
you need to take the lead. Suggest what you would do if it
were your problem. Urge him to talk to friends he trusts.
Discuss ways for him to heal by getting away from fear
and judgment. Buy him some good self-help books. If he
gains confidence in you, he not only has a better chance
of getting through his problem, but of building a deeper
relationship with you.

- For your relationship to work, it has to breathe. A certain
amount of privacy and independence has to be granted to
each partner. An ideal relationship can be defined as one
where each partner is not afraid to tell everything to the

other, but neither finds it necessary to do so. Each partner recognizes the need to grow and experiment outside of the relationship, to search out ever-shifting identities, interests and passions. Boundaries should be drawn by a couple (for example, no infidelity), then both can let go of inhibitions and fears. As good relationships mature, trust is essential to staying together. To meddle or interfere means there is no trust. To be controlling in any way is a short-term solution to one's own insecurity, and a long-term guarantee of both partners' unhappiness.

- Because emotional self-understanding in men often stops sometime in late adolescence, or whenever men "grow up" and become busy in the "real world," they are at a disadvantage when their adult relationships fall into crisis. Unable to articulate what he's really feeling, and forced to listen to his partner—who knows exactly what he did wrong—a man often lapses into anger or retreats into silence. Women can be quickly resented for the pain they cause. In *Sideways*, the two male friends, Jack and Miles, bond best when their world is free of worries about women and sex. Whenever women come into their lives or even their conversations, there is—underneath the wistful hope for happiness—conflict, jealousy, anxiety and disappointment. The two characters are attempting on their free-wheeling road trip to revisit, psychologically and emotionally, the point in time before they left adolescence and stopped growing emotionally. They want their past back, at least an idealized version of it, before life started to become too serious and full of responsibilities, including relationships. All men should try to remember the last time they felt truly happy, before the onset of settling down. Identifying that moment can provide the take-off point to start growing their emotions again. If not used, emotions, like a muscle, atrophy.

- To argue for a moment with Tolstoy, who wrote that all

happy families resemble one another, perhaps all happy couples do not resemble one another. A successful relationship is built on many things, one of which is understanding what makes your relationship unique. In addition to love, it's crucial to identify the common denominator that leads to the greatest happiness: a deep friendship; religious, ethical or family values; a shared passion; a work ethic; a type of intelligence; a tolerance and respect for the other's space; or an understanding of how to balance time together and time apart. What's important is knowing what works and why. If and when your relationship breaks down, connecting to your areas of strength is the first objective.

• For all the differences between men and women, in the end, no matter what their gender, the values we teach our children—compassion, tolerance, reason, honesty, love and faith—are what we need to re-teach ourselves.

Bibliography

Being a Man: The Paradox of Masculinity.
  Donald H. Bell. (Harcourt Brace Jovanovich)

In a Time of Fallen Heroes: The Recreation of Manhood.
  William R Betcher. (Atheneum)

Sex on the Brain: The Biological Differences Between Men and Women.
  Deborah Blum. (Viking)

Strong Mothers, Strong Sons: Raising the Next Generation of Men.
  Ann F. Caron. (Perennial)

Masculinities.
  R.W. Connell. (Berkeley: University of California Press)

The Men and the Boys.
  R. W. Connell. (Berkeley: University of California Press)

Stiffed.
  Susan Faludi. (Harper Collins)

The Myth of Male Power.
  Warren Farrell. (Simon and Shuster)

The Liberated Man: Beyond Masculinity.
  Warren Farrell. (Random House)

A Choice of Heroes: The Changing Face of American Manhood.
  Mark Gerzon. (Houghton Mifflin)

Manhood in the Making: Cultural Concepts of Masculinity.
    David D. Gilmore. (Yale University Press)

Fathering.
    Will Glennon. (Yale University Press)

The Hazards of Being Male: Surviving the Myth of Male Privilege.
    Herb Goldberg. (Penguin Books)

The New Male: From Self-Destruction to Self-Care.
    Herb Goldberg. (SelfHelpBooks.Com)

The Wonder of Boys.
    Michael Gurian. (Penguin Books)

Manhood in America: A Cultural History.
    Michael Kimmel. (Free Press)

Brain Sex: The Real Difference Between Men and Women.
    Ann and David Jesse Moir. (Dell)

The Men They Will Become: The Nature and Nurture of Male Character.
    Eli H. Newberger. (Persus)

Man Enough: Fathers, Sons and the Search for Masculinity.
    Frank Pittman. (Perigee Books)

Finding Our Fathers.
    Samuel Osherson. (McGraw Hill)

Real Boys: Rescuing Our Sons from Myths of Manhood.
    William Pollack. (Random House)

I Don't Want to Talk About It: Overcoming the Secret Legacy of Male Depression.
>Terrence Real. (Fireside)

Standup Guy: Manhood After Feminism.
>Michael Segell. (Villard)

The War Against Boys: How Misguided Feminism is Harming Our Young.
>Christina Sommers. (Simon & Shuster)

Raising Cain: Protecting the Emotional Life of Boys.
>Dan Kindlon and Michael Thompson. (Ballantine Books)

About The Author

Michael French is a businessman and author who divides his time between Santa Barbara, California, and Santa Fe, New Mexico. He is an avid high altitude mountain trekker, as well as a collector of first editions of Twentieth Century fiction.

Mr. French has published some twenty books, including fiction, young adult fiction, biographies and art criticism. His novel, *Abingdon's,* was a best seller and a Literary Guild Alternate Selection. His young adult novel, *Pursuit*, was awarded the California Young Reader Medal.

Why Men Fall out Of Love: The Secrets They Don't Tell is his most recent book.

Printed in the United States
39171LVS00003B/196-228